Peaudicaf

COLLECTION ANDRÉ BALLANDRAS
Inspecteur Général de l'Instruction Publique

7

SAY WHAT YOU MEAN

TERMINALES

A. GREMY
Agrégé de l'Université

R. LE BRETON-STILING
(B.A. Honours)
Agrégée de l'Université

B. GARBARZ-BERCOVITZ
Agrégée de l'Université

avec la collaboration de

C.L. CAMPOS
(Ph. D. Cantab.)

FERNAND NATHAN
18, rue Monsieur-le-Prince - Paris 6ᵉ

AVANT-PROPOS

Cet ouvrage est le troisième de la série ***Say What You Mean.*** La variété des documents présentés et la diversité de l'appareil pédagogique font qu'il s'adresse à la fois aux élèves de 1re et de 2e langues.

Nous sommes restés fidèles aux principes qui avaient guidé la conception des précédents manuels (Say What You Mean 2e et 1re). L'objectif premier demeure l'entraînement et l'enrichissement linguistiques, ce travail étant conçu en fonction des « besoins langagiers » prévisibles au moment des trois opérations auxquelles donne normalement lieu l'étude d'un document : **compréhension orale et écrite, exploration du contenu, exploitation.** C'est ce souci qui nous a conduits à ne pas adopter une classification par thèmes, mais à tenter de concevoir une organisation allant du plus simple au plus difficile au plan de la compréhension, et du plus urgent au moins urgent au plan de l'expression.

Pour atteindre ces objectifs nous nous sommes appuyés sur des textes accompagnés d'un appareil pédagogique, et sur un support audio-oral.

Les textes. Ils sont de quatre ordres : 1) des textes accompagnés d'un appareil pédagogique riche 2) des documents présentés sous la rubrique *« Spotlight on... »* dont l'appareil pédagogique est beaucoup plus léger 3) des poèmes 4) des textes français qui, dans quatre cas sur cinq, présentent le point de vue d'un Français sur les questions abordées dans le texte anglais précédent. Si nous avons introduit cette nouveauté, c'est que nous estimons que le travail auquel ces textes peuvent donner lieu présente une triple légitimité : au plan intellectuel, il y a là matière à comparaisons enrichissantes et stimulantes ; au plan linguistique, la compréhension étant résolue d'entrée de jeu, on peut concentrer les efforts sur l'expression orale et écrite et vérifier la disponibilité des éléments de langage acquis au cours de l'étude du texte anglais précédent ; enfin pour certains de ces élèves des classes terminales, ce travail constituera une initiation aux exercices qu'ils auront à pratiquer dans les classes préparatoires aux grandes écoles en vue des épreuves de concours.

Pour les deux premiers types de textes, notre choix a été dicté par un triple souci. Nous avons cherché des documents qui puissent être à la fois **outils pour l'expression** et **incitation à l'expression.** Cela signifie qu'ils offrent un modèle de la langue orale et écrite, qu'ils peuvent donner lieu à un entraînement et à un enrichissement linguistiques, et qu'ils sont suffisamment stimulants pour susciter le désir de s'exprimer. Nous avons veillé à ce que leur charge lexicale ne soit jamais trop lourde. Enfin — est-il besoin de le préciser — ces textes s'efforcent de présenter les aspects les plus significatifs de ce qu'il est convenu d'appeler la civilisation américaine. Nous avons, à cet égard, rassemblé sous le titre *The A.B.C.'s of the U.S.A.* certains termes dont il est indispensable de connaître le sens si l'on veut comprendre le mode de vie et de pensée des Américains.

Appareil pédagogique : il comporte des illustrations et des exercices. Comme dans les deux précédents ouvrages, les illustrations font partie intégrante de l'ensemble. Elles devraient pouvoir servir de support à un travail linguistique préalable ou postérieur à l'étude des textes.

Les exercices : leur gamme est étendue, mais nous avons essayé de les organiser de manière plus structurée en les groupant sous trois rubriques : ceux qui sont destinés à la compréhension *(Towards Comprehension)*, ceux qui permettent une exploration du contenu et une remise en forme des énoncés essentiels autour de structures ou de « notions » dictées par les contraintes internes du sens du texte *(Language Practice)*, et ceux qui ouvrent les voies de l'expression personnelle et invitent au jugement de valeur *(Towards Appreciation)*. Notre souci, dans cet ouvrage comme dans les précédents, est d'apporter aux élèves les moyens de conquérir leur autonomie langagière.

Notre approche des faits de langue est double : notionnelle — ou fonctionnelle — et syntaxique, ainsi qu'en témoignent les deux index.

Nous avons introduit une autre nouveauté : *les tests*. Ils sont au nombre de 5 et répartis à peu près également sur l'ensemble de l'ouvrage. Dans notre esprit, ils devraient contraindre à des révisions périodiques et permettre d'établir des bilans. Ils portent principalement sur trois aspects de la langue : 1) Les mots-outils, les mots de liaison, dont la maîtrise est indispensable à qui veut exprimer une pensée élaborée. 2) Quelques verbes de grande fréquence indispensables eux aussi à l'expression. 3) Les fonctions essentielles du langage. Dans ce dernier cas, nous avons donné les consignes en français car notre objectif est de vérifier la disponibilité d'éléments de « production » et non de contrôler la compréhension. Cette troisième partie a été conçue en fonction d'un principe pédagogique fondamental de cette collection, à savoir que **la même idée peut et doit s'exprimer de diverses manières.**

Enfin, sous le titre *« On your own »* on trouvera des documents destinés au travail individuel. Il s'agit de nouvelles ou d'extraits de roman permettant l'entraînement à la lecture personnelle, et également de textes éclairant certains aspects de la civilisation américaine. L'objectif est de persuader les élèves qu'ils peuvent comprendre rapidement l'essentiel d'un document, même si le sens de quelques termes isolés leur échappe. Là encore notre souci est de les acheminer vers l'autonomie.

Appareil audio-oral : tous les textes, à l'exception des documents présentés sous la rubrique *« Spotlight on... »* ont été enregistrés, si bien que les professeurs qui souhaiteraient aborder leur étude selon une approche audio-orale pourraient le faire.

Quelques textes pour une étude audio-orale : ils ont été « composés ». Ils ne figurent pas dans le livre de l'élève, mais seulement dans celui du professeur. Ils répondent à un double souci : développer l'aptitude à la compréhension orale, mais également servir à l'entraînement linguistique préalable à l'étude de certains textes du livre de l'élève, dont ils reprennent les éléments structuraux et lexicaux essentiels.

Quelques corrigés de compositions écrites ou orales (livre du professeur) : ils pourraient être dictés au magnétophone, voire faire l'objet d'une étude audio-orale pour des élèves dont l'oreille serait encore insuffisamment éduquée.

Comme pour les précédents manuels, un **Livre du professeur** offrira à ceux qui nous honoreront de leur confiance une réflexion méthodologique plus approfondie et, pour chaque texte, un inventaire des objectifs possibles accompagné d'une description des cheminements permettant de les atteindre.

INDEX GRAMMATICAL

Les numéros renvoient aux pages du livre où des exercices ont été prévus pour entraîner à la production du fait de grammaire répertorié. Lorsque le N° est en caractère gras, cela signifie qu'une explicitation a été proposée.
Terminologie : *BV = base verbale = infinitif sans to. To-infinitif = infinitif complet. Passé = prétérit. Parfait = present perfect.*

INDEX FONCTIONNEL

SUBJECTS

CONTENTS

MAJOR DATES

IN THE HISTORY OF THE U.S.A.

1607	Captain John Smith founds the first permanent settlement at Jamestown, Virginia. (Henry IV is king of France; James I, the son of Mary Queen of Scots (Mary Stuart), is king of England.)
1620	The Pilgrim Fathers, in search of religious freedom, found a colony at Plymouth, Massachusetts. (Louis XIII is king of France.)
1682	La Salle claims Louisiana for France. (Louis XIV is king of France.)
1770	The Boston Massacre. After several years of growing hostility towards British taxation, several Americans, including one Negro, are killed in a clash with British troops in Boston. (Louis XV is king of France; George III is king of England.)
1775	The Boston Tea Party. As a protest against a tax on tea, some Americans disguised as Indians board British ships in Boston harbour and throw their cargo of tea into the sea.
1775-1783	American War for Independence. (Louis XVI is king of France.)
1789	April 30th. George Washington is inaugurated President of the United States. (July 14th. The storming of the Bastille.)
1803	The Louisiana Purchase. Territory from the Mississipi to the Rocky Mountains is acquired for 80,000,000 francs from France. (Bonaparte is First Consul.)
1823	The Monroe Doctrine. President James Monroe declares that the United States will not intervene in European affairs and will not tolerate European intervention in the American hemisphere. (Louis XVIII is king of France; George IV is king of England.)
1861-1865	The American Civil War. Abraham Lincoln is elected President in 1861. (Napoleon III is emperor of France; Victoria is queen of England.)
1863	The Proclamation of Emancipation.
1865	President Lincoln is assassinated.
1867	The Dominion of Canada is constituted.
1876	Battle of Little Big Horn. General Custer is killed in a fight with Sioux.
1890	Sioux Chief Sitting Bull is killed in a fight with U.S. troops.
1913	Woodrow Wilson is elected President.
1914-1918	World War I.
1917	Bolshevik Revolution in Russia. America declares war.
1918	Treaty of Versailles.
1929	Crash of the Wall Street stock market and beginning of the Depression.
1932	Franklin Roosevelt, the Democratic candidate, makes his "New Deal" speech.
1933	(January) Hitler becomes chancellor of Germany. (March) Roosevelt is inaugurated President of the United States.
1939-1945	World War II.
1941	The U.S. declares war on Japan and Germany.
1945	The Atom bomb is dropped on Hiroshima.
1947	The Marshall Plan for economic aid to Europe.
1950-1953	Korean War. U.S. troops are sent to South Korea.
1954-1957	Beginning of the Negro Revolt : the first Civil Rights Act is passed to protect Negro voting rights; there are clashes over de-segregation in schools. (Eisenhower is President of the United States.)
1961	John Kennedy is elected President.
1963	President Kennedy is assassinated in Dallas, Texas.
1964	Civil Rights Act passed : it is designed to abolish all forms of segregation. (Johnson is President of the United States.) U.S. bombers attack North Vietnam in retaliation for attacks on U.S. warships.
1965	U.S. combat troops land in South Vietnam. Student protest begins
1968	Robert Kennedy and Martin Luther King, the non-violent black leader, are assassinated.
1969	Americans land on the Moon.
1973	End of the War in Vietnam.
1974	President Nixon forced to resign because of the Watergate Scandal.
1976	Bicentennial celebrations.

WHAT'S THE DIFFERENCE ?

U.S.	G.B.
the Administration	*the Government (Cabinet)*
an American citizen	*a British subject*
anyplace (everyplace, etc.)	*anywhere, etc.*
apartment	*flat*
ashcan (trashcan)	*dustbin*
bartender	*barman, barmaid*
a (dollar) bill	*a (pound) note*
billfold	*wallet* (portefeuille)
buck (colloquial) : dollar	*quid (coll) : pound*
bus	*coach (long distance)*
bum	*beggar, vagabond, tramp*
canned fruit	*tinned fruit*
centennial	*centenary*
a check (restaurant, etc.)	*bill*
check in (hôtel)	*register*
the Chief Executive	*the Prime Minister*
corn	*maize*
creek	*river (small)*
custom-made/built	*made to measure/order*
a dirt road	*an unpaved road*
dough (colloquial)	*cash, 'brass'*
draft	*military service*
elevator	*lift*
fall	*autumn*
filling station	*petrol station*
first floor	*ground floor*
the First Lady (the President's wife)	*no equivalent : the Prime Minister's wife.*
fix	*arrange, repair, etc.*
garbage	*rubbish* (ordures)
gas, gasoline	*petrol*
grade	*class, form*
guy	*fellow*
hood (car)	*bonnet*
hire (a person)	*engage*
icebox	*refrigerator*
a long distance call (telephone)	*a trunk call*
mob (ster)	*gang(ster)*
pack of cigarettes	*packet*
pants	*trousers*
parking lot	*carpark*
parking ticket	*parking fine* (contravention)
pass the buck	*shift the responsibility*
pavement	*roadway*
precinct	*electoral (or police) district*
public school	*state school*
purse	*handbag*
to quit *(+ gérondif)*	*to stop* (+ gérondif)
railroad	*railway*
a raise (in salary)	*a rise*
realtor	*estate agent*
sidewalk	*pavement*
subway	*underground, 'tube'*
superhighway, throughway	*motorway*
transportation	*transport*
truck, trucker	*lorry, lorry-driver*
trunk (automobile)	*boot (car)* (malle)
windshield	*windscreen* (pare-brise)

UNITED STATES OF AMERICA

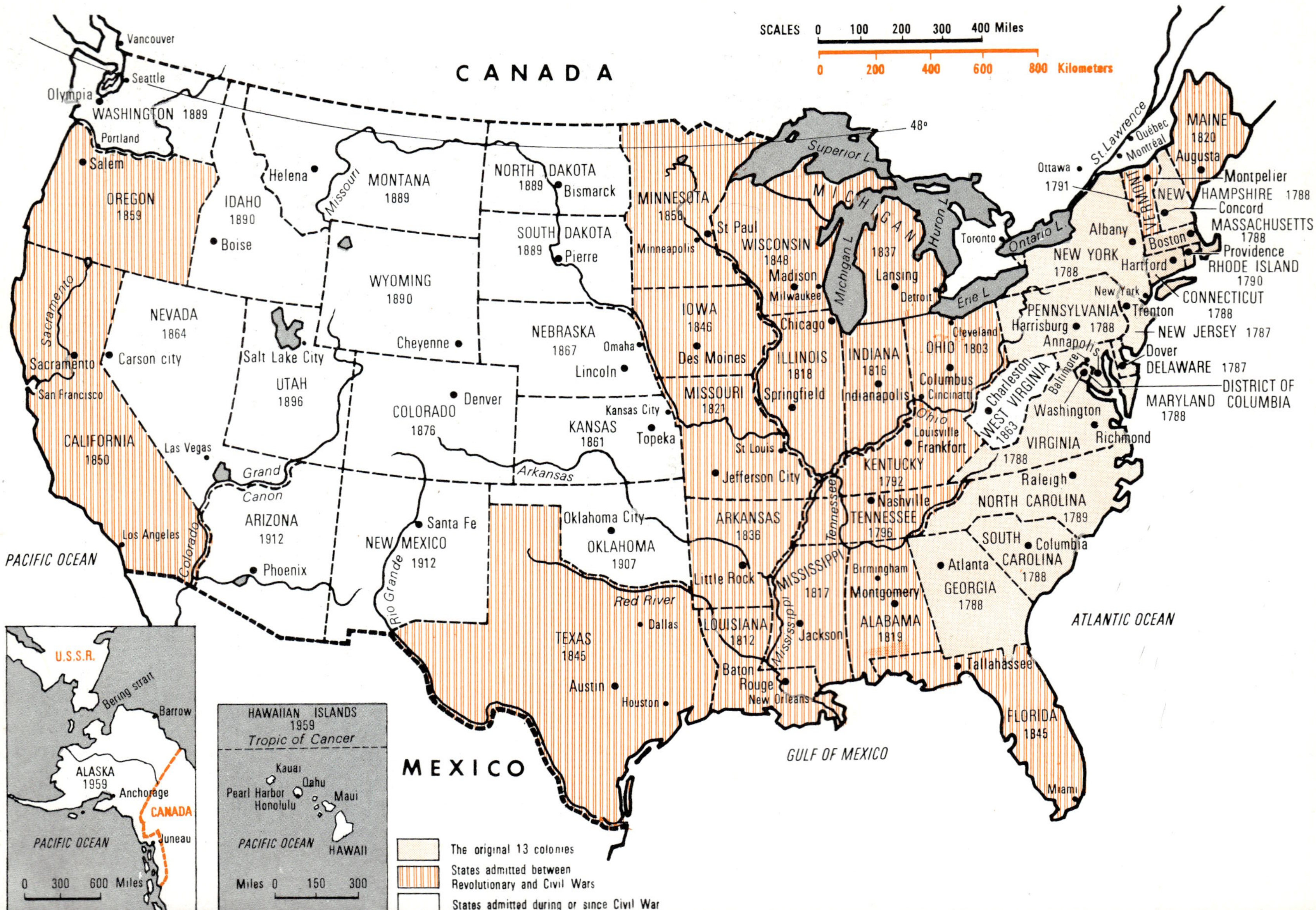

Meet the Americans

Varied ['vɛərid], vocabularies [və'kæbjuləriz], monosyllables ['mɔnə,siləblz], insult (noun) ['insʌlt], insult (verb) [in'sʌlt], accustomed [ə'kʌstəmd], courteous ['kə:tjəs], Japanese [dʒæpə'ni:z], informality [,infɔ:'mæliti], radiator ['reidieitə], pendulum ['pendjuləm], extremes [iks'tri:mz].

•BLUNT SPEECH

Because we Americans come from varied backgrounds, many of us lack full social graces and have remarkably small vocabularies. Don't think we are being rude if we tend to speak in monosyllables or answer with a mere "O.K.," "Sure," or "Nope," or greet you with "Hi." Our brevity is not a personal insult, though to those accustomed to gracious phrases we are (and will seem) •blunt. How much more courteous it is to use the Japanese phrase "Osore irimashita"—"I am •overpowered with admiration"—in a shop, for example, than just to say "Too expensive" and turn away. Both make it clear that since the price is too high the speaker is not going to buy, but the Japanese way is undoubtedly more gracious!

INFORMALITY

Although American informality is well known, many interpret it as a "lack of respect" when they first encounter it, especially in the business world. The almost immediate use of •first names, for example, •jars on nerves long accustomed to deference or respect from men of lower rank.

Don't be surprised if Americans do not shake hands. They often just nod or smile instead. A casual "Hi" or "How are you doing?" or "Hello" often takes the place of a formal handshake, but it means the same thing. Nor will you find Americans circulating about a group in the office or at a party giving each one a personal farewell. Instead [...] they will just wave a cheery "good-by" or say something informal to the whole group such as "Well, see you tomorrow" or "So long everybody." Then they will disappear. No handshakes.

Often you will see men working at office desks in shirt-sleeves, sometimes without their ties. They may lean far back in their chairs and even put their feet on the radiator or desk while they talk on the telephone. This also is not meant to be rude. Once we get out of the tense, hurried city streets, we are an informal, relaxed people.

Our pace is total—either totally hurried, intense, work-absorbed, and competitive (in play as well as work); or else totally at ease, relaxed, •"undone," and informal, our feet up, our manner •breezy. We tend to swing between these extremes. This is the pendulum you need to understand if you are to understand America and its people.

ALISON RAYMOND LANIER, *Living in the U.S.A.*
3rd edition, 1978.
Publisher by OVERSEAS BRIEFING ASSOCIATES

• **blunt** : frank, outspoken, not trying to be polite, abrupt • **overpowered** : *accablé* • **first names** : *le prénom* • **jars on** : irritates • **"undone"** : "unbuttoned" • **breezy** : *dégagée*.

TOWARDS COMPREHENSION

1 ***Complete with words from the two texts:***

1. He doesn't like ceremony, he prefers . . . . 2. He was not very polite, you could even say he was . . . . 3. Their informality is sometimes mistaken for . . . . of respect. 4. I'm sorry if I sounded rude, I didn't . . . . to be rude to you. 5. He doesn't have much regard for the feelings of others, he is . . . . and tactless.

2 ***Replace the words in italics by words from the two texts having the same or nearly the same meaning:***

1. Don't *mistake* his behaviour *for* a lack of regard for the feelings of others.
2. The way he tries to imitate American speech *gets on* my nerves.
3. That is what you need to understand if you *want to* understand America.
4. He *said clearly* that he saw things differently.
5. *From the moment* he leaves his place of work, the American becomes a different man.
6. Your *abrupt* question may have hurt his feelings.

3 ***Show that the meaning of the following words and phrases becomes clearer if we look a little further down or further up:***

1. Our brevity (l. 4). 2. Our pace is total (l. 25). 3. We tend to swing between two extremes (l. 27).

FROM THE CONTEXT

LANGUAGE PRACTICE

HOW TO COMPARE
AS - LIKE

1. LIKE : introduit une comparaison entre deux éléments différents et s'emploie lorsque le 2e terme de la comparaison est un nom ou un pronom : they were behaving like children *(ils se conduisaient comme des enfants, en enfants)*, he is just like everybody else, don't talk like that, people like me have got to work a lot to earn their living.

2. AS :

a) s'emploie dans la comparaison de l'adjectif : (as . . . as, not as . . . as) : they work as hard as we do;

b) s'emploie dans une comparaison lorsque le 2e terme est un verbe, une proposition (dont le verbe est exprimé ou non) : don't do as I do, *mais :* don't do like me. Here it is not as in the U.S.A. *(on trouve* like *en américain et parfois en anglais).*

N.B. Ne pas confondre : He behaves like an American *(mais il n'en est pas un)* et As an American, I must tell you... *(en tant qu'Américain, je...*; le locuteur est Américain).

4 ***Drawing on the text, compare:***

In the U.S.A. they . . . ., we . . . .
Americans . . . ., Europeans . . . .

HOW TO EXPRESS DIFFERENCES

5 ***Connect the above sentences with:*** whereas, while.

Example: They say "Hi" whereas we Europeans shake hands.

6 ***Written work: re-cast the above sentences as follows:***

Americans differ from us in that . . . .
Unlike Americans, we . . . .

IN THAT
= in the sense that

7 ***Make up as many sentences as you can to show that appearances may be misleading. Use the following patterns:***

MISLEADING APPEARANCES
(= trompeuses)

He seems rude, but . . . .
He appears unsociable, but . . . .
He may sound a bit blunt, but . . . .
He's got an unpleasant way of . . . ., but . . . .

8 ***Now make your sentences a little longer:***

Judging from appearances, you might think he/they . . . . but when you get to know him/them better, you'll realize . . . .

9 ***Drawing on the text, make a few sentences on the following pattern:***

INSTEAD OF + GERUND

Instead of . . . . Americans (merely/just) . . . .

TOWARDS APPRECIATION

10 ***Judging from these texts, would you say that what is called the golden mean or the happy medium*** *(le juste milieu)* ***is something typically American?***

11 ***What do you think of formality, informality, etiquette, manners, familiarity, etc. Do they make social behaviour easier or more difficult?***

12 ***Creative written work: show that generalities about foreigners may be misleading.***
(It is often said that the English are . . . ./Germans are . . . ./the French are . . . . but . . . ./Although . . . . once you know them better . . . .)

13 ***Written translation:***
Translate from: *Although American informality...* down to: *No handshakes.*

IMPROVE YOUR VOCABULARY

In what way?
How do you mean?
What is meant by...?
Could you make your meaning clearer?
Would you mind explaining...?
} *(when you need more detailed information)*

Now, do I make myself clear?
I wish to make it clear that...
To put it bluntly, I'll say that... *(pour parler net, carrément...).*
To put it mildly, ... *(pour m'exprimer en termes modérés...).*
To put the matter another way, ... *(in other words).*

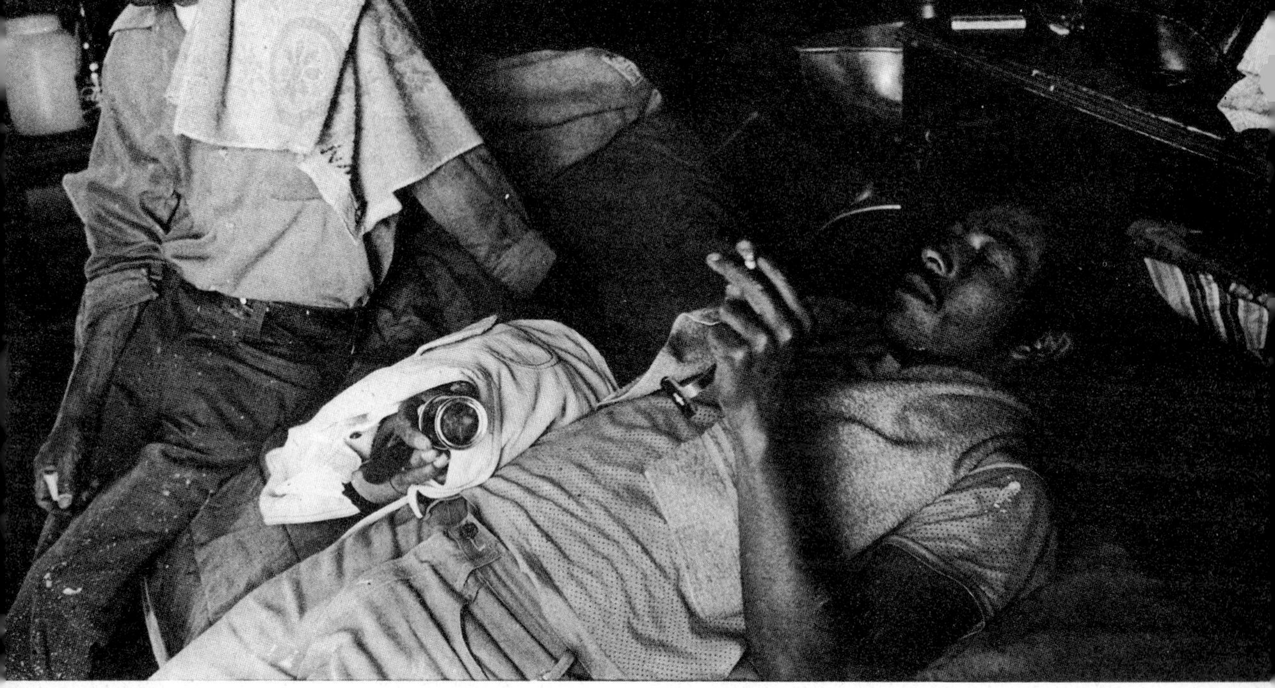

The American promise

Mind the stress :
On the first syllable : half a dozen smiles : [ˈhɑːfəˈdʌznˈsmailz], daughter [ˈdɔːtə], harvest [ˈhɑːvist], journey [ˈdʒəːni], creditors [ˈkreditəz], realized [ˈriəlaizd], people of great consequence [ˈpiːpl əv ˈgreit ˈkɔnsikwəns], figured [ˈfigəd], bargain [ˈbɑːgin], manage [ˈmænidʒ], passage [ˈpæsidʒ],
On the second : expected [ikˈspektid], exchange [iksˈtʃeindʒ], embarrassment [imˈbærəsmənt], estate [iˈsteit], adrift [əˈdrift], decided [diˈsaidid], suggested [səˈdʒestid], officials [əˈfiʃlz].

It was nearly a year and a half ago that Jurgis had met Ona, at a •horse-fair a hundred miles from home. Jurgis had never expected to get married—he had laughed at it as a foolish •trap for a man to walk into ; but here, without ever having spoken a word to her, with no more than the exchange of half a dozen smiles, he found himself, purple in the face with embarrassment and terror, asking her parents to sell her to him for his wife—and offering his father's two horses he had been sent to the fair to sell. But Ona's father proved as a rock—the girl was yet a child, and he was a rich man, and his daughter was not to be had in that way. So Jurgis went home with a heavy heart, and that spring and summer •toiled and tried hard to forget. In the •fall, after the •harvest was over, he saw that it would not do, and •tramped the full fortnight's journey that lay between him and Ona.

He found an unexpected state of affairs—for the girl's father had died, and his estate was •tied up with creditors ; Jurgis's heart leapt as he realized that now the prize was within his reach. There was Elzbieta Lukoszaite, Teta, or Aunt, as they called her, Ona's stepmother, and there were her six children, of all ages. There was also her brother Jonas, a dried-up little man who had worked upon the farm. They were people of great consequence, as it seemed to Jurgis, •fresh out of the woods ; Ona knew how to read, and knew many other things that he did not know ; and now the farm had been sold, and the whole family was •adrift—all they owned in the world being about seven hundred roubles, which is half as many dollars. They would have had three times that, but it had gone to court, and the judge had decided against them, and it had cost the •balance to get him to change his decision.

Ona might have married and left them, but she would not, for she loved Teta Elzbieta. It was Jonas who suggested that they all go to America, where a friend of his had gotten rich. He would work, for his part, and the women would work, and some of the children, doubtless—they would live somehow. Jurgis, too, had heard of America. That was a country where, they said, a man might earn three roubles a day ; and Jurgis •figured what three roubles a day would mean, with prices as they were where he lived, and decided •forthwith that he would go to America and marry, and be a rich man •in the bargain. In that country, rich or poor, a man was free, it was said; he did not have to go into the army, he did not have to pay out his money to •rascally officials—he might do as he pleased, and count himself as good as any other man. So America was a place of which lovers and young people dreamed. If one could only manage to get the price of a passage, he could count his troubles at an end.

UPTON SINCLAIR, *The Jungle*

Upton Sinclair (1878-1968) was born in Baltimore. He began writing at the age of 15 in order to pay his way through college. He wrote "The Jungle", from which this passage is taken, in 1906 after investigating conditions in the stockyards of Chicago, and it marks his conversion to socialism.

• **horse-fair:** *foire aux chevaux* • **trap:** *piège* • **toiled:** worked hard • **fall:** (Am.) autumn • **harvest:** *moisson* • **tramped:** walked • **tied up:** *(ses biens) étaient placés sous séquestre pour dettes* • **fresh out of the woods:** *qui arrivait tout droit de sa campagne* • **adrift:** *désemparée* • **balance:** the rest: i.e. 1,400 roubles • **figured:** imagined • **forthwith:** at once, immediately • **in the bargain:** *the usual phrase is:* into the bargain=in addition • **rascally officials:** dishonest civil servants *(fonctionnaires).*

TOWARDS COMPREHENSION

1 ***The 1st paragraph is mainly (chiefly, for the most part) about:***

— a father's love for his daughter?
— love at first sight?
— love of money?

2 ***Pick out the words and phrases justifying your answer.***

3 ***Express differently***
(you can use the prompts between brackets).

IN OTHER WORDS

1. Without ever having spoken a word to her. (he had never . . . .)
2. With no more than the exchange of half a dozen smiles. (they had only . . . .)
3. Purple in the face with embarrassment and terror. (he was so . . . .)
4. Ona's father proved as a rock. (Nothing could make him . . . .)
5. The girl was yet a child. (. . . . not yet . . . .)
6. His daughter was not to be had in that way (. . . . not the right way . . . . Jurgis would never . . . .)
7. He saw that it would not do. (He realized he could not . . . .)

4 ***Bring out the new elements to be found in the 2nd paragraph.***

5 ***Express the ideas differently*** *(in as many ways as you can).*

IN OTHER WORDS

1. He realized that now the prize was within his reach.
2. The whole family was adrift.

6 ***Find a title for the 3rd paragraph and justify your choice.***

7 ***3rd paragraph. Pick out all the words and phrases related to:***

a. money and money problems. b. freedom.

8 ***One adjective is used three times: which one?***

9 ***Test your memory: can you supply the end of the following sentences?***

1. It was nearly a year and a half ago that . . . .
2. He had laughed at it . . . .
3. But Ona's father proved as a rock . . . .
4. He found an unexpected state of affairs . . . .

5. It was Jonas who suggested . . . .
6. In that country . . . .
7. If one could only manage . . . .

10 ***Sum up each paragraph in one or two sentences.***

LANGUAGE PRACTICE

11 ***The following statements could be answers to questions. Imagine the questions*** *(there may be several solutions).*

Example : Jurgis met Ona a year and a half ago.
When/how long ago did Jurgis meet Ona?/How long have Jurgis and Ona known each other?

1. The horse-fair was a hundred miles away from home.
2. Jurgis had to walk to the horse-fair.
3. He walked there in order to sell two horses.
4. Jurgis wanted to marry Ona.
5. . . . . because she was too young.
6. In the fall, after the harvest was over, he realized he could not live without her.
7. The family had to sell the farm.
8. They had nowhere to go, so they decided to leave for America.
9. It was Jonas who suggested they all go to America.
10. If a man wants to make a fortune, he chooses America rather than Europe.

HOW TO SEEK INFORMATION

What, where, who, which, whose, why, what... for, how, how far, how long, how often...?

12 ***Make up a few sentences of your own beginning with :***

1. How far . . . . ?
2. How often . . . . ?
3. How long . . . . ?

PROPOSITION INFINITIVE

verbe + { nom / pr. pers. comp. } + to + b.v.

après les verbes exprimant une volonté, un souhait, un désir, un ordre, un conseil :
I don't want my daughter to go out with that boy. I'd prefer her to stay at home.

13 ***Drawing on the text, make as many sentences as you can beginning with :***

Ona's father didn't want . . . .
Jurgis didn't expect . . . .
Ona didn't want . . . .

14 ***Complete the following sentences :***

1. Ona's father refused to give Jurgis his daughter because she . . . .
2. He refused to give Jurgis his daughter because of . . . .
3. They decided to leave their country because they . . . .
4. They decided to leave their country because of . . . .
5. . . . ., that was why they left their country.
6. . . . ., that was why he went back again to Ona's place.
7. . . . ., that's why people still emigrate there.

HOW TO EXPRESS: REASON and CAUSE

— Because + clause *(proposition).*

— Because of + noun *(= à cause de, en raison de).*
I can't do it now because I'm too busy.
I didn't go out, because of the rain.

— That's why, that was why.
I've worked hard, that's why I'm tired.
He wanted to improve his English, that was why he left for Britain.

15 ***Complete the following sentences with clauses of purpose*** *(propositions de but) :*

1. Jurgis went to Ona's father's place . . . .
2. Jurgis worked hard all through the summer . . . .
3. They decided to leave for America . . . .
4. In America, they would all work very hard . . . .

HOW TO EXPRESS PURPOSE *(= le but)*

— to, so as to, so as not to
in order (not) to *lorsque le sujet est le même dans la principale et dans la subordonnée.*

— so that, so that... not
in order that, in order that... not *lorsque le sujet de la principale n'est pas le même que celui de la subordonnée.*
He went to Britain to/so as to/in order to improve his English.
He sent his son to Britain so that he should/might/could improve his English.

16 ***Fill in the gaps with*** must ***or*** have to ***in the correct tense :***

1. Jonas . . . . work hard in the summer, if he wants to have a good crop.
2. Jurgis . . . . walk all the way to the horse-fair, because there was no other way to go there.
3. They . . . . go to court, although they were very reluctant to do so.
4. Even children . . . . work in America if the family wants to make plenty of money.
5. In America, Jurgis . . . . go into the Army.
6. If they were in America, they . . . . give their money to rascally officials.
7. When Jurgis arrives in America, he . . . . find a job.
8. He . . . . buy a new house, but he hasn't made up his mind yet.

HOW TO EXPRESS OBLIGATION and ABSENCE OF OBLIGATION
must - have to

On utilise **have to** lorsque les temps font défaut à **must** : You'll have to learn all this *(il faudra que vous appreniez...).*

Au présent, on trouve les 2 formes. Elles ne sont toutefois pas toujours équivalentes : **must** implique que l'autorité de celui qui parle est en jeu : You must be back by 7. *(moi je dis que tu dois être de retour pour 7 heures, moi je veux que..., c'est un ordre).*

N.B. L'absence d'obligation ne s'exprime pas par **must not,** qui a valeur d'interdiction ou de vigoureux conseil, mais par : **don't have to.**

You don't have to go if you don't want to.

If you were British, you wouldn't have to do your military service.

HOW TO EXPRESS:
WILLINGNESS, INTENTION, INSISTENCE and THEIR OPPOSITES

I'm quite willing to .... (= *je veux bien, je ne demande pas mieux que de ....*)
He willingly/readily ....
I'm going to ....
I intend to ....
I'm determined to ....
He is eager to .... / anxious to .... } (=strongly desirous)

He is unwilling to ....
I won't ....
He would not ....
I've got no intention whatever of ....
He is reluctant to ....
He refused to ....

17 ***Using verbs or phrases from the box, express the opposite:***

1. Before meeting Ona, Jurgis was eager to get married.
2. Ona's father readily consented to sell him his daughter.
3. The family was willing to sell the farm.
4. The judge was eager to help them.
5. They were all reluctant to go to America.
6. They were determined not to forget their native country.

TOWARDS APPRECIATION

18 ***Imagine the young man's feelings:***

a. when he asked her parents to sell her to him,
b. when the father refused,
c. in the fall (autumn),
d. when he learned the father had died,
e. when he met all the members of the family ("people of great consequence"),
f. when all of them considered emigrating to the United States.

19 ***The American Dream.***

To Jurgis, leaving for America meant ....
He/they will have to ....
If he/they wanted to ...., it was in the hope of ....
He naïvely thought that ....

20 ***Written work: Jonas meets another immigrant in the street in New York City. Imagine what the man may tell him.***

Immigrant: ....?
Jonas: We are from Lithuania.
I.: ....?
J.: We came here in order to make money.
I.: ....?
J.: We are determined to set off for Chicago as soon as we can.
I.: ....?
J.: No, no relatives, but a friend of mine lives here.
I.: ....
J.: Yes, I know, my friend told me we had to be very wary (cautious, careful) in New York City. How about Chicago, is it as bad?
I.: ....
J.: That's why I want to go there. I'm eager to get my first pay in dollars.

21 ***Describe—either orally or in writing—what it feels like/how it feels to be an immigrant.***

a. what you had or have to endure?
b. the reason(s) why you leave your country and what you expect,
c. what you might be faced with.

22 ***Written translation:*** the last paragraph.

IMPROVE YOUR VOCABULARY

The great waves of immigration from Europe.
An immigrant, a settler.
They are considering settling in America/emigrating to America/expatriating themselves to .... (= *ils envisagent de ....*).
They will have to adapt themselves to a new climate, to adjust themselves to new living conditions. [ə'dʒʌst]
Uprooted: *déraciné*.
He hopes (that) they will ....
He has good hope (that) they will ....
His hopes may be disappointed. [,disə'pɔintid]
He has great expectations.
They stand to lose nothing ....
They stand to gain a lot ....
Credulous, credulity. Naïve, naïvely, naïvety. ['kredjuləs, kri'dju:liti. nɑ:'i:v]
He is under an illusion.
They will soon be disillusioned.

Tycoon or tyrant?

Tycoon [tai'ku:n], tyrant ['taiərnt], idealistic [ai,diə'listik], high moral standards ['hai'mɔrl 'stændədz] degenerate [di'dʒenərət], tremendous ability [tri'mendəs ə'biliti], indecisions [,indi'siʒnz], defects ['di:fekts], [di'fekts], assets ['æsets], he was obviously referring [,hiwəz 'ɔbviəsli ri'fə:riŋ], perquisites ['pə:kwizits], excesses [ik'sesiz], Lithuania [,liθju'einjə], tenement ['tenəmənt], promises ['prɔmisiz], winds up ['waindz'ʌp], determination [di,tə:mi'neiʃn], junkyard ['dʒʌŋkjɑ:d], courage ['kʌridʒ], succeeds [sək'si:dz], success [sək'ses], possessed [pə'zest], dominate ['dɔmineit], entertains [,entə'teinz], phenomenon [fi'nɔminən], emperor ['empərə], abuse (noun) [ə'bjus], tough [tʌf], recognize ['rekəgnaiz].

Dave, a young director, has come to Hollywood from New York to work for Harry P. Koenig, President of Magna Pictures and head of the world's largest studio. Grobe is a former professor of English literature now working for H.P. Koenig.

•"Lochinvar, you're a little too young and too idealistic to understand now. But if you stay around •this town long enough you will. Let me say only that •H.P. is a terrible person. And a marvelous man. He is a man of high moral standards. And a degenerate. He is a man of tremendous ability. And no talent. He is a man of great power. And of equally great conflicts and indecisions.

"What I am saying is that H.P. is a giant; his defects are as great as his •assets." Grobe got up and began to •pace. [...] "It's the job itself that keeps me here. That's what makes me •put up with H.P.'s rages and excesses." He paused and turned directly to Dave.

"If I didn't sense something in you, I wouldn't bother to talk to you like this. To understand this town, first you have to understand H.P. Koenig. You have to know where he came from and what he is. A young boy of eight comes to America from a small town in Lithuania and can't speak a word of English. He goes to live in a •tenement in the slums, and his mother and father both have to work to keep the family alive. At the age of ten he promises his mother that he'll make money for her, more money than the President of the United States!"

Grobe smiled. "Which mother hasn't heard some such •boast from her son? But which son •winds up making ten times what the President makes? You want to know what determination is, Dave? At the age of fourteen he owned his own •junkyard, his own horse and wagon. At the age of seventeen he owned three junkyards. Now, you want to know what •gambler's courage is? At the age of nineteen he sells it all to open a little movie theater on the East Side of New York. And of course he succeeds. But in him success only feeds ambition.

"At the age of twenty-seven he leaves his wife and two young children and goes West to make his own pictures. Once he gets here, he discovers this is the place he's searched for all his life.

"The first picture he ever made, he wrote the script himself. [...]

From the beginning he was possessed by this need to dominate people, to own them, to force them to his will. You can hate him for it, or admire him, or envy him. You can fight him or submit to him. But the one thing you can't do is deny that he built the studio that •entertains more people the world over than any man in history!"

Albert Grobe dropped into a chair. "I think of him as an institution. A phenomenon. Whatever it's done to him, to his wife, to his daughters, he has built himself a kingdom. He is an emperor who controls the finest actors, the greatest writers, the most talented directors and musicians. They •stand all kinds of •abuse from him. But in the end, even those who hate him respect him.

"How do you •contend with a man like that? You accept him. That •tough little junk dealer rules the world we live in, Dave. Accept it. And do the best you can at the same time. Because he'll recognize it. One thing that man knows, Dave: quality. Give it to him and you'll get along with him."

H. DENKER, *The Starmaker*, 1977.

Henry Denker is a Broadway play producer, and stage, screen, radio and television writer.

● **Tycoon** : magnate, wealthy and powerful businessman ● **Lochinvar** : romantic young hero ● **this town** : Hollywood ● **H.P.** : Harry P. Koenig ● **assets** : valuable qualities ● **to pace** : to walk with slow steps ● **put up with** : tolerate ● **tenement** : *(taudis)* ● **boast** : *Quelle mère n'a pas entendu son fils se vanter ainsi?* ● **winds up** : ends up ● **junkyard** : *dépotoir (de ferraille, etc.)* ● **gambler** : a man who plays games of chance for money ● **entertains** : provides amusement ● **stand** : endure, put up with ● **abuse** : insults ● **contend with** : struggle with ● **tough** : *tenace.*

TOWARDS COMPREHENSION

1 ***After listening to a recording of the text, or reading it carefully, choose the right answers and justify your choices:***

1. This passage is about
   a) the cinema in Hollywood.
   b) H.P. Koenig's career.
   c) the difficulties that immigrants encounter.
2. Grobe says all this to Dave because
   a) they have known each other for a long time.
   b) H.P. Koenig asked him to do so.
   c) he feels that Dave has a strong personality.
3. Grobe's purpose is
   a) to prevent Dave from making mistakes in Hollywood.
   b) to help him to succeed in the world of the cinema.
   c) to persuade him to accept H.P. as he is.

2 ***Test your memory. Finish the following sentences:***

1. Lochinvar, you're a little too young . . . .
2. What I am saying is that H.P. . . . .
3. If I didn't sense something in you, ...
4. To understand this town, ...
5. A young boy of eight . . . .
6. At the age of ten . . . .
7. At the age of fourteen . . . .

8. At the age of twenty-seven . . . .
9. From the beginning he was possessed . . . .
10. But the one thing you can't do . . . .

LANGUAGE PRACTICE

3 ***This text provides a great deal of information about H.P.'s life, past and present. Ask the corresponding questions:***
Example : Where was he from?

HOW TO SEEK INFORMATION
(comment interroger)
Voir p. 17

DISCOURS INDIRECT

Lorsqu'on rapporte les paroles de quelqu'un, on utilise le **discours indirect,** ou **style indirect** (indirect/reported speech). He told me (that) I was wrong. La proposition introductive (he told me, he said, he asked...) peut être sous-entendue. On parle alors de **style indirect libre.** She told him (that) he would never succeed. He didn't work enough. La seconde phrase est au style indirect libre.
Discours direct et **discours indirect** demandent souvent l'emploi des verbes **say** et **tell.** Il faut savoir bien les manier.
Say peut s'employer au discours direct et au discours indirect. Il peut s'employer avec ou sans complément au discours direct, mais seulement sans complément au discours indirect. S'il y a complément, **say** doit être suivi de la préposition **to.** Ex. : "I'm busy", he said, or : he said to me. He said he was busy, *mais :* he told me he was busy.
Tell peut être employé au discours direct ou indirect. Il est surtout employé au discours indirect, et obligatoirement lorsqu'il y a un complément, lequel suit le verbe sans préposition. He told me (that) he would come. C'est **tell** qui s'emploie lorsqu'on fait état d'un ordre donné par une tierce personne : he told us to keep quiet. Au style direct, on aurait l'impératif.
Le passage du discours direct au discours indirect impose certaines modifications, notamment dans les temps.

1) Énoncés déclaratifs : lorsque le verbe qui introduit l'énoncé (say, tell, remark...) est au présent — ce qui est rare — au parfait (present perfect) ou au futur, aucun changement de temps ne se produit au discours indirect :
"I'm hungry", he will say. ⟶ He will say (that) he is hungry.
"I know him", she has (just) said. ⟶ She has (just) said (that) she knows him.
Lorsque le verbe qui introduit l'énoncé est au passé, ce qui est le cas le plus fréquent, les changements suivants se produisent.

a. Temps des paroles du discours direct :	**Temps du verbe rapportant ces paroles :**
présent simple	passé
présent progressif	passé progressif
passé (simple past)	pluperfect
passé progressif	passé progressif
parfait	pluperfect
parfait progressif	pluperfect progressif
futur	conditionnel

Exemples :

She said, "I'm happy."	She said (that) she was happy.
She said, "I'm writing a letter."	She said (that) she was writing a letter.
She said, "he didn't come."	She said (that) he hadn't come.
She said, "I was living in London at that time."	She said (that) she was living in London at that time.
She said, "I've already done it."	She said (that) she'd already done it.
She said, "I've been waiting for him for 2 hours."	She said (that) she had been waiting for him for 2 hours.
She said, "I'll be twenty in November."	She said (that) she would be twenty in November.

b. Pronoms personnels :

"I'm twenty," she said to me.	She told me she was twenty.
«I've brought you a book," she said to him.	She told him she had brought him a book.
"We're going to help you," they said to her.	They told her they were going to help her.
etc.	

c. Compléments de temps :
yesterday devient *the day before, last week* devient *the previous week*, etc.

2) Questions :

Les mêmes changements de temps se produisent. De plus :

a. il n'y a plus de point d'interrogation.
b. la construction interrogative du verbe devient une construction de type affirmatif.
c. le verbe qui introduit la question doit devenir un verbe de sens interrogatif.
"Where did you buy your dress?" she said to my sister. She asked my sister where she had bought her dress.
d. si la question est une "yes or no question," il faut introduire **if** ou **whether.**
"Do you like tea?" he asked me. He asked me if (ou whether) I liked tea.

3) Ordres :

Outre les changements déjà mentionnés, on note :

a. L'emploi d'un verbe exprimant ordre ou requête.
"Show me your book," he said to me. He asked me (he ordered me, he told me) to show him my book.
"Please, lend me your dictionary." He asked me to lend him my dictionary.
(**N.B.** *Please* disparaît au style indirect.)
b. Lorsqu'il s'agit d'une défense, le verbe se met à l'infinitif négatif.
"Don't park here." He asked me (he told me, he ordered me) not to park there.

4 *Turn into reported speech :*

1. "You're a little too young and too idealistic", he said to Dave.
2. He added : "You can't understand now".
3. He said to Dave : "You will understand later".
4. "If you stay around this town long enough you will understand", he said.
5. "Bear in mind that H.P. is a marvelous man", he said to him.
6. "Never forget that H.P. is a man of high moral standards", he said to Dave.
7. "I must add that he is also a degenerate", he said.
8. He said to Dave : "If I didn't sense something in you, I wouldn't bother to talk to you like this."
9. "Do you know what he promised his mother", he asked Dave.
10. "Have you ever seen a man like him", he said to me.

5 ***Compare :***

He is wilful, he is hesitant.
He is wilful, but he is also hesitant.
He is wilful, and yet he is hesitant.
He is wilful, however he is hesitant too.
He may be wilful, but he is also/equally hesitant.
(Al)though he is wilful, he is (also/equally) hesitant.
He is both wilful and hesitant.
He is wilful and hesitant as well.
Strange as it may seem, he is both wilful and hesitant.
On the one hand he is wilful, on the other he is hesitant.

Using the above patterns, make up as many sentences as you can from the table below :

He is a terrible person He is a man of high moral standards He is a man of tremendous ability He is a man of great power People hate him People envy him	they admire him. he has no talent. he is a marvelous man. he is a degenerate. he can be hesitant. they respect him.

HOW TO EXPRESS CONTRAST and ADDITION

6 ***Compare :***

That's what makes me put up with H.P.'s rages and excesses.
That's why I put up with H.P.'s rages and excesses.

Give the other construction :

1. That's why people both hate and admire him.
2. That's why people put up with his tyranny.
3. That's what makes me endure his authoritarianism.
4. That's why people stand all kinds of abuse from him.
5. That's what makes so many people fawn on him (= flatter him in a servile way).

Imagine other sentences on the same patterns.

HOW TO EXPRESS REASON

Voir p. 18

MAKE + BV

On notera qu'à la forme active, **make** est suivi de **l'inf. sans to** (base verbale).

7 ***Using the patterns from the box, below imagine what H.P. may have thought when he lived in a tenement in the slums, then when he owned his own junkyard, and what he may think now that he has reached the top.***

I .... and yet I wish I { had .... / was .... / could ....

(N.B. *On notera que le verbe* wish *est suivi du verbe au preterit. Ce preterit n'exprime pas un fait passé, mais un souhait. Il a valeur d'irréel, on l'appelle preterit modal.*)

HOW TO EXPRESS COMPARISON

Twice, Three times
Four times
\+ { as + *adj.* / as much / this amount

I wish I was/were twice as rich as I am.

I wish I earned three times as much.

"Trying to make the presidency work these days is like trying to sew buttons on a custard pie."

8 ***Connect the following pairs as in the example below:***

Example: He is successful/his will to succeed is strong.
The more successful he is, the stronger his will to succeed (is).

1. He becomes rich/he wants to become rich.
2. He is powerful/he is happy.
3. He makes money/he feels powerful.
4. He makes people work/they admire him.
5. You argue with him/he respects you.
6. You stand up to him (=resist him)/he esteems you.
7. He tyrannizes over people/he feels powerful.

THE + COMP. ....
THE + COMP.
plus ... plus
The more he works,
the happier he feels.

9 ***Imagine Dave's thoughts as he listened to Grobe.***

The more I listen to him, the more I feel ....
If he thinks he's going to make me ....

10 ***Paragraph writing.***

Expand into a paragraph of about ten lines: *"But in him success only feeds ambition."*
Try and use the above pattern.

11 ***Creative written work*** (about 15 lines):

H. P. is a self-made man. What are the good qualities required in order to succeed when you begin life without money, education or influence?
(You've got to be .... it takes courage/determination/unflagging energy/perseverance .... you can't .... unless you ....)

SPOTLIGHT ON...

the immobile society

Immobile [i'məubail; U.S.:i'məubl], phenomenon [fi'nɔminən], mobile ['məubail. U.S.:'məubl], recreational facilities [,rekri'eiʃənl fə'silitiz], analysts ['ænəlists], executive transfer [ig'zekjutiv 'trænsfə:], initials [i'niʃlz].

Is America settling down in middle age?

• Alexis de Tocqueville was struck by the phenomenon during his nine-month visit to America in 1831. In the U.S., he wrote, a man "settles in a place, which he soon afterwards leaves to carry his changeable •longings elsewhere." In the intervening years, Americans have •lived up to their reputation as the most mobile people in the world, •tearing up roots and moving—across the nation or across town—at the slightest prospect of a better life. The average American family changes its residence every five or six years, much more frequently than the average European household. Now, however, there are signs that the great national •game of musical houses is slowing down. Since 1970, reports the Census Bureau, the percentage of Americans who move each year has dropped from 19.1% to 17.7%, the lowest rate in more than a generation. Says the bureau's Larry Long: "As incomes rise in the U.S., more people are unwilling to give up the place, climate and recreational facilities they like, simply for more money."

Some analysts attribute the trend to a housewives' revolt against •executive transfer. Michael Russell, a United Van Lines agent in Los Angeles, reports a spreading phenomenon: when the •van rolls up to a house to move a family, the wife abruptly announces she has changed her mind and will not go. Says Rosie Montgomery, a counselor at the Women's Center in Dallas: "Women always thought of going along as a wifely duty. Now they are saying, 'Wait a minute; it's my life too, and my children's lives.' "

Other possible explanations for the shift:

• Middle-class Americans are now more concerned with the quality of life, less determined to get ahead by moving to new jobs and new towns.

• The •corporate shift from the older industrial cities of the Northeast to the Sunbelt has spread employment more evenly around the country. White migration from South to North has •slowed to a trickle, and black migration has stopped entirely: since 1970 as many blacks have moved to the South as from the South.

• The trend to smaller families is eliminating one need for moving—a larger house.

TIME, *November 28, 1977*

Mobile society puts down roots

Young executives—and their families—resist the nomadic life

American executives are becoming increasingly interested in things money cannot buy, notably a stable home life, a safe environment, a wholesome community, sun, fun and culture. For example, Mark Burns, 42, a fast-rising IBM executive in Chicago, turned down three transfers in order to raise his three children in one place. But Burns is aware that his refusals limited his possibilities at IBM, whose initials, many employees joke, stand for I've Been Moved. Hence, Burns came to the conclusion he must switch careers and now is president of a small bank on Chicago's South Side.

TIME, *June 12, 1978*

• **Alexis de Tocqueville**: a French historian and politician who wrote "On American Democracy" • **longings**: aspirations • **have lived up to their reputation**: have acted in a typical manner • **tearing up roots** : leaving places and people that they are attached to • **the great national game of musical houses** : an allusion to the children's game of 'musical chairs' in which there is one chair fewer than the number of players. Each time the music stops, the players sit down and the one left without a seat is eliminated • **executive transfer** : *mutation des cadres* • **van** : *camion de déménagement* • **corporate shift** : the fact that the big firms (corporations) are moving to the South • **has slowed to a trickle** : has been reduced to a very small number of people.

1 ***Sum up in two sentences what this text is about.***

2 ***Pick out the five most significant words or phrases.***

3 ***Using the information given in the text, make as many sentences as you can beginning with:***

American executives are becoming less and less willing to . . . .
They are more and more reluctant to . . . .
Until a few years ago . . . . but since 1970 . . . .
More and more Americans are beginning to realize that . . . .
They are increasingly interested in . . . . and less and less concerned with . . . .
More and more women . . . .
The reasons for this change aren't hard to find . . . .

4 ***Express more clearly and expand the following ideas:***

Is America settling down in middle age?
At the slightest prospect of a better life.
Women always thought of going along as a wifely duty.
Middle-class Americans are now concerned with the quality of life.

5 ***Until quite recently the Americans were often depicted as a people on the move. How could such mobility be accounted for** (explained).?*

(The quest for opportunity . . . . the fear of being trapped . . . . the American Dream . . . .)

6 ***What other scheme of values** (échelle des valeurs) **seems to be emerging?***

7 ***What are your views on the two schemes? If you were offered a job abroad, would you accept it? Why?***

Extract from: The lonely lady

On the first syllable : perfume [ˈpəːfjuːm], echoed [ˈekəud], communist [ˈkɔmjunist], challenged [ˈtʃæləndʒd], client [ˈklaiənt], liquor [ˈlikə], Senator McCarthy [ˈsenətə məˈkɑːθi].
On the second : reproachfully [riˈprəutʃfuli], imagine [iˈmædʒin], apparent [əˈpærnt], committee [kəˈmiti], considered [kənˈsidəd], absorb [əbˈsɔːb], idea [aiˈdiə], maintain [meinˈtein], ability [əˈbiliti], divorce [diˈvɔːs].
Secondary stress on the first syllabe, main stress on the third : disapproval [ˌdisəˈpruːvəl], inconvenient [ˌinkənˈviːniənt], interrupted [ˌintəˈrʌptid].

John Randall looked over the top of his *New York Times* as his daughter came to the breakfast table. She came quickly around the table and kissed him on the cheek. He caught a quick scent of perfume as she went to her chair [...]

"Good morning, Daddy" [...]

"Something must be happening," he said.

She looked at him over the bottle of milk she was pouring on her cornflakes. "What, Daddy?"

"I said something's going on."

"Nothing special."

"Come on now," he said gently. "Has a new boy come into the class?"

She laughed, shaking her head. "Nothing like that."

"Still Bernie?"

She blushed but didn't answer.

"There has to be something."

"Daddy," she said reproachfully, "why does it always have to be a boy?"

"Because you're a girl."

"It's nothing like that," she said. "But I did meet someone yesterday. On the bus."

"On the bus?" he echoed, puzzled.

She nodded. "He sat down yesterday right next to me. Imagine that, Daddy? For three months he's been sitting next to me and I never knew who he was."

"He?" Now he was really puzzled. "Who?"

"Walter Thornton," she said. "I always thought he was only here for the summer. I never knew he lived here all the time."

"Walter Thornton?" he asked, a note of disapproval in his voice.

"Yes. America's greatest writer."

The disapproval in his voice became more apparent. "But he's a communist."

"Who said so?" she challenged.

•"Senator McCarthy, more than two years ago. •He took the fifth before the committee. And everybody knows what that means. When the news came out, the bank seriously considered asking him to take his business somewhere else."

"Why didn't you?"

"I don't know," he answered. "We felt sorry for him, I guess. After all, we are the only bank in town and it would be inconvenient to make him go out of town."

JeriLee had heard enough talk about the banking business to absorb an idea of how it was run. "Did he maintain heavy balances?" she asked •shrewdly.

He •flushed. She had put her finger on it. When all was said and done, the man probably had greater cash balances than any other client of the bank. The weekly •income was fantastic. "Yes," he admitted.

Having made her point, she was silent.

He stared at her. She was not like other girls or even other women he had known. Certainly her mother did not have the same ability to •cut through to the bone the way she did. In many ways she seemed to think like a man. Still there was nothing about her that was not female.

"What's he like?" he asked curiously.

"What's who like?" Veronica asked, bringing the eggs and bacon from the kitchen.

"Walter Thornton. JeriLee met him on the bus yesterday."

"Oh him? I read in the papers he's going through a divorce." [...]

Veronica turned to her daughter. "What is he like?" she asked. "Mr. Smith at the market says that whenever Mrs. Thornton came in she smelled of •liquor. At times he even suspected she might be drunk. They all felt sorry for him."

JeriLee shrugged her shoulders. "He seems very nice. Quiet. You wouldn't think he is who he is."

"Did you tell him you wanted to be a writer?" her mother asked.

JeriLee nodded.

"What did he say?"

"He thought it was nice. He was very polite."

"Maybe he will look at some of your things. He could give you advice."

"Oh, Mother!" JeriLee exclaimed. "A man like that wouldn't bother reading the work of a schoolkid."

"I don't know, you never-"

"I don't think she should trouble him," John interrupted. "JeriLee's right. The man is a professional. It would be very unfair to ask him. He's probably got more important things to worry about."

"But-" Veronica began.

Again he interrupted. "Besides he's not exactly the kind of person JeriLee should be associated with. He's very •different than us. He has different standards. Everyone knows that communists have very loose morals."

"He's a communist?" Veronica asked.

John nodded. "Mr. Carson says that the bank has to be very careful in our •dealings with him. We don't want anyone to get the wrong ideas about us."

Mr. Carson was president of the bank, the leading Republican and the most important man in Port Clare. For the past twenty years he had personally selected the mayor of the town, although he was too modest to want the office for himself.

Veronica was impressed. "Well, if Mr. Carson thinks so-"

"I think that's unfair!" JeriLee burst out. "There are many people who think that Senator McCarthy was worse than the communists."

"Senator McCarthy is a real American. He was the only one standing between us and the communists. The way Truman was acting, we were lucky we didn't give the whole country away." John's voice was positive.

"Your father is right, dear," Veronica said. "The less you have to do with him the better." Suddenly JeriLee found herself near tears. "I'm not doing anything with him,

Mother. He just sits in the seat next to me on the bus."

"That's all right, JeriLee." Her mother's voice was soothing. "Just be careful you don't let people see you talking too much to him."

HAROLD ROBBINS, *The Lonely Lady*

● **Senator McCarthy**: see A.B.C. ● **He took the fifth before the committee**: see A.B.C. ● **shrewdly** [ˈʃru:dli] : penetratingly ● **flushed** : became red in the face ● **income** : *revenu, rentrées d'argent* ● **to cut through to the bone** : *aller droit à l'essentiel* ● **liquor** : spirits such as whisky, gin, etc. ● **He's very different than us** : in good English you should say : different from... ● **dealings** : business relations.

TOWARDS COMPREHENSION

1 *Fill in the blanks with the verbs given below:*

(blush, consider, give away, go on, nod, stare at, worry about).

1. He didn't say anything, he just . . . . to show that he agreed.
2. He is so shy that he . . . . whenever a girl speaks to him.
3. How can you expect the rich to . . . . their money and property to the poor?
4. It's very rude to . . . . people.
5. She'll never be happy, she . . . . the slightest thing.
6. How can you know what's . . . . in the world if you never read the papers?
7. Our house is too small, we are . . . . buying a larger one.
8. He was . . . . by one of his accomplices.
9. Is it true that he's . . . . leaving the communist party?

2 *Choose the nearest equivalents to the words, phrases or sentences in italics:*

1. He echoed, *puzzled* (l. 18)
   a) angry *b*) perplexed *c*) interested.
2. *Did he maintain heavy balances?* (l. 35)
   a) Were the sums of money he deposited in the bank large?
   b) Was he a very important man?
   c) Was he the bank's best client?
3. *Having made her point,* she was silent. (l. 39)
   a) Having said what she had to say . . . .
   b) Having proved that what she said was true . . . .
   c) Her argument being accepted . . . .
4. *He has different standards.* (l. 66)
   a) His moral values and principles are different from ours.
   b) He is in favour of revolution.
   c) He is against social conventions.
5. *Communists have very loose morals.* (l. 67)
   a) They are easily discouraged.
   b) They are immoral.
   c) They are not courageous.

3 *Are you sure you understand the details and the ideas? Say why:*

1. She nodded. (l. 19)
2. The writer says: "she challenged". (l. 27)
3. The writer says: "she asked shrewdly". (l. 35)
4. He flushed. (l. 36)
5. She shrugged her shoulders. (l. 51)

(Ex.: she nodded to indicate that it was on the bus that she had met Mr Thornton.)

4 ***In a nutshell.***
Fill in the blanks without looking at the text:

John Randall realizes that . . . . but he is wrong in thinking that . . . . If she is excited, it is because . . . . but her parents disapprove of her . . . . because . . . . and they'd rather she . . . .

5 ***Pick out all the words and phrases showing that JeriLee disagrees with her parents.***

LANGUAGE PRACTICE

6 ***Imagine all that Mr and Mrs Randall could say to their daughter:***

A banker's daughter should (not) . . . .

A banker's daughter should be careful who she . . . . / where she . . . . / how she . . . .

A banker's daughter is supposed to . . . .

7 ***Now imagine what JeriLee could retort:***

Who said that a banker's daughter . . . .
I'd like to know why a banker's daughter . . . .
Why shouldn't a banker's daughter . . . .

8 ***To express their disapproval, Mr and Mrs Randall could also have said:***

We don't want you to . . . .
Or: We'd rather you didn't . . . .

Using the above constructions, imagine what they could say.

SHOULD

(à toutes les personnes) peut exprimer une obligation à laquelle, souvent, on se soustrait, d'où son sens conditionnel, d'où également sa valeur de conseil.
You shouldn't go out with that man (= *vous ne devriez pas sortir...*)
You should be more careful (about) what you say (= *vous devriez faire plus attention à ce que...*).

PROPOSITION INFINITIVE

Voir p. 17

HOW TO EXPRESS PREFERENCE

On peut employer :
had rather.
would rather

Ils sont équivalents, mais c'est **would rather** qui est employé à l'interrogation :
Would you rather stay at home? *(Aimeriez-vous mieux rester...).*
Lorsque le sujet de **had rather/would rather** n'est pas le même que celui de la proposition qui suit, on emploie le preterit modal :
She'd rather you didn't tell her father about it *(elle aimerait autant que vous n'en parliez pas à...).*

TOWARDS APPRECIATION

9 ***What could be said in defence of the parents?***

(They're afraid their daughter may . . . . they don't want . . . . it's understandable (up to a point) if we bear in mind that . . . .)

10 ***Perhaps they made some mistakes.***

(They should (not) have . . . .)

11 ***The case for, the case against McCarthyism: what could be said in favour of, then against McCarthy*** (oral or written work).

(In defence of McCarthy, it could be said that .... I'll say that ....
Thanks to him .... he saved them/us from .... He put a stop to ....
But for him (=if he had not done what he did) ....

I'm dead against witch-hunting because .... it paves the way for ....
As a democrat I can't .... He was a dangerous enemy of civil rights .... the international image of the nation .... He appealed to people's baser instincts ....)

12 ***Written work:***

JeriLee keeps a diary *(tient un journal)*. Imagine what she may have written after this conversation with her parents.

13 ***Could you suggest a title for this passage?***

IMPROVE YOUR VOCABULARY

1. He has no morals.
   He has loose morals.
   He is a man of loose morals.
   He does not lead a moral life.

2. He is a conformist.
   She is a nonconformist.
   Her nonconformity to the established rules (her refusal to conform to ....).
   She doesn't care what people say.
   They are very sensitive to gossip.
   You'll get yourself talked about.

3. I have a right to ....
   You have no right to ....
   By what right do you ....?

4. Children and parents sometimes find it hard to communicate and to understand each other: it is called the generation gap.

Barter

● **Barter**
Life has loveliness to sell-
   All beautiful and splendid things,
Blue waves whitened on a •cliff,
   Climbing fire that •sways and sings,
And children's faces looking up
Holding wonder like a cup.
Life has loveliness to sell-
   Music like a curve of gold,
•Scent of pine trees in the rain,
   Eyes that love you, arms that hold,
And for your spirit's •still delight,
Holy thoughts that star the night.
Spend all you have for loveliness,
   Buy it and never count the cost,
For one white singing hour of peace
   Count many a year of •strife well lost,
And for a breath of ecstasy
Give all you have been or could be.

SARA TEASDALE, "Barter" from *Love Songs* by Sara Teasdale. Reprinted by permission of The Macmillan Company, publishers

Sara Teasdale (1884-1933) was born in St Louis. She wrote several volumes of lyric poetry.

● **barter**: exchange ● **cliff**: *falaise* ● **sways**: *ondule* ● **scent**: perfume ● **still**: quiet ● **strife**: combat.

1 ***What different sorts of loveliness does Sara Teasdale value?***
2 ***Do you agree with her conclusion? Are the things she enumerates really worth sacrifice?***

HARDWARE
LOCKSMITH
PAINTS

Diary of a Harlem schoolteacher

Lively ['laivli], energetic [,enə'dʒetik], pronounced [prə'naunst], psychologist [sai'kɔlədʒist], retarded [ri'tɑ:did], area ['ɛəriə], combed [kəumd], laughter ['lɑ:ftə], Thailand ['tailænd], pronunciation [prə,nʌnsi'eiʃən], communicate [kə'mju:nikeit], address [ə'dres], refer [ri'fə:], emergency [i'mə:dʒənsi], operator ['ɔpəreitə], deprivation [,depri'veiʃən], substantial [səb'stænʃəl].

Joe is a lively, energetic youngster with a pronounced speech defect. From the psychologist's report and my teaching experience with him, he is retarded. [...]

The boy has never known his real father. He has lived with his mother in many different one-room flats in the same area, attending the same school. His mother does day work downtown ; she is illiterate and in poor physical health, and recently had to have all her teeth pulled. She does her best to keep Joe neat and clean, and he does have a few extra cents to spend on himself.

He is proud on Fridays when he gets the chance to wear his white shirt to •assembly. On these days he is all shiny and new looking and does not play with the other boys for fear they will get his shirt dirty. If they touch him he brushes himself and •frowns.

Joe has a •humped-over, old-man walk which he is unable to correct. He moves •in long strides, swinging his arms wildly, when he is in a hurry. When I remind him that he has not combed his hair he tells his mother that he needs a haircut, even if he has had one the week before. He seems more eager to get his hair cut than to comb it. He has been going to a female barber, whose name he doesn't know, for a year or more.

His •over-all behavior within the class situation is good, even though he has great difficulty in expressing himself. This sometimes evokes laughter from the other children. When I ask him, "Joe, what did you like about the story I read, or didn't you like it?" he seems very •confused, as if he is having trouble understanding plain English. His mother also has a speech defect but he seems able to understand her. To a phrase like "Say finger, Joe," he responds, "Inger" ; to "Let Joe," his response is "Et."

When the class guest from Thailand gave the children post cards of the country's •landmarks it was Joe who, after long thought, asked her for her •zip code so he could write to her. When she explained that Thailand does not need zip codes because the country is very small, Joe said, "Ooks ig to me." (Looks big to me.)

The doctor who has checked Joe says the child's tongue is not tied and there are no other physical defects. He is simply retarded and slow to learn. Possibly his early learning was based on his mother's defective speech pattern and he finds it difficult to change over, for fear he might be incapable of mastering the correct pronunciation and •thereby lose all ability to communicate.

Joe is not sure of his present address. Like many children in my class, he has his name and address on the cover of his composition book, which he will refer to when he is asked where he lives.

Like all but three of my children, Joe has never had a telephone at home. During a class unit on the use of the telephone he was excited at playing "emergency calls." He wanted to be the policeman "because my father is." He was referring to his mother's boy friend, who is not a policeman but a security guard with a police-like uniform. The police image evokes a fantasy world in which Joe can project himself into some big, important position. (Joe, like the other children, was reluctant to allow the others to take their turns at the telephone. They enjoyed calling the fire department and the police department but they had great difficulty understanding that they could not start talking until after the phone at the other end of the room rang. I finally got them to just dial "O" for operator and ask her to get whatever emergency number they wanted to reach.)

Joe's mother came in during the winter to ask me for the number to call to make her •landlord give some heat. I gave her the emergency telephone number which was constantly in the daily press and on radio and television.

It is clear that Joe's mother, through no basic fault of her own, has been a major instrument contributing to his retardation, as is the case of so many other parents of retarded children. Add the factor of social deprivation resulting from his own lack of experience and we have some reason for a substantial portion of his problems.

Little if anything can be done for his mother. She works long and hard in order to support her son and herself. It looks hopeful that Joe can be helped to overcome many of his difficulties. He has made tremendous growth in important areas and is continuing to do so. He will need a lot of help. Some he will receive ; some he will not, mainly because of the educational system's deficiencies.

JIM HASKINS, *Diary of a Harlem schoolteacher*

Jim Haskins was born in Alabama in 1941, and had various jobs before becoming a teacher. He wrote this passage when he was teaching 5th grade (10-year-olds) in a public school in Harlem.

• **assembly** : assembly of the whole school to hear announcements made by the headmaster • **frowns** : *fronce les sourcils* • **humped-over** : bent • **in long strides** : *à grandes enjambées* • **over-all behavior** : *comportement général* • **confused** : disconcerted, embarrassed • **landmarks** : important buildings or natural features (mountains, etc.) • **zip code** : *code postal* • **thereby** : so ; in this way • **landlord** : the person from whom she rents her flat.

TOWARDS COMPREHENSION

1 ***Are you sure you have understood everything? Right or wrong?***

A. 1st half of the text (down to: *his response is "Et"*) :

1. Joe has never known his father.
2. He has changed schools several times.
3. His mother can't read.
4. She's in good health.
5. Joe likes to be well-dressed.
6. He hates going to the barber.
7. He seems to feel ill-at-ease in class.
8. The other children never mock (at) him.
9. His mother also has a speech defect.
10. He has trouble understanding her.

B. 2nd half of the text:

11. Joe asked the guest from Thailand for her zip code.
12. He did not understand why there was no zip code in Thailand.
13. If Joe can't speak properly, it's only because he is retarded and slow to learn.
14. If he is retarded, it may be due to his mother's speech defect.
15. He wants to be a policeman because his best friend's father is a policeman.
16. He does not know how to use a telephone.
17. Joe will receive all the help he needs.

2 ***Find in the text words, phrases or sentences having the same meaning, or approximately the same meaning, as the following:***

1. A *backward* child.
2. What kind of school does he *go to?*
3. She is unable to read or write.
4. She is often ill.
5. Has a doctor *examined* him?
6. He is a slow learner.
7. Who is he *speaking of?*
8. They are *unwilling* to come to school.
9. I *persuaded* him to say what he wanted to say.

3 ***Express differently:***

IN OTHER WORDS

1. He seems more eager to get his hair cut than to comb it.
(. . . . prefer . . . .)
2. This sometimes evokes laughter from the other children.
(. . . . make . . . .)
3. He seems very confused, as if he is having trouble understanding plain English.
4. . . . . for fear he might be incapable of mastering the correct pronunciation. (afraid that . . . . afraid of . . . .).
5. It is clear that Joe's mother, through no basic fault of her own, has been a major instrument contributing to his retardation. (If Joe is retarded . . . .)

4 ***Test your memory. Can you supply the end of the following sentences?***
A. 1st half of the text:

1. Joe is a lively, energetic youngster with . . . .
2. Joe has lived with his mother in . . . .
3. His mother is illiterate and in poor physical health, and recently . . . .
4. His over-all behavior within the class situation is good, even though he has difficulty . . . .
5. His mother also has . . . .

B. 2nd half of the text:

6. He is simply retarded . . . .
7. Like many children in my class . . . .
8. Joe, like the other children, ...
9. Joe's mother came in during the winter . . . .
10. She works long and hard . . . .
11. He will need a lot of help . . . .

5 ***Test your memory. Fill in the blanks with words from the text, but don't look at it.*** (Every 5th word has been deleted.)

The boy has never . . . . his real father. He . . . . lived with his mother . . . . many different one-room flats . . . . the same area, attending . . . . same school. His mother . . . . day work downtown; she . . . . illiterate and in poor . . . . health, and recently had . . . . have all her teeth . . . . She does her best . . . . keep Joe neat and . . . ., and he does have . . . . few extra cents to . . . . on himself.

IMPROVE YOUR VOCABULARY

1. Don't confuse
- **laughter** (uncountable): ['lɑ:ftə;U.S.:'læftə]
  We need laughter in our lives almost as much as love.
  I heard sounds of laughter in the kitchen *(éclats de rire).*
  When they saw the comic, they burst into laughter.
- **laugh** (countable): [lɑ:f,*am*:læf] :
  She answered with a laugh.
  We've had many good laughs over it *(çà nous a fait bien rire).*
- **laugh** (verb) { **at** a person, a joke, a story. / **about** a person, a thing.
  It's not a matter to laugh about *(il n'y a pas de quoi rire).*
  It's no laughing matter.
  When they saw the comic, they burst out laughing.
  I hate being laughed at *(j'ai horreur qu'on se moque de moi).*
  He laughs best who laughs last.
  He is the laughing-stock *(risée, tête de Turc).*

2. Difficulty.
They had a lot of difficulties, she is having financial difficulties.
But: he has difficulty (in) recognizing the different aspects of situations, she had little difficulty in convincing him, he answered the question with (some) difficulty/without (any) difficulty.

3. Fault.
Whose fault is it? Whose fault is it that he is retarded? (who's to blame).
It is our (own) fault if they think that . . . .
It's no one's fault. It's never his fault. It's always somebody else's fault.

4. Lack (verb): (=be without, not have enough). He lacks the qualifications for such a post. He lacks experience. He lacks confidence. They lack the necessities of life. They lack for nothing.
Lorsque l'on fait référence aux qualités d'une personne on trouve parfois :
be lacking in: he is lacking in courage/taste/manners.
(noun): lack of money/time/experience/training *(formation).*

LANGUAGE PRACTICE

6 ***Drawing on the text, make as many sentences as you can beginning with:***

1. Joe had difficulty (in) . . . .
2. It was hard for him to . . . .
3. It was fairly easy for him to . . . .
4. It was not easy for the teacher to . . . .
5. Joe has trouble . . . .

Then, re-cast some of the above sentences, using the pattern:

He found it hard to . . . .

IT + FOR + PROP. INF.

La proposition infinitive peut être introduite par **for.** On rencontre cette construction après :

a. un attribut (adj. ou nom) : is it necessary for me to go? *(= est-il nécessaire que j'y aille?).* It is hard for them to understand that. It is time for you to leave. *(= Il est temps que vous partiez).*

b. un adj. précédé de *too* ou suivi de *enough :* this tea is too hot for me to drink.

7 ***Written work: make up a few sentences beginning with:***

HOW TO EXPRESS LACK

1. His retardation makes it difficult for him to . . . .
2. His speech defect makes it difficult for him to . . . .
3. His inability to . . . . makes it difficult for him to . . . .

8 ***Complete the following:***

1. What these children need is . . . .
2. What they lack is . . . .
3. If they had more/better . . . .
4. If their parents had the time to . . . .
5. If . . . ., it is because they are deprived of . . . .

TOWARDS APPRECIATION

9 **"It is clear that Joe's mother, through no basic fault of her own, has been a major instrument contributing to his retardation."**
React as in the example:

HOW TO EXPRESS AGREEMENT AND DISAGREEMENT

A. Why didn't she read stories to her son?
B. Yes, you're right, she should have read stories to her son.
C. Well, I don't see how/I wonder how she could have read stories to her son, she was illiterate/she could not read.
A. Why didn't she teach him how to write? B. . . . . C. . . . .
A. Why didn't she correct his speech defect? B. . . . . C. . . . .
A. Why didn't she show him how to use a telephone? B. . . . . C. . . . .
A. Why didn't she explain to him what he didn't understand at school? B. . . . . C. . . . .
A. Why didn't she take him to a doctor? B. . . . . C. . . . .
A. Why didn't she play with him? B. . . . . C. . . . .

MODAL + HAVE + PART. PASSÉ

s'emploie lorsque je prends position, dans le moment présent, sur un fait ou un événement passé.
She should have been more attentive *(elle aurait dû être plus . . . .).*
He may have forgotten *(il se peut qu'il ait . . . .).*
He can't have seen you *(il n'a pas pu, pas dû vous voir).*

10 ***Creative oral work:***

The teachers gather to complain about their working conditions.
(Over-large classes/they need individual attention/to establish a good relationship with the pupils, with their parents/to lack time, training, experience/if we received a more appropriate training . . . .)

11 ***Creative written work:***

The teachers decide to send a petition to the Board of Education. Draw up this document (about 20 lines).

Education makes a people easy to lead, but difficult to drive; easy to govern, but impossible to enslave.
–Lord Brougham
House of Commons, 1828

Hey, Spic!

Arrangements [ə'reindʒmənts], menace ['menəs], desperately ['desprətli], vultures ['vʌltʃəz], I swore revenge [ai'swɔ:ri'vendʒ].

When we arrived in New York, it was wintertime. My •stepfather had made arrangements for us to stay with Tio Santos on Monroe Street until we found a place of our own. I remember the first time we looked out and saw snow fall. Carlos, Nellie, and I ran out to the backyard. And I couldn't believe my eyes, the whole world was being covered with white cotton. We started making snowballs, but after only a few minutes our hands were frozen. We ran in and put them under the hot-water tap. But instead of •easing the pain our hands felt like they were on fire.

Soon Carlos and I had to go to school where they spoke *inglés*. But there were quite a few kids who didn't know English either, and those who did used to •show off with their newly learned phrases. When we •lined up for the cloakroom after class, I soon learned to •chime in, "Open thee door." And since Moms had to work, we'd walk ourselves to an after-school center where we stayed until she came for us.

Carlos and I were walking under the bridge at Monroe Street on the way to the center when I heard somebody calling, "Hey, •spic." That was the first time I had heard the word. About six •cats were saying it all at the same time like a melody: "Hi ya, spic, ya... Hi, spic..." I didn't know the meaning but I caught the menace intended. Get to 80 Monroe, instinct told me. It was only one-block away but I looked at my little brother and knew we wouldn't make it. They were •gaining on us and getting bigger as they got closer.

"Hey, spic, ya got any money?"

What were they saying? •"*Si te dan, dales para tra*". I remembered the •*macho* training my mother had given me: An eye for an eye, a tooth for a tooth. That was the unwritten law in Puerto Rico. Bring two sacks, one to give and one to receive. So I prepared myself.

?"*Qué dicen ?*" Carlos asked, ready to cry.

•"*No se*, but it looks, like they want a •*pelea*. •*Sigue*, keep walking."

"C'mon, spic... spic." I heard that same word again and then a black fist was smashing my face. I fought back desperately. When I looked to •check on Carlos I saw him running up ahead with a few •*morenos* on him like vultures. So I ran up alongside to try to give my brother protection. *Caramba*, my tall boots weighted me down like a thousand pounds. I had to stop and let the *morenos* •beat up on me to get my boots off because I couldn't fight with them on. But then I was punching away and threw those boots hard at those •bastards.

I don't know how it happened, but we •made the block unharmed except for the heat on my face from the punches I'd taken. But I remembered and I swore revenge. And looking back, I guess I was beginning not to be such a good •*muchacho* anymore. Mami wanted us to defend ourselves, to be *macho*, and to protect each other. But she couldn't understand us getting into a fight and not even knowing what it was all about. Things just seemed to go from bad to worse in this America.

LEFTY BARRETTO, *Nobody's Hero A Puerto Rican story*

Lefty Barretto lives in Manhattan. He is executive director of Aquarius, a nonprofit multiracial group involved in the production of plays and films. As a boy, he knew the life of the human jungle of New York's ghetto, running with street gangs and becoming a thief. He even went to prison.

● **stepfather**: his mother had remarried ● **easing the pain**: lessening it, making it less acute ● **show off** : *crânaient* ● **lined up** : queued up ● **chime in** : join in the chorus ● **spic** : a Spanish-American (offensive language) ● **cats** : (colloq) guys, men ● **gaining on us** : drawing closer to us (because they were walking faster) ● **Si te dan...** : *S'il te frappe, il faut le frapper aussi* ● **macho training** : his mother had brought him up, educated him in such a way that he should become a *macho*, a **he**-man ● **No se** : I don't know ● **pelea** : a fight ● **sigue** : follow ● **to check on Carlos** : to see where he was ● **morenos** : black boys ● **beat up on me** : *me donner une raclée* ● **bastards** : *salauds* ● **we made the block unharmed** : we reached the block unhurt (without being hurt) ● **muchacho** : child.

TOWARDS COMPREHENSION

1 *Right or wrong. Justify your answers.*

1. It's a young Puerto-Rican who is speaking.
2. He is looking back upon his past.
3. When they arrived in New York, they bought a house.
4. At school, the languages spoken were English and Spanish.
5. All the pupils except the narrator and his brother knew English.
6. After school the two boys came home straight away.
7. They were insulted on their way home.
8. It was the first time they had heard the word "Spic".
9. The muggers *(agresseurs)* outnumbered them (were more numerous).
10. The narrator's first reaction was to run away.
11. He went to his brother's rescue.
12. He was badly hurt.

LANGUAGE PRACTICE

2 *Complete the following sentences in any way you like :*

1. I've never been to New York, so I can't . . . .
2. I've bought a map of New York, so now I . . . .
3. He has learnt English, so now he . . . .
4. I've never heard that word before, so I . . . .
5. He has never seen snow before, so he . . . .
6. My stepfather has made arrangements for us to stay with friends, so we . . . .
7. They have been taught how to defend themselves, so they . . . .

3 *Using the verbs and phrases given below, make dialogues like this :*

A. Have you ever been insulted?
B. Yes, I have (or: Yes, I've often been insulted).

C. When did it happen? (or: When was that? or: How did it happen.)
D. It happened a few years ago (a long time ago, or: when I was ....) I was insulted by a friend of mine, he called me a liar/a coward.... I was very angry with him ....
(be insulted/go to New York/see snow fall/make snowballs/call someone names/be called a fool/box somebody's ears/receive a beating-up/have to defend oneself/take punches.)

PARFAIT ou PRESENT PERFECT

GÉNÉRALITÉS

1. Formation : have + part. passé.
Sa forme réduite est **'ve ou 's.** Même lorsque **have** est en forme pleine, il se prononce [əv] (forme faible), sauf lorsqu'il porte un accent d'insistance. I've already told him about it *(je lui en ai déjà parlé).* He's never been to New York.

Cas du verbe go : go a 2 formes de parfait : *have gone, have been.* Comparez : he's gone to New York (=he is still in N. Y., or he is on his way to N. Y. = *il est à, il est parti pour N. Y.*) et he's been to N. Y. (=he once visited N. Y. but he isn't there now).

2. Emplois : pour éviter les erreurs les plus fréquentes, les Français devraient retenir les quatre points suivants :

a) Ce n'est pas parce que le parfait anglais ressemble, par sa forme, au passé composé français que ces deux formes verbales ont les mêmes sens et emplois.

b) En français, le passé composé est de plus en plus le temps du récit, alors que c'est le preterit (passé) en anglais.
je l'ai rencontré hier, nous avons bavardé quelques instants dans la rue, puis nous avons pris un verre. I came across him (I met him) yesterday, we talked ...., then we had a drink.

c) Alors qu'en français on emploie le présent pour exprimer la durée avec les expressions *il y a, ... depuis ....,* en anglais on emploie le parfait avec *for* ou *since* :
je travaille avec elle depuis 3 ans ; il y a 3 ans que je travaille avec elle. I have worked (been working) with her for 3 years... since 1976.

d) Le parfait anglais est un **présent passé** (on l'appelle parfois **present perfect**) ; il établit des liens entre **l'actuel** et le **révolu,** entre le **présent** et le **passé,** alors que le preterit s'emploie lorsqu'on fait référence à une action qui est considérée comme terminée, classée, située, donc sans liens avec le présent.

On peut résumer ainsi les emplois du parfait :
— Lorsque l'action se termine à l'instant, donc lorsqu'elle n'est pas encore située : How long have you been waiting for me? *(Vous m'attendez depuis longtemps?)* I've just seen him (**passé immédiat :** *je viens de le voir).*
— Lorsqu'elle n'est pas située : **passé indéfini :** Have you been to Russia? I've seen you before, but I can't remember when or where.
— Lorsqu'elle peut se renouveler, donc n'est pas encore classée : I've often been to London. Several people have phoned this morning *(le matin n'est pas terminé)* and I expect there will be some more calls before lunch.
— Lorsqu'on considère le **résultat présent, le retentissement :** they have arrived (=they are now here). He has been given a watch (=he now has a watch) I've taken a bath (=I'm clean now).
— Le parfait est souvent associé à certains adverbes ou expressions de temps (already, ever, never, so far, up to now, lately, recently) ainsi qu'avec : it's the first time.

Remarque : en Américain, on trouve parfois le preterit là où en British English on a le parfait : Did you sell your old car yet?

4 ***React as follows:***

REPORTED SPEECH

Voir p. 23

A. You've been to New York before, haven't you?
B. No, it's the first time I've been to New York.
A. You've spoken English at school before, haven't you? B. . . . .
A. They've seen snow fall before, haven't they? B. . . . .
A. They've made snowballs before, haven't they? B. . . . .
A. The boy has heard the word Spic before, hasn't he? B. . . . .
A. Their mother has had to work before, hasn't she? B. . . . .
A. The children have been to the after-school center before, haven't they? B. . . . .

5 ***Turn the sentences from the above exercise into reported speech:***

Example: I asked him if he had been to New York before. He answered me/he told me it was the first time he had been to New York.
or: He asked me if I had been to N. Y. before. I answered/told him it was the first time I had been to N.Y.
or: He/she asked him if he had been to N. Y. before. He/she answered/told him it was the first . . . .

TOWARDS APPRECIATION

6 ***Lefty Barretto writes to a friend, complaining about America:***

HOW TO EXPRESS CONTRAST
Whereas

Example: Here we have to stay with our uncle, whereas in Puerto Rico we used to have our own house.

1. In New York, we have to wear warm clothes in winter, whereas . . . .
2. In America, Carlos and I have to study English . . . .
3. . . . . we used to know everybody.
4. . . . . in Puerto Rico she used to stay at home.
5. . . . . whereas . . . .

USED TO

Ne pas confondre :

1. Used to exprimant la **répétition** d'une action dans le passé, et souvent **l'opposition** entre passé et présent (voir p. 52) : I used to ['ju:stə] go for a swim every day when I was your age. A la forme négative et interrogative **used to** se comporte généralement comme un verbe ordinaire : he used to live there, didn't he?

2. Be/get used to ['ju:stə] + **noun or gerund.** Exprime une **habitude** : I'm used to hard work. I'm used to working hard *(j'ai l'habitude de... je suis habitué à...).* You'll soon get used to living in a big city.

3. Used [ju:zd] pret. ou part. passé du verbe *use (utiliser) :* What's this thing used for? *(à quoi sert cet objet?).*

7 ***The new-comers will have to get used to a lot of things. Using the prompts given below, make dialogues like this:***

HOW TO EXPRESS OBLIGATION
have to

Voir p. 18

A. We aren't used to snow.
B. Well, you'll have to get used to it.
A. We aren't used to speaking English.
B. Well, you'll have to get used to it: *you could also say:* Well, you'll soon get used to it, *or:* It won't be long before you get used to it.

(snow, speak English, big cities, to be insulted, to be called a Spic, to live in the open air, to be looked upon as a foreigner, to be cramped for room (=to have insufficient space, to travel on crowded buses, to be cooped up in a small room, to be attacked by muggers).

8 *Imagine some of the reasons why the new-comers will have to . . . .*

You'll have to . . . . or you'll . . . .
You'll have to . . . . or you won't . . . .
You'll have to . . . . or you won't be able to . . . .
Unless you . . . . you won't be able to . . . .
If you are to stay here, you'll have to . . . . or you . . . .

9 *Using the phrases from the box, say how the mother would have reacted if:*

1. The children had behaved like cowards.
2. They had been disrespectful to her.
3. They had come back home with their clothes torn to pieces.
4. They had called the Black boys "niggers".
5. They had associated with bad boys.
6. If the elder brother had not protected his younger brother.

THE FUTURE

Voir p. 52

HOW TO EXPRESS CONDITION

... or ... if (*sinon*)
unless = if ... not
be to: peut exprimer à la fois la condition et le but dans les **if-clauses:**
If we are to become rich, we must work hard (= if we intend to become rich, if we are going to... in order to become rich... *(si nous voulons...)*.

HOW TO EXPRESS DISAPPROVAL
(= *la désapprobation*)

1. Tactfully:
Did you have to . . . . ?
Did you need to . . . . ?
Did you *really* have/need to . . . . ?
Why did you do a thing like that?
I wonder if you were right to . . . . ?
I wonder if you were right in + gerund?
I'm not sure you were right to . . . ./in . . . .
Don't you think it would have been better if . . . .

2. More forcefully:
I don't like the way you . . . .
I don't like you to . . . .
I don't want you to . . . . *(prop. inf.,* voir p. 17).
It would have been better, I think, if you had/hadn't. . . .
I think you were wrong to . . . .
I think you were wrong in + gerund . . . .
You shouldn't have . . . . (*vous n'auriez pas dû,* voir p. 40).
I *did* hope you wouldn't . . . .
I disapprove of . . . . + gerund.
(I disapprove of children being rude to adults, ...)

10 *Creative written work: compose a dialogue between Lefty and his mother after the first day at school:*

A. Lefty speaks of the difference between Puerto Rico and America.
B. He tells her about the mugging: how he felt frightened and how he fought back.
C. The mother is cross because he has ruined his new clothes and she scolds him.

FOR FURTHER INFORMATION

Now 19 million, and growing fast, Hispanics are becoming a power

That extraordinary vessel, the American •melting pot, is bubbling once again. The source of ferment: American residents of Spanish origin, whose official numbers have increased by 14.3% in the past five years alone. ...According to 1978 census estimates, there are 12 million Hispanic Americans in the U.S....

Even the most reliable census figures, however, fail to take into account the enormous numbers of Hispanics who are living and working in the U.S. illegally. •At a conservative estimate, some 7.4 million • "undocumented" Hispanic aliens raise the actual total to more than 19 million, and the Hispanic proportion of U.S. population to around 9%, vs. 12% for blacks. Because the rate of natural increase (births over deaths) among Hispanics is higher than that for Blacks, and because Hispanic immigration (legal and illegal) is running at the •staggering rate of an estimated 1 million people a year, Hispanics may outnumber American blacks within the next decade. Already the two groups are competing fiercely for jobs and Government aid...

Of the officially recognized Hispanics, the largest single group is the chicanos (short for Mexicano), comprising some 7.2 million people of Mexican origin concentrated largely in the U.S. Southwest. An estimated 1.8 million Puerto Ricans live chiefly in the northern-central states, particularly in the Northeast. Some 700,000 Cubans, mostly refugees from Fidel Castro's regime, are now in the U.S., mainly concentrated in Florida. But there are also Dominicans, Ecuadorians, Colombians and natives of other Latin American countries or of Spain itself scattered all over the U.S., totaling another 2.4 million Hispanics.

As has happened with almost every ethnic group in America, the Hispanics are learning that growing numbers and •assertiveness often produce growing hostility... As America's latest great wave of immigrants, Hispanics are learning another hard lesson: latecomers start at the bottom... Hispanics are the most undereducated of Americans—despite their own deep belief in the maxim, *Saber es poder* (Knowledge is power)... Language is an obvious handicap, but the •vocal Hispanic demand for bilingual education raises particular problems... Critics attack bilingual programs on several grounds: that extra efforts should not be made for Spanish-speaking children unless they are also made for French-speaking or Hebrew-speaking or Vietnamese-speaking children; and, perhaps most •cogently, that Hispanic students who speak mostly Spanish at home will never really learn to compete in American society as a whole. ... What is more, the perpetuation of a large subculture with little or no skill in English could lead to something the U.S. has so far managed to avoid: the rise of a nation-within-a-nation...

The "Illegals"

Many thousands have come from Central and South American countries like Guatemala, Colombia and Ecuador, but about 90% are Mexican. On foot, by air or in autos, they filter across the 2,000-mile-long southern U.S. border. Last year nearly I million illegal entrants were apprehended and deported by the Immigration and Naturalization Service... Behind the mass influx are some stark economic figures: half of Mexico's 18 million-member labor force is unemployed; a devalued peso has sent prices there spiraling; the country's 3.5% population growth is one of the world's highest. Says Border Patrolman Michael S. Williams: "They're starving to death down there."...

Sooner rather than later, Congress is going to have to confront the problem of halting the flow of illegals. Meanwhile, there are millions of legal Hispanics in the U.S., and it no longer matters whether they or their ancestors arrived as •wetbacks splashing across the ankle-deep Rio Grande or as political refugees in fishing boats from Cuba, or in the trunks of, •'coyote' cars... What does matter is that they—and their fellow Americans—now face another problem: writing a new chapter in the perpetually unfinished story of American pluralism...

Time, *October 16, 1978*

• **melting pot** : see A.B.C. • **at a conservative estimate** : *au bas mot* • **undocumented** : without legal documents : illegal immigrants • **staggering** : shocking • **assertiveness** : *la volonté de s'affirmer* • **vocal** : insistent • **cogently** : convincingly • **wetbacks** : *ouvriers agricoles mexicains (entrés illégalement)* • **'coyote'** : illegal transporter.

TEST YOUR ENGLISH - TEST YOUR ENGLISH – TEST YOUR ENGLISH

A. Choose the right answer:

1. She works hard . . . . support her son and herself.
   a) for *b*) so that *c*) in order to *d*) so as not to.
2. She showed him how to use the telephone . . . . he should not feel different from the other boys.
   a) to *b*) in order to *c*) so as to *d*) so that.
3. . . . . you explain to him what he is supposed to do, he won't do it.
   a) whereas *b*) because *c*) while *d*) unless.
4. . . . . a Frenchman, I find it hard to understand American informality.
   a) when *b*) whereas *c*) as *d*) unless.
5. . . . . do you go to the cinema: once or twice a month?
   a) how long *b*) how often *c*) how far *d*) how.
6. I wish I . . . . all that he owns.
   a) own *b*) will own *c*) owned *d*) would own.
7. You . . . . told me about it before, I wouldn't have come.
   a) must *b*) should *c*) must have *d*) should have.
8. You'll have to . . . . hard if you want to succeed.
   a) be used to work *b*) get used to working *c*) get used to work *d*) be used to working.
9. Have you . . . . New York?
   a) ever been at *b*) never been at *c*) ever gone to *d*) ever been to.
10. Don't worry, I . . . . arrangements for our journey to America.
    a) had made *b*) should have made *c*) have made *d*) I wish I could make.

B. Fill in the gaps with verbs from the following list

(adjust oneself to, be lacking in, intend, lack, laugh at, mean, need, say, tell, want).

1. Is it true you . . . . leave for America next month? 2. Do you think you'll be able to . . . . new living conditions? 3. Those immigrants are not . . . . courage, but what they . . . . is better working conditions. 4. I don't think he'll be chosen, he . . . . the qualifications for the post. 5. Don't . . . . them, they're to be pitied. 6. He . . . . me I was the director he . . . ., but I didn't believe him. 7. Everyone . . . . he is the most powerful man in Hollywood. 8. He . . . . us he . . . . to become President, and he certainly . . . . what he . . . . 9. If you . . . . him to engage you, don't . . . . him where you are from. 10. What do you . . . . when you . . . . he . . . . generosity? I think you're wrong, he *is* generous, but he . . . . everyone to do their best.

C. Dans l'exercice suivant, vous proposerez le plus de solutions possible :

1. Que dites-vous lorsque vous ne comprenez pas ce que l'on cherche à vous expliquer?
2. Que dites-vous lorsque vous voulez savoir :
   a) Combien de temps vous allez devoir attendre.
   b) Combien de temps l'un de vos amis a l'intention de rester aux U.S.A.
   c) Pourquoi l'un de vos amis veut émigrer aux U.S.A.
   d) Si l'un de vos amis a déjà été aux U.S.A.
3. Que dites-vous :
   a) Lorsqu'on vous dit de vous hâter et que vous estimez avoir le temps.
   b) Lorsque vous estimez que vous n'auriez pas dû vous moquer de quelqu'un.
   c) Lorsque vous voulez absolument que quelqu'un vous accompagne.
   d) Lorsque vous estimez que le travail qu'on vous demande de faire est trop difficile.
4. Un de vos amis a été très impoli envers une personne âgée. Comment réagissez-vous pour marquer votre désapprobation?

TEST YOUR ENGLISH - TEST YOUR ENGLISH – TEST YOUR ENGLISH

A land for free men

Colleen [kɔ'li:n], lantern ['læntən], rancid steerage ['rænsid 'stiəridʒ], urine ['juərin], majority [mə'dʒɔriti] cholera ['kɔlərə], famine fever ['fæmin 'fi:və], tuberculosis [tju,bə:kju'ləusis], pneumonia [nju'məunjə] Xavier Armagh ['zæviə ɑ:'mɑ:], Sean [ʃɔ:n], perpetually [pə'petʃuəli], bowl [bəul], melancholy ['melənkəli] murmurous ['mə:mərəs], Viaticum [vai'ætikəm], voyage ['vɔiidʒ], fragrance ['freigrəns], janitor ['dʒænitə] repletion [ri'pli:ʃən], execrated ['eksikreitid], exposure [iks'pəuʒə].

"Joey, Joey? Oh God! Joey?" [...]

"I'm here, Mum," said Joseph, holding her thin small hand tighter. "I won't leave you, Mum." She stared at him in the •dimness, her eyes bright and distended with terror. [...] Her fingers squeezed his hand until they were tight on his flesh. "Oh, Mum," he murmured. "You'll be well, Mum." He was thirteen years old.

"I'm dying, Joey," she said, and her •weary young voice was hardly audible. "There's Sean, Joey, and the little •colleen. You'll take care of them, Joey, for •himself? You'll mind them?"

"Sure, and I'll mind them, Mum," he said. "Dad will meet us. You'll be well then."

"Good Joey," she whispered. "You were always a good boyeen. You're a man, Joey."

"Yes, Mum," he said. The fingers that clutched his hand had become icy, and not only the tips. His mother's thick black hair faintly shone in the light of the stinking and •swaying lantern which hung from the wooden ceiling. That ceiling and the wet wooden walls sweated and the big masted ship creaked all about them. It was still light outside the four small •portholes but little light entered here in the rancid •steerage where fifty women and children slept on •noxious •bunks under thin blankets. The broken floor was soiled with the urine of children and scattered with •sawdust. It was very cold. The portholes were blurred with •spray. The ship was a fourmaster which had left Queenstown, Ireland, over six weeks ago. By standing on tiptoe the tallest could see the shoreline of New York, the faint gloomy illumination of lamps. Some of the steerage passengers had been rejected twenty-four hours ago in Boston. They were Irish.

The majority of women and children on the hard bunks were sick with cholera, famine fever, tuberculosis and pneumonia. Joseph Francis Xavier Armagh felt and saw nothing but his dying mother, who was hardly thirty years old. He heard bitter crying near him and he knew it was his little brother, Sean, who was scarcely six. Sean was crying because he was perpetually hungry and cold and frightened. He had had his supper ten minutes before, a bowl of thin •oatmeal and a slice of coarse dry bread which smelled of mice... A heavy mist was rising from the cold sea and melancholy horns began to moan in the harbour. The ship rocked. "I'll take ye to your home again," sang the men beyond the curtain, "to where the grass is fresh and green!" They sang of the land they had left because there was no bread there any longer to satisfy the body, and only •rotting and blackened potatoes in the wet and •ravished fields.

A murmurous sound rose, the Litany for the Dying. The priest administered the Sacrament of Extreme Unction and Viaticum to the dying woman, whose white lips barely moved in her extremity. Then the priest said, "Go forth from this world, O Christian soul..."

Joseph did not hear this. He was saying to his father, Daniel, who was to meet them in New York, "I brought her to you, Dad, and Sean and the little colleen, and now you and I will take care of them, in the house you provided, and we'll be free and never hungry or homeless again. No one will hate us and drive us from our land and tell us to starve... Dad, we've come home to you."

It was real to him, for he had dreamt that scene a thousand times on this sorrowful voyage. His father would meet his family on the dock and •enfold them all, and then he would take them to the "flat" in the Bowery where he lived with his brother, Jack, and it would be warm and there would be soft beds and a hot stove and joy and the fragance of boiling potatoes and •turnips and beef or lamb and safety and comfort and peace and hope. Had they not received letters from him, and money, and had he not told them of this? He had a good job as •janitor in a small hotel. He ate to repletion for the first time in years. He worked hard, and he received money for his labour. He would provide for his family, and no more would they be hunted like vermin and •despised and execrated for their Faith, and thrown from their land to die on the highways of •exposure and hunger. "Ah, and it is a land for free men," Daniel had written in his careful hand. "The lads will go to school, and the little one will be born in America, and we will be Americans together, and never part again."

TAYLOR CALDWELL, *Captains and the Kings*

Taylor Caldwell is an English woman by birth but has lived in America since her family emigrated to New York State in 1906. She writes historical novels and her first book was published in 1938. "Captains and the Kings", from which this passage is taken, has been made into a successful television series.

● **dimness** : in the bad light ● **weary** [ˈwiəri] : tired ● **colleen** : (Irish) young girl ● **himself** : (Irish coll.) head of the household ; here : your father ● **swaying** : swinging, oscillating ● **portholes** : *hublots* ● **steerage** : *(entrepont)*, 3rd class ● **noxious** : harmful, bad for the health ● **bunk** : sleeping-place fixed on the wall ● **sawdust** : *sciure* ● **spray** : *embrun* ● **oatmeal** : *farine, bouillie d'avoine* ● **rotting** : *pourrissantes* ● **ravished** : desolate ● **enfold** : embrace, put his arms round them ● **turnips** : *navets* ● **janitor** : doorkeeper, porter ● **despised** : ≠ esteemed ● **exposure** : (here) cold.

TOWARDS COMPREHENSION

A. 1st part (down to : "*which smelled of mice*").

1 ***After reading the text carefully, pick out all the words and phrases creating an atmosphere of horror and death.***

2 ***Sum up the facts in 3 or 4 sentences.***

B. 2nd part.

3 ***Right or wrong. Justify your answers :***

1. The passengers are emigrating to the U.S.A. because they were persecuted in their own country.
2. Joseph didn't hear what the priest said when his mother died.
3. He was carrying on an imaginary conversation with his father.
4. He had imagined what he would say to his father several times during the voyage.
5. He expected to find a comfortable home.
6. His father had often written to them.
7. He didn't know how his father made a living. (He knew nothing about his father's job.)
8. Joseph seems to have suffered from hunger.

IMPROVE YOUR VOCABULARY
(useful verbs)

- **Flee, fled, fled** (=run away from...).
  They fled their country because . . . .
  If they fled their country, it was because . . . .
- Don't confuse
  - **escape** death, starvation, punishment, notice *(éviter de se faire remarquer)*,
  - **escape from** prison, from one's captors, from a burning building, from a sinking ship (=break out of, get away from, get free of).
- **Suffer:**
  They must have suffered from hunger.
  But They must have suffered great hardships (=they must have experienced/gone through great hardships = *connaître de rudes épreuves*).
- Don't confuse
  - **provide for...**
  - **provide someone with...**

  He'll provide for his family *(= subviendra aux besoins...)*.
  He is provided for *(à l'abri du besoin)*.
  Does your firm provide you with a car? *(vous fournit...)*.
- **Die:**
  They died of hunger, but he died from a wound *(des suites d'une blessure)*, the illness from which he died . . . .
- **Mind:**
  1. Mind the step (=be careful of the step = *attention à la marche*).
  2. Who's going to mind the neighbour's dog while they are on holiday (=take care of, look after).
  3. Do as you like, I don't mind at all (=it's all the same to me = *ça m'est égal*).
  4. Do you mind if I open the window? (=do you object).
     Would you mind shutting the door?
  5. Never mind=it doesn't matter.

LANGUAGE PRACTICE

4 ***This text provides information about a group of immigrants. Ask as many questions as you can about:***

a. their past b. their present living conditions c. their future, or their hopes.

5 ***Pick out all the verbs in the past and read them aloud.***

HOW TO SEEK INFORMATION

Voir p. 17

LE PASSÉ OU PRÉTÉRIT

Il peut être régulier, et se termine alors par le suffixe **-ed.** Il peut être irrégulier (voir liste).

1. Prononciation du suffixe -ed :

a) **[id]** : après les bases verbales se terminant par *d* et *t* : added ['ædid], hated ['heitid];

b) **[d]** : lorsque la base verbale se termine par une consonne *sonore* : b, g, v, z, ʒ, m, n, ŋ, l : frightened ['fraitnd], soiled ['sɔild] lived : après les voyelles et les diphtongues : cried [kraid], stared [stɛəd] stayed;

c) **[t]** : lorsque la base verbale se termine par une consonne *sourde* : p, k, ʃ, f, s, worked [wə:kt], clutched [klʌtʃt].

LE PASSÉ OU PRÉTÉRIT (continued)

2. Il s'emploie pour décrire une action **révolue, située :**

a) dans l'histoire : the war broke out in 1939 ;

b) dans le passé même récent : she phoned a few minutes ago. (*Mais on dira :* she has just phoned = *elle vient de téléphoner*).

c) dans son décor : they took the boat in Ireland ;

d) dans l'esprit des personnes qui y font allusion : did everything go as planned? *(est-ce que tout a marché comme prévu?).*

C'est le temps de la **narration,** alors qu'en français c'est souvent le passé composé. On le rencontre avec les marqueurs de temps suivants : yesterday, last week/month/year.../, ... ago, the other day, in those days, in + date.

15 sept

6 ***Compare :*** They may be turned back. / Perhaps they will be turned back.

Give the other form :

1. Perhaps they will be allowed to disembark.
2. Perhaps the priest will be allowed to go on shore.
3. They may be refused admittance.
4. Perhaps they will be hunted like vermin once again.
5. Perhaps they will be despised in America as they were in Ireland.
6. Perhaps they will never be humiliated again.
7. Perhaps they will not be allowed to leave the ship.

MAY

exprime une éventualité ou une hypothèse portant sur le présent ou sur l'avenir. Il a une valeur de **futurité.** They may be rejected = perhaps they will be rejected.

VOIX PASSIVE

Généralités

Formation : **be** + **part. passé** (+ **by** + **comp.** d'**agent**).

- Elle peut s'employer à tous les temps : They have often been despised (= *on les a souvent méprisés*), they will be rejected.
- Elle peut être associée à un auxiliaire modal : they may be rejected *(il se peut qu'ils soient, ils seront peut-être rejetés).*

On la rencontre fréquemment sans complément d'agent.

LA FUTURITÉ

Elle peut s'exprimer de plusieurs façons :

1. présent simple : a un caractère de certitude, soit parce qu'un calendrier a été établi, soit parce que le locuteur n'a pas le pouvoir de modifier le cours de l'événement :
We leave for Britain to-morrow. To-morrow is Monday.

2. présent progressif : implique que des dispositions ont été prises en prévision de l'événement futur. Il est presque toujours accompagné d'une expression de temps.
When are you leaving? I'm leaving to-morrow. I'm seeing him to-night.

3. going to : très fréquent. Exprime généralement l'intention du locuteur, ou la certitude que celui-ci a qu'une action va se produire :
I'm going to tell him what I think of his behaviour *(je vais lui dire ce que je pense de sa conduite).*
If you stay in the rain, you're going to catch cold.

LA FUTURITÉ (continued)

4. **Be to :** (encore appelé futur d'intention ou de convention).
I am to see him this afternoon *(je dois le voir cet après-midi).*

5. **shall/will :** il est difficile d'établir des distinctions très rigides entre ces deux auxiliaires, dont l'emploi peut varier selon les régions, voire selon les individus. On peut s'en tenir aux constatations suivantes :

a) dans la conversation on emploie les formes contractées : **'ll.** I'll see to it to-morrow *(= je m'en occuperai demain),* he'll see to it to-morrow ;

b) **shall :** à la forme affirmative (1res personnes), peut exprimer la constatation d'un fait, sans intention particulière de la part du locuteur : I shall be forty seven in April ;

c) aux 1res personnes de la forme interrogative, **shall** a valeur « d'offre de service ». Shall I buy you the paper (= would you like me to . . . .) ;

d) **won't** est parfois ambigu. Il peut exprimer un **refus** : I won't answer that question (= I refuse to answer that question), une **promesse** : I won't do it again (= I promise not to do it again). A **la forme progressive.** l'ambiguité disparait :
he won't come with us
peut signifier *il ne veut pas . . . .*, mais :
he won't be coming with us = *il ne viendra pas*;

e) **will you** peut exprimer une **requête polie** : will you pass the butter, please?

f) A ces considérations particulières, on peut ajouter que cette forme de futurité (shall/will) ne marque aucune intention particulière de la part du locuteur. C'est un **futur « neutre »**, une sorte de constat par avance, parfois aussi une forme de **prédiction :** One day I'll die. I'll be forty-seven in April. In 20 years'time, he'll retire on a pension *(= il prendra sa retraite).* Cette forme est très fréquente dans les propositions principales associées aux « if-clauses ». If you press this button, the door will open. I'll write to him this afternoon if I've got time. Mais si le locuteur veut marquer son intention, il dira : I'm going to write to him this afternoon.

TOWARDS APPRECIATION

7 ***Suppose Joey has succeeded in meeting his father. He gives him an account of the voyage.***

8 ***Complete the following sentences as in the example :***

NEVER . . . . AGAIN

So far they have often been hungry, but now it's over ; they will never be hungry again, or at least they hope so.

1. So far they have been homeless . . . .
2. So far they have been hunted like vermin . . . .
3. So far they have often suffered from hunger . . . .
4. So far they have often been despised . . . .

Go on . . . .

SO FAR + PARFAIT

Voir p. 43

9 ***Now take a slightly less optimistic view and imagine what an easy prey those frightened immigrants must have been for unscrupulous people.***

10 ***Drawing on the text, make up as many sentences as you can beginning with :*** What will happen if . . . ., ***then try and answer them.***

11 ***Creative written work :*** Expand into a paragraph of ten lines *"it is a land for free men"*.

12 ***Oral or written translation :*** the last paragraph.

Prince of peace

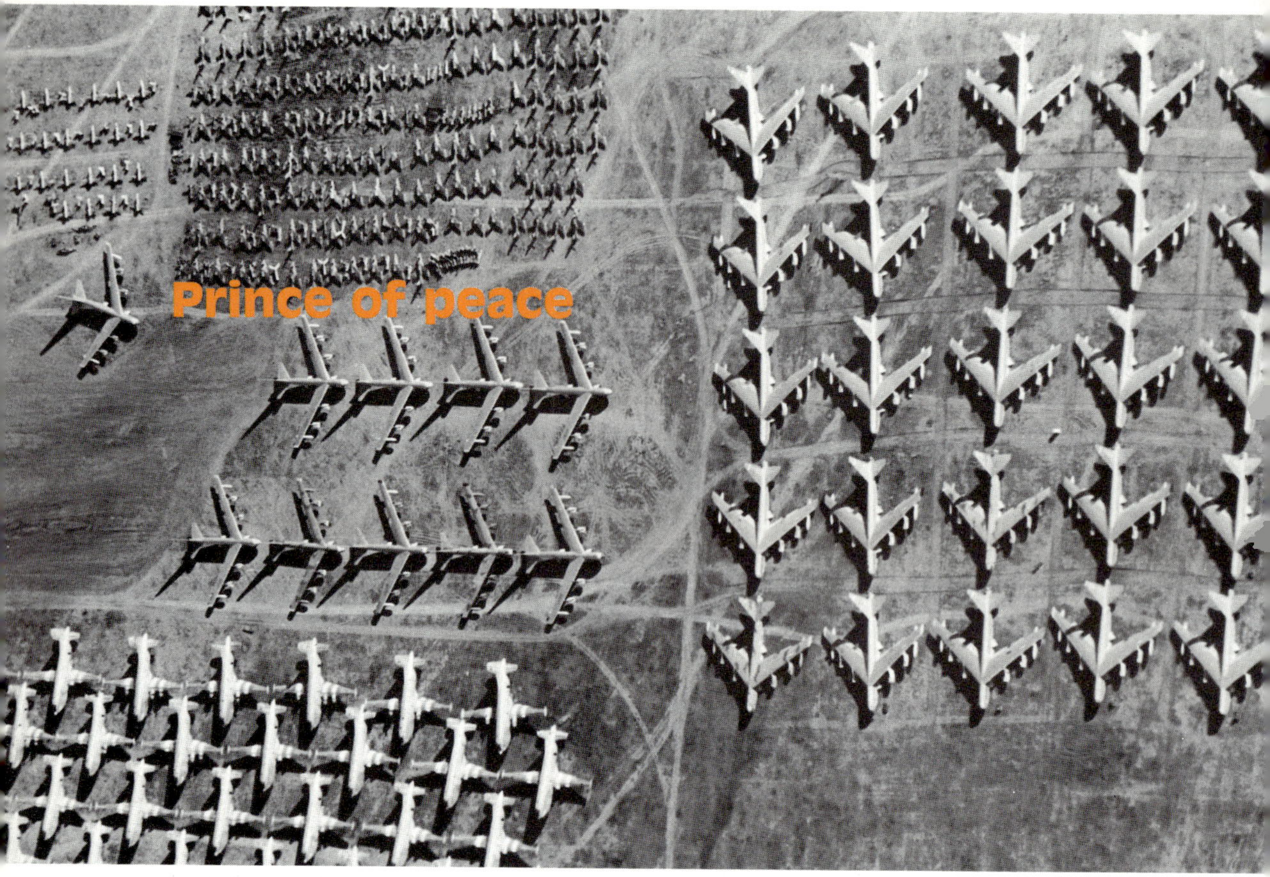

•Andrew Carnegie
was born in Dunfermline in Scotland,
came over to the States in an immigrant
ship worked as •bobbinboy in a textile factory
fired •boilers
•clerked in a bobbin factory at $2.50 a week
ran round Philadelphia with telegrams as a Western Union
messenger
learned the Morse code was telegraph operator on the
•Pennsy lines
was a military telegraph operator in the Civil War and
always saved his pay ;
whenever he had a dollar he invested it.
Andrew Carnegie started out buying Adams Express and
Pullman stock when they were •in a slump ;
he had confidence in railroads,
he had confidence in communications,
he had confidence in transportation,
he believed in iron.
Andrew Carnegie believed in iron, built bridges Bessemer
plants •blast furnaces •rolling mills ;

Andrew Carnegie believed in oil;
Andrew Carnegie believed in steel;
always saved his money
whenever he had a million dollars he invested it.
Andrew Carnegie became the richest man in the world and died.
•Bessemer Duquesne Rankin Pittsburgh Bethlehem Gary
Andrew Carnegie gave millions for peace
and libraries and scientific institutes and •endowments and
•thrift
whenever he made a billion dollars he endowed an institution
to promote universal peace
always
except in time of war.

JOHN DOS PASSOS, *U.S.A.*, The 42nd Parallel

Dos Passos (1896-1970) was born in Chicago. His grandfather was a Portugese immigrant. His great trilogy "U.S.A.", published between 1930 and 1936, illustrates his revolutionary technique of novel-writing. The story is conducted on three different levels so as to give an all-round view. We follow the lives of a certain number of characters but these narrations are interspersed with brief biographies of famous Americans, with "news reels" recalling contemporary happenings and "Camera Eye" passages containing Dos Passos' own reflections.

• **Andrew Carnegie** (1835-1919). Was born in poverty in Scotland. His family came to Pittsburgh, Pennsylvania, in 1848 and Andrew began life as a bobbin boy. He succeeded in creating a monopoly in steel and became a multi-millionaire. He retired from business and became world-famous for his philanthropy • **bobbin boy** : *bobineur, rattacheur* • **boilers** : *chaudières* • **clerked** : worked in an office • **Pennsy** : Pennsylvania • **in a slump** : when the price was low *(quand le cours était en baisse)* • **blast furnace** : *haut fourneau* • **rolling mills** : *laminerie* • **Bessemer, Duquesne, ...** : names of steel towns • **endowments** : foundations • **thrift** : Carnegie gave millions to promote peace, etc. and habits of economy.

1 ***How does Carnegie illustrate the American Dream?*** (see A.B.C.)

2 *"Prince of Peace"* ***is the title given to the Messiah. Find words or phrases showing that it is used ironically here. What did Carnegie really believe in? Why did he give away so much money?***

3 ***What makes the last line so forceful?***

FOR FURTHER INFORMATION

Immigration

For the first century of its existence, the U.S. had no immigration policy at all. Thomas Jefferson stated the prevailing view of the matter when he asked: "Shall we refuse to the unhappy fugitives from distress that hospitality which the savages of the wilderness extended to our fathers arriving in this land?" No, we shall not, was the answer, and so there came the thousands of Irish starved by the potato famine of 1845, and thousands more of Germans oppressed after the uprisings of 1848, and still more thousands of Russian Jews afflicted by the czars' pogroms, and then in 1882 Congress passed the first immigration laws barring lunatics, convicts and Chinese laborers. The principle of "selectivity" had been born.

The tide of immigration, which built the railroads and cattle towns of the West, flowed on for another generation. Some 8.8 million arrived during the first decade of this century, and in 1907, the inspectors at Ellis Island processed an alltime daily record of some 6,500 Italian peasants and Greek fishermen and various other humble souls, many of them wide-eyed children clinging anxiously to the hands of their mothers.

But selectivity—meaning the native-born Americans' •know-nothing inclination to exclude anyone unlike themselves—proved victorious. In 1921 a new immigration law introduced the principle of national quotas. They were based, somewhat inaccurately, on the different national groups in the U.S. in the 1890s. The figures were changed every few years, but the basic principle was clear in the quotas set for the British (about 34,000), Italians (3,800) and Chinese (105). Even in the Hitler era, when millions needed a sanctuary, the U.S. admitted only about 115,000 refugees from Nazi Germany throughout the 1930s.

It was perhaps the incalculable enrichment of America by those refugees—by Albert Einstein and Thomas Mann, Artur Schnabel and Paul Tillich—that started the process of change. By special legislation in 1948, the U.S. began admitting more than 400,000 "displaced persons." Then came 32,000 refugees from the Hungarian revolt of 1956 and some 650,000 from Fidel Castro's seizure of Cuba in 1959. But only under President John F. Kennedy, great-grandson of an immigrant farmer from Ireland's County Wexford, did overall reform begin. According to the Immigration Act of 1965, which finally took effect in 1968 national quotas were abolished. A ceiling now limits immigration to 170,000 from the Eastern Hemisphere (and no more than 20,000 from any one country) and 120,000 from the Western Hemisphere, for an annual total of 290,000...

TIME, *July 5, 1976*

• **Know-nothing** : a semi-secret political party of the 1850's whose members always replied "*I know nothing*" when questioned. It appealed to racial and religious prejudices and was born of hostility towards German and Irish immigrants.

Only one nation in the world

Foreign policy ['fɔrin 'pɔlisi], successes [sə'ksesiz], interest ['intrist], Annapolis [ə'næpəlis], focus ['fəukəs], morality [mə'ræliti], inadvertently [,inəd'və:tntli], effectuated [i'fektjueitid], Pakistan [,pɑ:kis'tɑ:n], Chile ['tʃili], Cambodia [kæm'bəudjə], exemplified [i'gzemplifaid], commitment [kə'mitmənt], embarrassing predicament [im'bærəsiŋ pri'dikəmənt], secrecy ['si:krisi], ethics ['eθiks], characteristic [,kæriktə'ristik], inherently [in'hiərəntli], competent ['kɔmpitnt], compassionate [kəm'pæʃənit], capable ['keipəbl], distrust [dis'trʌst].

Every concerned American has given thought in recent years to this nation's foreign policy, both its •flaws and successes. It has been a field of keen interest to me since my days at •Annapolis, when my awareness of American military power helped •focus a more general concern on the United States' role in the world.

Recently I met with about a dozen of our nation's top political writers for several hours of discussion about subjects of current interest and major importance. During a heated exchange, one of the reporters exclaimed, "There is no place for morality in foreign policy!" Although he later modified his position, he perhaps inadvertently described the feelings of many Americans about foreign policy as effectuated in recent years.

As it has related to such areas as Pakistan, Chile, Cambodia, and Viet Nam, our government's foreign policy has not exemplified any •commitment to moral principles. Furthermore, each time we have become •embroiled in an embarrassing •predicament, it has become apparent that our leaders have often departed from the more honest inclinations of the American people. This has required varying degrees of secrecy and •outright lying.

A nation's domestic and foreign policies actions should be derived from the same standards of ethics, honesty and morality which are characteristic of the individual citizens of the nation. The people of this country are inherently unselfish, open, honest, decent, competent, and compassionate. Our government should be the same, in all its actions and attitudes.

There is only one nation in the world which is capable of true leadership among the community of nations, and that is the United States of America. Many citizens of other countries know this to be true, and have looked with concern and consternation on our •fumbling and •heavy-handed administration of ill-advised international policies during the last few years. During my own travels in the Far East, Europe, the Americas, and the Mideast, I have found a natural friendship toward the American people, but a growing distrust of our government.

JIMMY CARTER, *Why not the Best*

• **flaws** : defects • **Annapolis** : the Naval Academy • **focus** : (here) clarify • **commitment** : engagement • **embroiled** : mixed up • **predicament** : difficult situation • **outright** : pure and simple • **fumbling** : (here) incompetent • **heavy-handed** : *maladroit.*

TOWARDS COMPREHENSION

1 ***Was this text written before or after Carter became President? Justify your answer.***

2 ***This text is about :***

a. America's domestic policy. b. America's foreign policy. c. both foreign and domestic policy.

3 ***Express the ideas differently, in simpler words if you can :***

IN OTHER WORDS

1. It has been a field of keen interest to me since my days at Annapolis.
(use : be interested)
2. When my awareness of American military power helped focus a more general concern on the United States' role in the world.
(there I became aware . . . .)
3. Our government's foreign policy has not exemplified any commitment to moral principles.
4. A nation's domestic and foreign policies actions should be derived from the same standards of ethics, honesty and morality that are characteristic of the individual citizens of the nation.

4 ***Try and sum up Carter's views in a couple of sentences.***

IMPROVE YOUR VOCABULARY
concern, concerned

It doesn't concern me = it's no concern of mine.
As far as I am concerned . . . .
As far as foreign policy is concerned . . . . Where foreign policy is concerned.
As concerns foreign policy . . . . = as regards, regarding . . . .
All the people concerned should be notified *(= il faudrait aviser tous les intéressés).*
We are not concerned with that matter *(nous n'avons rien à voir...).*
The people concerned in the riot (= implicated) have been arrested.
You'd better not concern yourself about that problem (=mind your own business).
He is concerned about his wife's health (=worried).
Don't be concerned about me (=don't worry).
He looked very much concerned (very anxious).

EXPRESSION DE LA DURÉE

a. *Pour interroger :* **how long.**
How long have you known her? *(depuis combien de temps la connaissez-vous?)*
How long did you stay there? *(combien de temps êtes-vous resté là-bas?)*

b. **ago + passé :** l'action est terminée, aucun lien entre le passé et le présent, entre l'actuel et le révolu. On exprime ainsi combien de temps s'est écoulé depuis la fin de cette action.
I met her two days ago *(je l'ai rencontrée il y a 2 jours).*

c. **for + parfait :** l'action n'est pas terminée au moment où je parle, ou vient de se terminer. Il y a lien entre le passé et le présent.
How long have you been waiting for me? *(= depuis combien de temps m'attendez-vous?)*
I've been waiting for you for three hours.

d. **parfait simple ou progressif :** On peut trouver l'un ou l'autre. Le parfait progressif exprime notamment que l'on veut laisser entendre que l'action va déborder sur l'avenir, ou que l'on considère le déroulement de l'action et non son achèvement.
I have been working for three hours and I must still go on. *(= Cela fait 3 heures que je travaille et il faut que je continue.) Comparez :* I've been repairing my car all the afternoon, my clothes are dirty and I'm tired, *et :* I have repaired my car, I won't need to take it to the garage.

e. **parfait + since :** met l'accent sur le point de départ de l'action et exprime la durée écoulée depuis ce point de départ.
I've known her since (yesterday, 1976, last week, her mother's death) *(= je la connais depuis...).*

5 *Drawing on the text make a few sentences on the following patterns:*

1. When I was at Annapolis, I became aware of. . . .
2. During my stay at Annapolis, I came to realize that. . . .
3. I . . . . since . . . . at Annapolis.

SHOULD

Voir p. 32

MODAL + PASSIF

6 *Drawing on the text, make as many sentences as you can beginning with:*

1. A nation's foreign policy should (be) . . . .
2. Our government should (not) . . . .

7 *Put the verbs between brackets into the right tenses (past or perfect):*

1. I (often, give thought) to this problem. 2. I (not, become aware) of the importance of this problem until I (go) to Annapolis. 3. I (travel) a lot, and I can tell you that the United States is held in high esteem abroad. 4. I (travel) a lot before I (become) President and each time I (go) to a foreign country I (be struck) by a growing distrust of our government. 5. As concerns foreign policy, our government (often, make) blunders which (tarnish) our reputation abroad. 6. A number of mistakes (be made) during the last few years.

LES ARTICLES

Ils se présentent sous 3 formes :
1. article zéro (∅) : he lacks courage, I hate dinner parties, 2. **a(n)**. 3. **the.**

Pour éviter les erreurs les plus fréquentes, on retiendra 4 grands principes :

1. Un nom peut être dénombrable (ou comptable), **ou indénombrable** (ou non comptable).
Un nom abstrait peut être dénombrable : patience *(indénombrable)* is a virtue *(dénombrable).*
Un nom concret peut être indénombrable : I like beer.
Un indénombrable peut se comporter comme un dénombrable : I could do with a beer *(= je boirais bien une bière).* He showed a courage he had never shown before.

2. **Un nom ou un groupe nominal peuvent avoir une valeur générique,** c'est-à-dire désigner toute une catégorie d'objets, d'animaux ou de personnes. Ils peuvent également avoir une **valeur spécifique** et désigner un ou plusieurs éléments de cette catégorie.

a) Valeur générique : avec les indénombrables, seul l'article zéro est la forme possible : wine is expensive, courage in the face of death is rare.
Avec les dénombrables, les 3 formes sont possibles, mais c'est ∅ qui est la forme la plus fréquente :
I hate dinner parties. A dinner party can be very boring. Lions are dangerous animals. The lion is a dangerous animal. A lion is a dangerous animal.
Exception : **man, woman** ; is man really different from woman?

b) Valeur spécifique : un nom peut alors être indéfini ou défini.
i. indéfini : I know a specialist in plastic surgery. His father is a specialist in plastic surgery.
ii. défini : the specialist you're speaking of is a friend of mine.

3. La détermination peut être :

a) Explicite : si le nom est suivi d'un complément ou d'une sub. relative (un adj. ne suffit généralement pas ; ex. : modern life, public opinion) : the man in the black mac over there is the specialist I told you about. The courage he showed is very unusual. The books you've bought must be very expensive.

b) Implicite : si le contexte permet au locuteur et/ou à l'interlocuteur d'identifier, de reconnaître l'objet ou la personne : you didn't seem to like the tea (c'est-à-dire le thé que vous venez de boire). Actually, I don't like tea (on retrouve ici la valeur générique).

c) Naturelle : si l'objet est unique : the sun, the moon, the sky.
N.B. On comprendra mieux ce phénomène de détermination si on sait que *the* est une forme atténuée de *this* et qu'il garde, de ce fait, une certaine valeur démonstrative.

4. The + adj. + verbe au pluriel = valeur générique :
the rich and the poor are equal in the face of death (= les riches, toute la catégorie des riches...). Si l'on veut passer du générique au spécifique, on devra dire : a/the rich man/boy/girl...
Cette règle s'applique aux adjectifs de nationalité terminés par -ch et -sh : the French like wine, mais : the Frenchman I met the other day hates wine.

N.B. On remarquera que le nom à valeur générique est souvent suivi d'un présent simple (valeur de généralité, d'habitude).

8 ***Supply the article*** (∅, a(n), the) ***and justify your choice (in French):***

1. I have always been interested in . . . . foreign policy. 2. . . . . morality in . . . . foreign policy is . . . . subject worth debating. 3. . . . . nation's foreign policy is sometimes conditioned by . . . . considerations which have no bearing on . . . . international questions. 4. Does it take . . . . courage to become . . . . diplomat? 5. . . . . citizens of this country have . . . . growing distrust of . . . . foreigners. 6. . . . . decision you're talking about has been prepared in . . . . secrecy. 7. Do you think . . . . English really want to join . . . . Common Market? 8. . . . . American people is fundamentally different from . . . . French people, and yet. . . . . Americans and . . . . French like and esteem one another.

TOWARDS APPRECIATION

9 ***Complete the following:***

1. It's quite natural for a candidate to the White House . . . .
2. It's quite natural that a candidate . . . .
3. What he says is all the more important as the President . . . .
4. That he should put emphasis on morality is . . . .

10 ***How does Carter see the average American? And how does the rest of the world see him?***

11 ***Can you think of examples of America's*** *"fumbling and heavy- handed administration of ill-advised international policies"*, ***then imagine what an opponent of America's foreign policy could say:***

a. ***As regards the past:***
They should (not) have . . . .
Instead of . . . . they should have . . . .

b. ***To-day:***
Instead of . . . . they'd better . . . .

MODAL

Voir p. 32

12 ***Creative written work:***

Carter has become President. How far has he changed the world image of America? Is it a change for the better or for the worse?

At a dinner a very pompous American woman was seated next to a rabbi. Wishing to impress him she said rather grandly, "One of my ancestors signed the Declaration of Independence." "Indeed," replied the rabbi, "one of mine wrote the Ten Commandments."

Extract from: Roots

Secret ['si:krit], excuse [iks'kju:s], efficiently [i'fiʃəntli], noticed ['nəutist], sweated ['swetid], issue ['iʃu:], gauging ['geidʒiŋ], capable ['keipəbl], poleaxed ['pəulækst].

Kunta was kidnapped in 1767 at the age of 16 and sold as a slave in Virginia. On arriving at the plantation, he escaped after half strangling the head slave, Samson. He was recaptured, brutally whipped and kept in chains for four days as a punishment. The second time he escaped, Samson captured him again but not before Kunta had tried to kill him. After that Samson kept a close watch on him.

Through the days that followed, it was as if he and Samson shared some secret pact of hatred. Kunta knew how closely he was being watched; he knew that Samson was waiting for any excuse to hurt him in a manner the •toubob would approve. Kunta responded by •going through the motions of doing whatever work he was given to do as if nothing had happened—but even faster and more efficiently than before. He had noticed how the •"oberseer" paid less attention to those who worked the hardest or did the most •grinning. Kunta couldn't bring himself to grin, but with •grim satisfaction he noted that the more he sweated, the less often the •lash fell across his back.

One evening after work, Kunta was passing near the barn when he spotted a thick iron •wedge lying half concealed among some of the sawed sections of trees where the "oberseer" had two men splitting firewood. Glancing around quickly in all directions, and seeing no one watching, Kunta snatched up the wedge and, concealing it in his shirt, hurried to his hut. Using it to dig a hole in the hard dirt floor, he placed the wedge in the hole, packed the •loose dirt back over it, then beat it down carefully with a rock until the floor looked completely undisturbed.

He spent a sleepless night worrying that a wedge discovered missing might cause all of the cabins to be searched. He felt better when there was no outcry the following day, but he still wasn't sure just how he might employ the wedge to help himself escape, when that time came again.

What he really wanted to get his hands on was one of those long knives that the "oberseer" would •issue to a few of the men each morning. But each evening he would see the "oberseer" demanding the knives back and counting them carefully. With one of those knives, he could cut •brush to move more quickly within a forest, and if he had to, he could kill a dog—or a man.

One cold afternoon almost a moon later—the sky •bleak and •slaty—Kunta was on his way across one of the fields to help another man repair a fence when, to his astonishment, what looked like salt began to fall from the sky, at first lightly, then more rapidly and thickly. As the salt became a flaky whiteness, he heard the blacks nearby exclaiming, "Snow!" and guessed that was what they called it. When he bent down to pick some of it up, it was cold to his touch—and even colder when he licked it off a finger with his tongue. It stung, and it had no taste whatever. He tried to smell it, but not only did there seem to be no odor either, it also disappeared into watery nothingness. And wherever he looked on the ground was a whitish film.

But by the time he reached the other side of the field, the "snow" had stopped and even begun to melt away. Hiding his amazement, Kunta •composed himself and nodded silently to his black partner, who was waiting by the broken fence. They set to work—Kunta helping the other man to •string a kind of metal twine that he called •"wire." After a while they reached a place almost hidden by tall grass, and as the other man hacked some of it down with the long knife he carried, Kunta's eyes were •gauging the distance between where he stood and the nearest woods. He knew that Samson was nowhere near and the "oberseer" was keeping watch in another field that day. Kunta worked busily, to give the other man no suspicion of what was in his mind. But his breath came tensely as he stood holding the wire tight and looking down on the head of the man bent over his work. The knife had been left a few steps behind them, where the •chopping of the brush had stopped.

With a silent prayer to Allah, Kunta clasped his hands together, lifted them high, and brought them down across the back of the man's neck with all the violence of which his slight body was capable. The man crumpled without a sound, as if he had been •poleaxed. Within a moment, Kunta had bound the man's ankles and wrists with the wire. Snatching up the long knife, Kunta suppressed the impulse to •stab him—this was not the hated Samson—and went running toward the woods, bent over almost double. He felt a lightness, as if he were running in a dream, as if this weren't really happening at all.

He came out of it a few moments later—when he heard the man he had left alive yelling at the top of his lungs. He should have killed him, Kunta thought, furious with himself, as he tried to run yet faster. Instead of fighting his way deeply into the underbrush when he reached the woods, he •skirted it this time. He knew that he had to achieve distance first, then concealment. If he got far enough fast enough, he would have time to find a good place to hide and rest before moving on, under cover of the night.

ALEX HALEY, *Roots*

Alex Haley was born in 1921 at Ithaca, New York. "Roots", his first novel, is the story of Kunta Kinte, his African ancestor. It is based on an oral tradition in his mother's family and was written after twelve years of research that finally took him back to Kunta's village in Gambia.

• **toubob** : white man • **going through the motions of doing** : mechanically doing • **oberseer** (=overseer) : *contremaître* • **did the most grinning** : *avaient le plus large sourire* • **with grim satisfaction** : *avec une satisfaction farouche* • **lash** (whiplash) : *fouet* • **wedge** : *coin* • **loose** : *meuble* (adj.) • **issue** : distribute • **brush** : *broussailles* • **bleak** : *morne* • **slaty** : *couleur d'ardoise* • **composed himself** : controlled himself • **string** : *tendre* • **wire** : *fil* • **gauging** : estimating • **chopping** : cutting • **as if he had been poleaxed** : *comme s'il avait été terrassé d'un coup de merlin* • **stab** : *poignarder* • **skirted** : went round.

TOWARDS COMPREHENSION

1 ***Fill in the gaps with the following verbs:*** conceal, hurry, search, reach, melt away, lift, bind, glance (a) round, escape, notice, (be) missing.

1. There was no time to lose, so he . . . .
2. This box is too heavy, I'll never be able to . . . . it.
3. If you . . . . his legs together, he won't be able to . . . .
4. You can . . . . the house from top to bottom, you'll never find where the treasure is . . . .
5. The overseer issued 20 knives; but there are only 15 left; 5 are . . . .
6. If I could . . . . the wood over there, I would be safe.
7. If he had . . . . he would have . . . . that he was being watched.
8. If the snow doesn't . . . . they will easily follow his tracks.
9. When the overseer came back, he found that a slave was . . . .
10. He managed to . . . . without being . . . . by the overseer.

2 ***Right or wrong? Justify your answer.***

1. Kunta didn't conceal his hatred for Samson.
2. He worked hard because he was afraid of Samson.
3. He found an iron wedge.
4. The next morning all the cabins were searched.
5. What he needed most was a long knife.
6. He asked the overseer for one.
7. One afternoon, as he was working with a white man, he escaped into the woods.
8. He had to kill the man he was working with.
9. The wedge proved very useful.
10. If he had not had a knife he could not have escaped.

3 ***Test your memory. Did these events happen in this order?***

1. One evening after work, Kunta passed near the barn.
2. He glanced around quickly in all directions.
3. He spotted an iron wedge.
4. He dug a hole.
5. He concealed the wedge in his shirt.
6. He placed the wedge in the hole.
7. He spent a sleepless night.

"A moon later" :

8. It started snowing.
9. He went to the fields to help another man repair a fence.
10. He picked up a long knife.
11. He struck the other man.
12. The man yelled at the top of his lungs.
13. Kunta bound the man's ankles and wrists.
14. He ran towards the woods.

LANGUAGE PRACTICE

4 ***Compare:***

A. He went through the motions of doing whatever work he was given. He did not want to attract the overseer's attention.

B. He went through the motions . . . . so as not to attract the overseer's attention.

A. He worked even faster than before. He wanted the overseer to pay less attention to him.

B. He worked even faster than before so that the overseer should pay less attention to him.

HOW TO EXPRESS PURPOSE

Voir p. 18

Give the B-pattern:

1. He behaved as if nothing had happened. He did not want to be watched closely.
2. He worked hard. He did not want to get whipped.
3. He worked as usual. He did not want Samson to get an excuse to strike him.
4. He concealed the wedge in his shirt. He did not want the others to know what he was planning.

5 ***Using information from the text, make a few more sentences on the same pattern.***

FOR FEAR OF/FOR FEAR THAT

expriment également le but, mais impliquent qu'il y a crainte parce qu'il y a risque :
He glanced in all directions for fear of being seen (le sujet est le même dans les deux propositions).
He glanced in all directions for fear that the others might/should see him (il y a deux sujets différents).

6 *Connect the following pairs of sentences, using either* for fear of *or* for fear that:

1. He behaved as usual. He did not want the overseer to suspect something.
2. He beat the dirt down carefully. He did not want the others to see he had dug a hole.
3. He worked busily. He did not want to arouse suspicion.
4. He kept silent. He did not want to give himself away. (betray himself)

Go on...

MODAL + HAVE + PART. PASSÉ

Voir p. 40

7 *Re-cast the above sentences as follows:*

If he had not glanced in all directions, he might have been seen.
If he had not glanced in all directions, the others might have seen him.

HOW TO EXPRESS APPEARANCES
AS IF/AS THOUGH

Ces deux conjonctions sont interchangeables. Elles sont parfois suivies d'un prétérit modal, ce qui souligne le caractère incertain de ce qui est dit et met en évidence l'opposition entre l'apparence et la réalité :
he walks as if he were drunk (but he is not).
Mais on trouve également le présent :
he walks as if he is drunk (= judging from the way he walks, he is drunk).
Elles sont souvent associées à *going to* :
it looks as if it is going to rain. He looks/sounds as if he is going to kill the overseer.

8 *Compare:*

A. He did whatever work he was given to do as if nothing had happened.
B. He did whatever work he was given to do, you might have thought (that) nothing had happened.

Give the other form:

1. He worked very hard, you might have thought he was trying to find favour with the overseer.
2. He struck the man's neck as if he wanted to kill him.
3. The man crumpled without a sound, you might have thought he was dead.
4. Through the days that followed, it was as if he and Samson shared some secret pact of hatred.
5. Kunta worked even faster and more efficiently as if he enjoyed his work.

TOWARDS APPRECIATION

9 *Appearances may be deceptive/misleading. Complete the following:*

1. He went through the motions of .... but actually/in fact ....
2. .... as if nothing was the matter.

10 *Show that it must have been very hard for a slave to run away:*

(slaves were constantly .... judging from what Haley says, we can easily ....)

11 *How far were the circumstances favourable on that cold afternoon?*

(Kunta must have thought he stood a good chance of .... as/since ....)

12 *What do you think of the "the snow episode". Is Kunta's amazement well-rendered? Could the passage be cut out? Isn't the snow likely to ruin his plans?*

13 *Creative oral work:*

You are a film director shooting this scene. Explain to the actors what is expected of them.

14 *Debate:*

Do you think Kunta should have killed the man? In other words, does the end justify the means?

15 *Creative written work:* Imagine what happened next.

16 *Find a suitable title for the passage.*

FOR FURTHER DISCUSSION

Racines

Vous n'oublierez plus Kounta Kinté, ce noir de Gambie qu'enlèvent, à 16 ans, des marchands d'esclaves. Ils le jettent dans les cales du « Lord Lionier », un bateau négrier. Quelques semaines plus tard, « La Gazette du Maryland » — ce Maryland qui n'est encore qu'une des colonies anglaises d'Amérique — annonce l'arrivée, le 29 septembre 1767, dans le port d'Annapolis, du navire négrier. La mise en vente, aussi, « contre argent comptant ou lettre de change, d'une cargaison d'esclaves sains et de premier choix ».

Deux siècles plus tard, jour pour jour, le Noir américain Alex Haley pleure sur l'un des quais d'Annapolis. Voilà cinq ans qu'il est parti à la recherche de ses ancêtres. Journaliste à « Play Boy », écrivain — on lui doit la rédaction de « L'Autobiographie de Malcolm X », le leader des Musulmans noirs — il sait maintenant qu'il est le lointain descendant de Kounta Kinté l'Africain. Qu'entre eux il n'y a que sept générations d'hommes et de femmes dont les vies représentent un pan caché ou mal connu de l'Histoire américaine. Sept générations arrivées sur le sol d'Amérique avant même que naissent les États-Unis et qui ont donné aujourd'hui un peuple de 25 millions de Noirs, dont les ancêtres ont été, comme Kounta Kinté, *déracinés*. Ainsi naît « Racines », le livre d'Alex Haley, quête et création d'un passé dont le peuple noir a été dépossédé. Publié en 1976, le livre devient en deux mois un phénomène social : près d'un million d'exemplaires vendus. Des vitrines de librairies brisées pour voler les livres. Huit épisodes d'un feuilleton télévisé, dont le dernier est regardé par 80 millions d'Américains. Record jamais égalé. Un choc émotionnel : les images, les phrases sont brutales. Les Blancs volent, violent, mutilent, tuent. Les Américains découvrent le passé de violence et d'oppression que cache l'Histoire de chaque État. Et ils osent le connaître : des centaines d'établissements scolaires inscrivent « Racines » à leur programme.

Max GALLO, *L'Express*, 13-19 juin 1977

1 ***Read the text carefully once or twice, then answer the following questions:***

1. What was Alex Haley's purpose when he wrote *Roots?*
2. Do you remember the details showing that this book was what M. Gallo calls a *"social phenomenon"?*
3. What kind of past did the Americans discover through *Roots?*
4. Did television play a part in that discovery? (a serial in 8 instalments.)
5. What were, according to M. Gallo, the reactions of the Americans to the discovery of such a past? What does he mean by *"They dare to become acquainted with it"*. What was *"daring"* about their reactions?
6. Do you think that the book and the film may have an influence on the relations between the whites and the blacks? (increase the whites' sense of guilt/make for better relations, better understanding)

2 ***Make a prècis of the text (in English) in not more than 100 words, then in not more than 50.***

Extract from: Black boy

Series ['siə,ri:z], attitude ['ætitju:d], doubted ['dautid], impatient [im'peiʃənt], leisurely ['leʒəli], concern [kən'sə:n], triumphantly [trai'ʌmfəntli], noticed ['nəutist].

I held a series of •petty jobs for short periods, quitting some to work elsewhere, being driven off others because of my attitude, my speech, the look in my eyes. I was no nearer than ever to my goal of saving enough money to leave. At times I doubted if I could ever do it.

One jobless morning I went to my old classmate, Griggs, who worked for a Capitol Street jeweler. He was washing the windows of the store when I came upon him.

"Do you know where I can find a job?" I asked.

He looked at me with scorn.

"Yes, I know where you can find a job," he said, laughing.

"Where?"

"But I wonder if you can hold it," he said.

"What do you mean?" I asked. "Where's the job?"

"Take your time," he said. "You know, Dick, I know you. You've been trying to hold a job all summer, and you can't. Why? Because you're impatient. That's your big fault."

I said nothing, because he was repeating what I had already heard him say. He lit a cigarette and blew out smoke •leisurely.

"Well," I said, •egging him on to speak.

"I wish to hell I could talk to you," he said.

"I think I know what you want to tell me," I said.

He clapped me on the shoulder, his face was full of fear, hate, concern for me.

"Do you want to get killed?" he asked me.

"Hell, no!"

"Then, for God's sake, learn how to live in the South!"

"What do you mean?" I demanded. "Let white people tell me that. Why should you?"

"See?" he said triumphantly, pointing his finger at me. "There it is, *now*! It's in your face. You won't let people tell you things. You rush too much. I'm trying to help you and you won't let me." He paused and looked about; the streets were filled with white people. He spoke to me in a low, full tone. "Dick, look, you're black, black, *black*, see? Can't you understand that?"

"Sure. I understand it," I said.

"You don't act a damn bit like it," he spat.

He then •reeled off an account of my actions on every job I had held that summer.

"How did you know that?" I asked.

"White people make it their business to watch niggers," he explained. "And they pass the word around. Now, my boss is a Yankee and he tells me things. You're marked already."

Could I believe him? Was it true? How could I ever learn this strange world of white people?

"Then tell me how must I act?" I asked humbly. "I just want to make enough money to leave."

"Wait and I'll tell you," he said.

At that moment a woman and two men stepped from the jewelry store ; I moved to one side to let them pass, my mind intent upon Griggs's words. Suddenly Griggs reached for my arm and jerked me violently, sending me stumbling three or four feet across the pavement. I •whirled.

"What's the matter with you?" I asked.

Griggs •glared at me, then laughed.

"I'm teaching you how to get out of white people's way," he said.

I looked at the people who had come out of the store ; yes, they were *white*, but I had not noticed it.

"Do you see what I mean?" he asked. "White people want you out of their way." He pronounced the words slowly so that they would sink into my mind.

"I know what you mean," I breathed.

"Dick, I'm treating you like a brother," he said. "You act around white people as if you didn't know that they were white. And they *see* it."

"Oh, Christ, I can't be a slave," I said hopelessly.

"But you've got to eat," he said.

"Yes, I got to eat."

"Then start acting like it," he •hammered at me, •pounding his fist in his palm. "When you're in front of white people, *think* before you act, *think* before you speak. Your way of doing things is all right among *our* people, but not for *white* people. They won't •stand for it."

RICHARD WRIGHT, 1937, *Black Boy*
Published by Harper and Row

Richard Wright, one of the most talented Negro Writers, was born in Mississipi in 1908 and died in Paris in 1960. He was abandoned by his parents and had a very unhappy childhood. He succeeded in leaving the South as a teenager and went to live in Chicago. "Black Boy" (1937) is autobiographical and recalls conditions in the South in 1925, that is, when segregation was still legal.

● **petty** : unimportant ● **leisurely** : unhurriedly ● **egging him on** : trying to make him... ● **reeled off** : *débita* ● **whirled** : turned round quickly ● **glared** : looked furiously ● **hammered** : *en martelant ses mots* ● **pounded** : hit his palm with his fist, using the latter like a hammer ● **stand for** : tolerate.

TOWARDS COMPREHENSION

1 ***Pick out the sentence that best expresses his old classmate's feelings.***

2 ***Express differently :***

IN OTHER WORDS

1. He looked at me with scorn. (.... scornful look ..../scornfully)
2. One jobless morning. (.... when I was ....)
3. His face was full of concern for me. (he looked ....)
4. Griggs glared at me. (.... looked ....)

3 ***Right or wrong. Justify your answer.***

1. His present aim in life is to save money.
2. He needs money because he wants to buy a house.
3. He has had lots of jobs but he could not hold them because the work was too hard.
4. According to Griggs, Dick's big fault is his lack of patience.
5. Griggs wants to teach him how to live in the South.
6. Griggs speaks loudly so as to be heard by white people.
7. Dick thinks that Griggs does not understand him.

4 ***Test your memory. Finish the sentences without looking at the text:***

1. I was no nearer than ever to my goal of . . . .
2. One jobless morning . . . .
3. I said nothing, because he was repeating . . . .
4. He clapped me on the shoulder, his face was . . . .
5. I'm trying to help you and . . . .
6. How could I ever learn . . . .

LANGUAGE PRACTICE

GET + PART. PASSÉ

Cette construction a valeur de passif. On pourrait également avoir : *be + part. passé :*
He was knocked down on his way home
or : he got knocked down on his way home.
Cette dernière construction est plus familière. Elle n'est pas suivie d'un complément d'agent.

5 ***React as follows:***
(Suppose that 2 boys are trying to caution Dick.)

A. You'd better be careful, or they'll kill you.
B. Yes, you behave as if you wanted to get killed.

A. . . . . careful, ... punish . . . . B. . . . .
A. . . . . work more . . . . fire . . . . B. . . . .
A. . . . . be more polite . . . . beat . . . . B. . . . .
A. . . . . not say that . . . . lynch . . . . B. . . . .
A. . . . . not say what you think . . . . send you to prison. B. . . . .
Go on

HOW TO EXPRESS ADVICE
you'd better + bv

6 ***Drawing on the text—or not—make a few sentences beginning with:***

Being black means that { you've got to . . . . / you may . . . . if . . . . / you aren't allowed to . . . . }
Working for a white man . . . .
Living in the South . . . .
Rebelling against white people . . . .

GERUND
Voir p. 142

7 ***Turn into reported speech:***

1. "Do you know where I can find a job?", I asked.
2. "I know where you can find a job", he said.
3. "I wonder if you can hold it", he said.
4. "What do you mean?", I asked.
5. "I think I know what you want to tell me", I said.
6. "Do you want to get killed?", he asked me.
7. "Learn how to live in the South", he said to me.
8. "You won't let people tell you things", he said.
9. "I'm trying to help you and you won't let me", he concluded.
10. "How did you know that", I asked.

REPORTED SPEECH
Voir p. 23

8 ***Compare:***

"I'll never be able to stay in the South."
He thought he'd never be able to stay in the South.
He doubted if he'd ever be able to stay in the South.
or: He wondered if he'd ever be able to stay in the South.

Give the other forms using: I doubt, I wonder, I'm not sure, ... if/whether...

"I'll never be able to get a job/work for a white man/learn to behave myself/hold this job/save enough money to leave."
Go on.

EVER

s'emploie dans les énoncés interrogatifs. Il a souvent le sens de « at least once » :
Have you ever been to Britain.
On le trouve aussi après les semi-négatifs :
I hardly ever talk to them *(je ne leur parle presque jamais).*

9 ***Drawing on the text, say what Griggs reproaches Dick for.***

He reproaches him for { being . . . . doing. / not being . . . .

10 ***Compose dialogues like this:***

A. I think you're too impatient.
B. And I think you're too patient/you aren't impatient enough.

A. I think you rush too much. B. . . . .
A. I think you speak too much. B. . . . .
A. You've got to learn to wait. B. . . . .
A. You lack moderation. B. . . . .
Go on...

TOO/ENOUGH

TOWARDS APPRECIATION

11 ***Griggs' attitude. Make a few sentences on this pattern.***

It looks as if he were on the white people's side, but he can't be on their side.
He looks as if he hated Dick, but . . . ., if he . . . . he . . . .
He looks as if he were against . . . . but . . . ., if he . . . . he . . . .

CAN'T

sert à exprimer la déduction logique à la forme négative. Il a donc un sens contraire à celui de *must* exprimant une forte probabilité.
He must be English ≠ he can't be English *(il ne peut pas, il ne doit pas être...; il n'est pas possible qu'il soit anglais).*

12 ***Now explain what he is trying to do:***

A. Isn't he trying to teach him how to live in the South?
B. Yes, what he is trying to teach him is how . . . .
Go on...

13 ***Compare the two boys:***

. . . . hates as much . . . . but if he showed . . . . he . . . .

So one . . . . whereas the other . . . .

14 ***Creative written work.***

Expand into a paragraph of 15 lines: *"... being driven off others because of my attitude, my speech, the look in my eyes."*

15 ***Creative oral work:*** Dick gets a job, tries to follow his friend's advice until the day when...

16 ***Choose the most suitable title and justify your choice.***

This strange world of white people. Learning how to live in the South.
A lesson in hypocrisy. A tricky master.
The art of dissembling (=hiding one's true feelings).

Extract from: The consumer

Advertising ['ædvətaiziŋ], indispensable [,indis'pensəbl], occupy ['ɔkjupai], associate [ə'səuʃieit], the auto industry [ði 'ɔ:təu 'indəstri], a cereal advertiser [ə 'siəriəl 'ædvətaizə], analyse ['ænəlaiz], opposite ['ɔpəzit], products ['prɔdʌkts], particular [pə'tikjulə].

Advertising plays upon the consumer's emotions and motivations. Advertisers know that people buy goods and services, not because these are indispensable, but because most goods and services are also symbols of the station in society one occupies or one wishes to occupy. Since many of these are bought because one wishes to conform, to be one of the crowd, advertisers cater to this wish. They tell us, for example, that at one time those who smoked a filter cigarette were "alone in the world" and go on to suggest that, today, smoking a filter cigarette is the thing to do because "everybody's doing it." Some advertising caters to our desire to be different (most people want to be only a little different). Most of us are probably snobs: we want to associate with "our own kind"—that is, with people we think are better or different. Advertisers make effective use of "snob appeal," as when they urge the consumer to "get away from the crowd," and go off on his own in a smart sports car sold by one of the giants of the auto industry.

Advertisers also know that many consumers like to do what they think well-known people are doing. A cereal advertiser will tell children, and through children their parents, that a famous football player eats Tiger Breakfast Food and that "you too" can grow up to be a tiger if you sit down and have a bowlful each morning. Few of us are immune to the blandishments of the advertisers. There are intellectual appeals to those who are, or think they are, scholars, and who, therefore, "never read advertising." There are appeals to our desires to protect our loved ones and to preserve motherhood, fatherhood, and family life. One mouthwash advertises that grandpa will be loved by his granddaughter, and she will sit in his lap, if only he would regularly use the mouthwash that "kills germs." Insurance companies effectively show an actor playing the part of the all-knowing insurance agent, whose only desire is to analyze a family man's financial picture to provide him with the insurance that will give the family a reasonable living standard even if the breadwinner should die. Advertisers cater to everyone's desire to be attractive to the opposite sex, and they do this most effectively by showing their products being used by beautiful men and women. One hair dressing advertises that "a little •dab will do you" and adds that the girls will •go wild. Another suggests that hair rinsed in a particular hair coloring and shampoo will make all the men take notice. Another advertiser has a •sultry girl advise men to "take it off, take it all off"—their •whiskers, that is—by using a particular brand of shaving cream!

GERALD LEINWAND, *Problems of American Society. The Consumer*

• **a little dab:** *une légère application* • **go wild:** go mad (about you) • **sultry:** ardent and sexy
• **whiskers:** *barbe.*

TOWARDS COMPREHENSION

1 *Understanding some key-words:*

1. symbols of *the station* in society. (l. 3)
   a) profession. *b*) (social) position. *c*) success.
2. advertisers *cater to* this wish. (l. 5)
   a) exploit. *b*) try to satisfy. *c*) analyze.
3. we want *to associate with...* (l. 9)
   a) look like. *b*) do better than. *c*) be often in the company of.
4. *our own kind.* (l. 9)
   a) people different from us. *b*) people of our social class. *c*) people wealthier than we are.
5. when they *urge* the consumer. (l. 11)
   a) ask. *b*) advise. *c*) try to persuade.
6. the *blandishments* of the advertisers. (l. 17)
   a) menaces. *b*) dangers. *c*) flattery.

2 *Pick out the words and phrases referring to:*

a. the consumer's emotions.
b. the consumer's motivations.

3 *Make a list of the reasons why people buy goods and services.*

4 *Test your memory (after reading or listening to the text): finish the following sentences without looking at the text:*

1. Advertisers know that people buy goods and services, not because . . . .
2. Most of us are probably snobs: we want . . . .
3. Advertisers also know that many consumers like . . . .
4. Few of us . . . .

LANGUAGE PRACTICE

5 *Make as many sentences as you can on this pattern:*

HOW TO PERSUADE PEOPLE TO DO SOMETHING
GET + OBJ + TO-INF

The main	purpose concern	of advertisers is to get	people consumers women children motorists	to...

BY + GERUND

6 *By what means do they get people to . . . .?*

Advertisers try to get . . . . to . . . . by . . . .

7 *Make as many sensible sentences as you can, read them aloud, then translate them:*

Example: Advertisers badger people into buying things they don't need. (Les annonceurs forcent/amènent les gens à acheter des choses dont ils n'ont pas besoin en les harcelant/en les importunant sans cesse/par la technique de harcèlement...)
On notera que le verbe qui suit "into" indique le résultat, tandis que celui qui précède indique le moyen utilisé pour atteindre ce résultat.

Advertisers	badger humiliate cajole talk irritate shame trick	people consumers parents motorists women	into	buying purchasing changing	lots of useless things. their cars every year. things they don't need. foodstuffs in large quantities.

8 ***Written work: Imagine all the possible beginnings:***

.... into purchasing something he may not have thought of buying.
.... that you had never dreamt about.

ONE

1. Peut être un numéral : How many envelopes do you need? One is enough. They came in by ones and twos *(ils arrivèrent un par un ou deux par deux).*

2. Peut servir à souligner l'unicité. Il est alors accentué. There's only one way to tackle the problem *(il n'y a qu'une seule façon de s'attaquer au problème).*

3. Peut être l'équivalent de : **a certain.** I have met one Mr. Johnson (on peut également dire : a Mr. Johnson).

4. Peut renvoyer à un nom ou à un pronom, peut être précédé d'un article : I have forgotten my pencil. Have you got one? Don't take this book, take that one, take the one I've just read. Here are some books. Which one (s) do you want? She's got one red dress and two blue ones.
N.B. Ne peut s'employer ni après un possessif ni après **own.** He never uses his father's new car, he always takes his own. Mais on peut dire : your father's new one is very expensive.

5. Peut avoir pleine valeur d'indéfini = **I and others.** Il équivaut souvent alors au pronom français : **on.** Il peut être sujet, complément, s'employer avec un génitif. One has to do one's best *(il faut faire de son mieux).* A room of one's own *(une pièce bien à soi).* His past makes one wonder whether one can trust him *(son passé fait que l'on se demande si on peut avoir confiance en lui).* One doesn't like to make a fool of oneself *(on n'aime pas se couvrir de ridicule).*

9 ***Use*** one ***wherever possible in the following sentences:***

1. My pair of shoes is still serviceable, I can wait to buy a new pair.
2. Have you seen their new refrigerators? You should order a refrigerator while they are being sold at such a low price.
3. The consumer is constantly confronted with problems of this kind: of two different shirts selling at the same price, is the first shirt any better than the second shirt?
4. A consumer is a person who consumes, that is a person who uses up goods and services.
5. "Have you tried this brand of toothpaste?" "No, I haven't tried this brand, but that brand, the brand they advertise on T.V."
6. The difference between those two brands of shaving-cream is only a difference of packaging.
7. The more you have, the more you want.
8. Not only have the poor the problems that face any consumer, but they also have special problems of their own.

On 9 December 1958, the *New York Times* carried this memorable front-page headline: Dangerous decline found in U.S. natural resources*.

"We Americans have used more of the world's resources in the past 40 years than all the people of the world had used in the 4,000 years of recorded history up to 1914... Man is becoming aware of the limits of the earth"—FAIRFIELD OSBORN*.

10 ***This text raises economic and moral problems. What are they?***

(Advertising encourages .... housewives .... wastefulness .... plays upon our weaknesses .... manipulates small children .... exploits our deepest .... develops an attitude of ....)
Don't forget to use: by + gerund.

11 ***What can be said in defence of advertising?***

(Advertising does have a useful function .... at its best, it can .... informative .... helps .... make up one's mind .... without advertising .... would/could not ....)

12 ***Creative written work:***

"Few of us are immune to the blandishments of the advertisers." What about you? Do you object to being manipulated? How do you react when you feel you are being manipulated?

13 ***Written translation:***

Translate from: *"One mouthwash..."* down to the end.

IMPROVE YOUR VOCABULARY
How to present your arguments

To begin with/in the first place ..../first of all ....
Secondly ....
What's more ..../Moreover ..../In addition to ....
In many cases, ... as a result ....
For example, ...
However, as is too often the case, ...
For their part, manufacturers ....
A second reason for .... is ....
According to this view ....
Those who hold this view contend that ..../forget that/overlook the fact that ....
It has often been said that ....
There is no denying that .... and yet ....
It is my feeling that ....
It is my belief that ....

14 ***Find a suitable title for this passage.***

"A society in which consumption has to be artificially stimulated in order to keep production going is a society founded on trash and waste, and such a society is a house built upon sand." DOROTHY L. SAYERS, in *Creed or Chaos**

* (All the quotations are taken from *The Hidden Persuaders* by Vance Packard.)

You're not hitting me, nigger

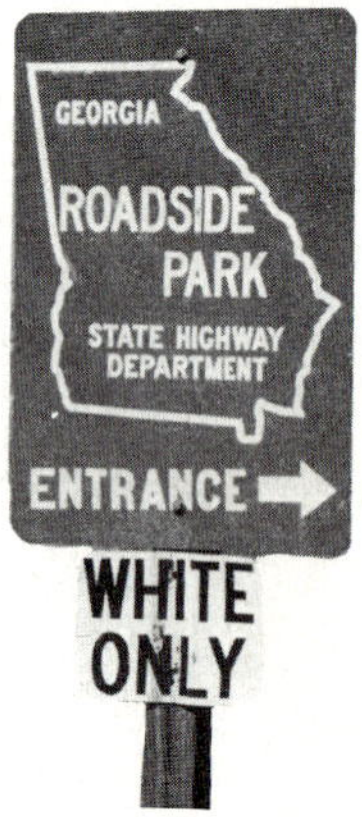

Abruptly [ə'brʌptli], naked ['neikid], collide [kə'laid], emitting [i'mitiŋ], paralysed ['pærəlaizd], seized [si:zd], traversed ['trævə:st], aisle [ail], fronting ['frʌntiŋ], humility [hju'militi], pawed [pɔ:d], scalded ['skɔ:ldid], injured ['indʒəd], salve [sɑ:v], imitated ['imiteitid].

Cross watched the waiter place a •tumbler of orange juice before the woman, then a platter of ham and poached eggs. The waiter was about to lift a silver pot of steaming coffee to fill her cup when the woman turned abruptly with her whole body, opening her mouth to speak. Cross saw the woman's •plump, naked elbow describe a tiny, swift arc and collide with the coffee-pot as it left the tray. There was a •ringing clatter of metal and a brown •spout of boiling coffee, emitting a cloud of vapor, splashed over the woman's bare arm and onto her •bosom. The waiter's movements froze and the woman leaped to her feet and screamed, her face distorted with fury and pain.

"You nigger, you're burning me!" she yelled.

The waiter stood paralyzed, his mouth open. The woman's •frantic eyes swept the •dining car, then rested upon the table. In one flowing movement, she seized the handle of a silver water pitcher and raised it above her head, her eyes •bulging and her darkly rouged lips curled in pain.

Cross was on his feet before he knew it and had traversed the •aisle and was standing between the woman and the waiter, fronting the woman, blocking her action with his uplifted right hand, which still clutched his napkin. The woman lowered her hand.

"You're not hitting me, nigger," the woman said quietly.

"You're not hitting anybody either," Cross said.

The priest rushed to the side of the woman, put his arm about her, then looked from Cross to the waiter. The dining car was full of the rumble of the train speeding over steel rails. In the middle of the car a tall, hard-faced man stood up and •glared.

"What's the matter down there?" the man called.

"I'm sorry, lady," the waiter •crooned in humility.

The woman •pawed at her arm, which gleamed a brick red where the coffee had •scalded it. Steam still rose from her dress. She began to weep.

"I got something for that burn, Ma'm." The waiter found his tongue and ran toward the rear of the car. The tall, hard-faced man rushed to the side of the priest and now two men were holding the woman and looking at Cross. Cross's hand fell to his side. He was surprised to find that he was smiling; he had acted before he had known it. Another white woman came forward and took hold of the •injured woman.

"Darling, I've got something in my purse for burns," the woman said and led her from sight, toward the women's lavatory. The waiter came running with a tube of •salve and stood staring helplessly at the backs of the two retreating women.

"It wasn't my fault," he said, looking at the silent, thoughtful faces in the car. "She turned round—like this." He imitated the woman's movement. "And she knocked the pot out of my hand."

RICHARD WRIGHT, *The outsider*
Published by Harper and Row

Richard Wright, one of the most talented Negro writers, was born in Mississipi in 1908 and died in Paris in 1960. Like the rest of his work, "The Outsider" (1953) is full of a burning sense of injustice. The hero of the novel is Cross, a Negro, and we find him in the restaurant car of a train bound for New York.

● **tumbler** : a glass ● **plump** : *potelé* ● **ringing clatter** : *un bruit métallique résonna* ● **spout** : *jet* ● **bosom** : *poitrine* ● **frantic** : mad with anger ● **bulging** : *exorbités* ● **aisle** : passage between rows of seats ● **glared** : he was angry and it showed (was visible) in his eyes, looked furiously at the scene ● **crooned** : in a soothing *(apaisant)* murmur ● **pawed** : *se tâta le bras* ● **scald** : burn with hot liquid ● **dining car** : railway coach equipped as a restaurant ● **injured** : hurt ● **salve** : *pommade*.

TOWARDS COMPREHENSION

1 *The facts : justify your answers.*

1. The action takes place :
   a) in a restaurant.
   b) on a train.
   c) in the street.

2. The main characters are :
   a) 3 men and a woman.
   b) 2 men and 2 women.
   c) 4 men and a woman.

3. The violent incident broke out because :
   a) the black waiter pushed the white woman roughly.
   b) the black waiter spoke to her rudely.
   c) burnt her with hot coffee.

4. Cross :
   a) pretended he had seen nothing.
   b) hesitated before interfering.
   c) interfered spontaneously.

2 *Test your memory : put the sentences in the right order.*

1. The waiter placed a platter of ham and poached eggs before the woman.
2. Then he placed a tumbler of orange juice.
3. The woman turned round abruptly.
4. The waiter was about to fill her cup.
5. The woman insulted the waiter.
6. Her elbow collided with the coffee-pot.
7. The coffee splashed over her arm and badly burnt her.

3 *After reading the text carefully, or listening to it, complete the following sentences :*

1. In order to show he was ready to help, the priest . . . .
2. People could hardly hear each other because . . . .
3. Another man interfered, he . . . .
4. The waiter humbly . . . .
5. The woman started . . . .
6. The waiter offered to help, he said . . . .
7. A white woman interfered, she . . . .
8. When the waiter returned with the tube of salve, he saw . . . .

LANGUAGE PRACTICE

4 *Complete the following sentences without looking at the text :*

1. The waiter lifted the coffee-pot . . . .
2. The woman opened her mouth . . . .
3. She called him nigger . . . .
4. She raised a water pitcher . . . .
5. Cross stood up . . . .

HOW TO EXPRESS PURPOSE
to, in order to, so as to

Voir p. 18

5 ***Drawing on the text, make as many sentences as you can:***

1. The woman couldn't help . . . .
2. Cross couldn't help . . . .
3. The priest couldn't help . . . .
4. The hard-faced man couldn't help . . . .

...COULDN'T HELP + GERUND

6 ***Give the ing-form:***

1. I refuse to tolerate rudeness.
2. I refuse to put up with your bad manners.
3. I refuse to take orders from you.
4. I refuse to eat in this dining-car.
5. I refuse to accept your excuses.
6. I won't allow you to speak rudely to me.
7. I won't allow him to touch my plate.
8. I won't allow her to insult me.

Imagine a few more sentences on the same patterns:

7 ***Supply the missing prepositions:*** (about, at, for, in, out of, with).

1. They stood glaring . . . . each other.
2. She was beside herself . . . . fury.
3. He was wild . . . . rage.
4. She was very angry . . . . the waiter . . . . spilling coffee.
5. When she scalded her hand . . . . hot coffee, she cried out . . . . pain.
6. He felt indignant . . . . her behaviour, and rightly so.
7. I wasn't speaking seriously, I only said it . . . . fun. You looked as though you were speaking . . . . anger.
8. Her hatred . . . . black people showed in her behaviour.
9. Would you go so far as to say that she acted . . . . this way . . . . hatred . . . . black people.
10. I don't know if she hates them, but what I'm sure . . . . is that she feels contempt . . . . them.
11. It's nothing to get excited . . . .
12. It's nothing to get worked up . . . .
13. It's not a matter to laugh . . . .

HOW TO EXPRESS REFUSAL

Voir p. 52

PRESENT CONTINUOUS

Si l'on compare ces deux phrases : « you nigger, you're burning me » « you're not hitting me, nigger », on découvre deux valeurs du présent progressif.

- Dans le 1er cas, il s'agit de l'aspect progressif classique, c'est-à-dire que l'action (décrite par le locuteur) s'inscrit dans une situation, qu'elle est vue comme commencée, mais non achevée (aspect imperfectif). A cela s'ajoute une valeur modale, dans la mesure où cet énoncé exprime une certaine irritation.
- Dans le second cas, ce présent progressif a d'abord une valeur modale, c'est-à-dire que le locuteur exprime son point de vue, prend position sur ce qu'il dit. C'est, en quelque sorte, un refus, une interdiction, une affirmation de volonté qui sont ainsi exprimés. Ce présent progressif comporte également une valeur de futurité. *(Tu ne vas tout de même pas me frapper.)*

On notera que **going to**, également à la forme négative, exprime la même idée de refus :
I'm not answering your stupid questions *(je refuse de répondre, ne comptez pas sur moi pour que je réponde . . . .).*
I'm not going to answer any more questions *(je ne vais répondre à aucune autre . . . . je refuse de répondre à toute autre . . . .).*
You're not going out with that boy. (=I won't allow you to . . . .).
You're not going to see him again (I won't allow you to . . . . I won't let you . . . .).

8 ***Compare :***

Perhaps he did it on purpose (=intentionally).
He may have done it on purpose.

AUX. MODAL + HAVE + P.P.

Voir p. 40

Give the other pattern :

1. Perhaps he did it out of hatred.
2. Perhaps he wanted to show the white woman how much he despised her.
3. Perhaps he thought it would impress Cross.
4. Perhaps the white woman was a bit too arrogant (contemptuous...).

9 ***Taking each of the above sentences, react as follows :***

What makes you think he did it on purpose? If he had done it on purpose, he would (not) have . . . .

IF-CLAUSES

10 ***Imagine the waiter's thoughts :***

(*you may use the prompts :* humiliate/hit/give her a piece of my mind/ fling the plates at . . . ./. . . .)
How I wish I could . . . .

HOW TO EXPRESS A WISH

Voir p. 25

11 ***Show that the waiter can't do anything. Use the patterns :***

If he . . . . he would . . . .
If he had . . . . he would have . . . .
He is well aware that he would have . . . . if he had . . . .
The only thing he can do . . . .

12 ***Imagine what would have happened if the waiter had been white.***

13 ***Creative oral work :***

a. The waiter and Cross talk about the incident.
b. Two white people ask each other questions about and comment upon the incident.

14 ***Creative written work : the writer's point of view.***

Whose side is he on? How are we made to feel whose side he is on? Does he comment upon the characters' reactions? Does he impose his views upon the reader? Is the reader left completely free to form his or her own opinion?

A *Choose the right answer:*

1. Why are you so angry .... him?
   a) against. *b*) for. *c*) with. *d*) over.
2. It's nothing to get excited ....
   a) at. *b*) for. *c*) on. *d*) about.
3. I don't know if you are right, but what I'm sure .... is that I'm not wrong.
   a) of. *b*) to. *c*) over. *d*) at.
4. He has the reputation .... very efficient.
   a) for being. *b*) not to be. *c*) of being. *d*) at being.
5. He apologized .... her.
   a) to burn. *b*) while burning. *c*) for burning. *d*) in order to burn.
6. They must have suffered .... hunger.
   a) with. *b*) of. *c*) because. *d*) from.
7. So far they .... very unhappy, but things .... look up. (=get better)
   a) were .... must. *b*) will be .... won't. *c*). have been .... may. *d*) are .... don't.
8. "When .... them?" "Two weeks ago."
   a) have you seen. *b*) did you last see. *c*) have you ever seen. *d*) will you see.
9. I .... they emigrated to the States.
   a) did not see them while .... *b*) haven't seen them since .... *c*) won't see them before. *d*) shouldn't see them after ....
10. Most of them .... persecuted in their country, that was why they .... it.
    a) will be .... will leave. *b*) are .... have left. *c*) can't be .... leave. *d*) were .... left,

B. Fill in the gaps with verbs from the following list: (allow, concern, escape, escape from. expect, let, look upon, mind).

1. Do you .... if I buy a new dress? 2. He is rightly .... as the best player in the world. 3. He only just .... being killed. 4. Don't .let. them trick you into buying that old car. 5. Would you .... moving aside to .... them pass. 6. It can't be easy to .... that prison. 7. All the people .... should have been notified a long time ago. 8. How can you .... them to win a match, they don't train regularly. 9. I can't .... her to do that, it's too dangerous. 10. I don't .... what you do so long as you don't make a noise.

C. Dans l'exercice suivant, vous proposerez le plus de solutions possible :

1. Que dites-vous lorsque vous voulez avoir des renseignements sur le passé de quelqu'un?
2. Vous demandez poliment à quelqu'un de parler plus fort.
3. Vous racontez que vous avez essayé de persuader quelqu'un d'acheter une voiture de sport en le flattant, mais que vous n'y êtes pas parvenu.
4. Que dites-vous pour persuader quelqu'un de changer d'avis.
5. Que dites-vous si vous estimez qu'il y a longtemps que l'on aurait dû interdire de fumer dans les endroits publics.
6. Que dites-vous si vous avez l'impression qu'il va pleuvoir, si l'un de vos amis vous a donné l'impression qu'il était ivre.

SPOTLIGHT ON...

the american system of education

Community [kə'mju:niti], responsibility [ris,pɔnsə'biliti], academic [,ækə'demik], communicating knowledge [kə'mju:nikeitiŋ 'nɔlidʒ], recognizes ['rekəgnaiziz], supplement ['sʌplimənt], aesthetic judgment [i:s'θetik 'dʒʌdʒmənt], emotional stability [i'məuʃənl stə'biliti], vocational [vəu'keiʃənl], avocational [,ævəu'keiʃənl].

Philosophy of Concord Public Schools and the Concord-Carlisle Regional School District

Education is a shared task of society involving the community, the family, the student and the school system. Formal schooling is one facet of the larger educational process. Among the many elements of society which contribute to education, the public school system plays the leading role and holds the major share of responsibility for teaching and training students in:

Academic skills—the means of acquiring and communicating knowledge.
Problem solving—the ability to apply knowledge with discrimination.
Significant information about:
- our cultural heritage,
- cultures and languages of other peoples,
- human behavior,
- the physical world,
- world affairs,
- the world of work.

In addition, the school system recognizes its responsibility to supplement the home and community by maintaining an environment, offering programs, and practicing methods which foster:
- aesthetic judgment,
- civic responsibility,
- desire for knowledge,
- emotional stability,
- moral integrity,
- physical health,
- positive person-to-person relationships,
- vocational and avocational skills.

Concord-Carlisle high school

Character and academic ratings for ....

In making the following ratings keep in mind that they will be used to compare this student with other very able students. Please make them as realistically as you can in comparison with your college preparatory students.

Below Average	Average	Good	Excellent	Superior		No basis for judgment
					Motivation	
					Creative Qualities	
					Self-discipline	
					Growth Potential	
					Leadership	
					Self-confidence	
					Warmth of Personality	
					Sense of Humor	
					Concern for Others	
					Energy	
					Emotional Maturity	
					Personal Initiative	
					Reaction to Setbacks	
					Respect Accorded by Faculty	
					Academic Ability	
					Written Expression	
					Oral expression	
					Originality	
					Independence	
					Personal Responsibility	

The main factors contributing to the respect accorded the applicant seem to be :

.... Superiority in studies
.... Accomplishment in activities
.... Success in athletics
.... Interest in other students
.... Leadership in activities
.... Personality

The main factors contributing to his not being respected seem to be :

.... Superiority in studies
.... Conceit
.... Lack of interest in other people
.... Not well known
.... Manners and personal habits
.... Other (please specify)

COMMENT : ....

Date .... Name .... Dept. ....

Student Signature

TOWARDS COMPREHENSION

1 ***Pick out the three verbs which best sum up the philosophy of Concord Public Schools.***

2 ***Spot the words which show that at least 2 aspects of this philosophy are dealt with.***

3 ***Understanding some key-words:***

1. .... *involving* the community, the family, the student and the school system. (l. 1)
   a) in favour of. *b*) in which the community .... take part. *c*) for the benefit of.
2. *Formal* schooling. (l. 2)
   a) formalistic. *b*) ceremonious. *c*) academic.
3. .... *to supplement* the home and the community. (l. 15)
   a) to replace. *b*) to do better than. *c*) to complete what is done at home ....

4 ***Right or wrong? Justify your answer.***

1. The community and the school system play the same role in education.
2. Training seems to be more important than teaching.
3. The school system plays two major roles of equal importance.

LANGUAGE PRACTICE

5 ***Complete the following:***

Our objectives are to help students (to) develop a capacity for ...., a sense of .... a continuing desire for ...., a feeling for ....

6 ***Say how the school system can supplement the home and community.***

BY + GERUND
exprime le moyen.

It can develop civic responsibility by ....
According to the Americans .... is not enough, we must also ....
It is the responsibility of .... to ....
Go on.

TOWARDS APPRECIATION

7 ***This system should produce good American citizens in so far as ....***

The American system attaches more importance to ..../places more emphasis on .... than we do.

8 ***Can such a system play a leading part in the process of assimilation called the Melting Pot?***

9 ***Creative oral work:***

a. Should or shouldn't the school system supplement the home?
b. Do you think that schools concentrate on more practical career training these days?

Anxious moments - a shared problem

Polled [pəuld], events [i'vents], pressure to succeed ['preʃə tə sək'si:d], anxieties [æŋ'zaiətiz], involved in school activities [in'vɔlvdən 'sku:l æk'tivitiz], extracurricular ['ekstrəkə'rikjulə], scheduled ['ʃedju:ld U.S.:'skedjuld], exhaustion [ig'zɔ:stʃən], process ['prəuses], entrance exams ['entrəns ig'zæmz], tedious ['ti:djəs], adult ['ædʌlt], maturity [mə'tjuəriti], decisiveness [di'saisivnis], unwinding ['ʌn'waindiŋ], concentrate ['kɔnsəntreit], a fast-paced society [ə'fɑ:st'peist sə'saiəti].

Roger Inhorn of James Madison Memorial High School polled his classmates about the kinds of senior year events that cause a lot of anxious feelings. He reports:

For many students, pressure to succeed in that final year of high school—plus uncertainty about the future—fills senior year with all sorts of tensions and anxieties. Some seniors feel that time is running out, and this is their last year to get really involved in school activities. Many get so caught up in •extracurricular things that they don't have time to relax from the •pace of school. Jenny, a Madison senior who's involved in the •track team, the newspaper and other activities, said, "My time gets so scheduled with meetings and things that I struggle just to get by." Simple exhaustion can make things a whole lot harder.

Meanwhile, the not-so-simple process of applying to college can be another major source of stress. Writing essays, getting recommendations, applying for financial aid and taking entrance exams are tedious tasks that further weigh down busy schedules. "Filling out five pages of forms for 10 different schools—and wondering if they'll like what I say—can be very •nerve-wracking," one college-bound senior said wearily.

Parents can often produce a lot of tension by simply wanting things to go smoothly for their children. "My parents often remind me that I'm going to be an adult soon," says Ted, another Madison senior. "They expect total maturity and decisiveness from me." Everyone seems to want you to make up your mind, and make it up now. It isn't easy.

For some people, even the "good times" of high school can produce a lot of pressure and tension. Many seniors—especially boys—seem to feel that this is their last year to have a lot of fun. "I realize that my time in high school is getting short," reasoned Dave. "I want to experience a lot of things before I go off to college." For this reason, many people try too hard to have a good time and feel a little bit let-down when day-to-day life is not as much fun as they expected.

All this stress and tension can produce some physical side-effects. One senior told me that after trying a number of different acne medicines, he realized his skin problems were directly related to the amount of stress he was under. Other students report headaches and stomachaches during tests or other tense moments.

Many seniors cope with stress through physical activity—jogging, shooting baskets or simply taking a long walk around the block to cool off. One senior reports that he plans his daily schedule each morning, including several breaks for just relaxing and unwinding. "My leisure time is very important to me," he explained. "It helps me concentrate on my work better."

I think learning to cope with senior stress is a valuable lesson. After all, we live in a fast-paced society. Pressures and tensions will always be with us. The stress-reducing habits we learn now will help us handle problems later on.

Roger Inhorn

● **extracurricular** : outside ordinary school work ● **pace...** : *rythme de la vie scolaire* ● **track team** : *équipe d'athlétisme* ● **can be very nerve-wracking** : can cause great nervous tension.

TOWARDS COMPREHENSION

1 ***Fill in the gaps with verbs from the following list:*** apply for (something), apply to (somebody), cool off, cope with, make up one's mind, remind, succeed.

1. I know I have to make a decision, but I can't . . . . just now.
2. I wonder how he is going to . . . . so many difficulties.
3. If I forget, please . . . . me.
4. I hope you will . . . . in your exam.
5. You're an adult now, it's for you to decide, we can't . . . . for you.
6. Please . . . . me that I have to write a letter of application.
7. If you have money problems, why don't you . . . . financial aid?
8. Who could I . . . . if I need financial aid?
9. He is excited and angry, wait until he . . . . before asking him for money.
10. I can't remember what it . . . . me of.

2 ***Right or wrong?***

1. This text is about students in the final year of high school.
2. The final year of high school is called the senior year and the students seniors.
3. The text is about seniors' problems.
4. The only thing that preoccupies them is their future.

3 ***Two words suggesting their anxious feelings are repeated several times. Find them.***

4 ***Choose the nearest equivalent.***

IN OTHER WORDS

1. Some seniors feel that time is *running out.* (l. 5)
   a) they feel that their days at high school are numbered.
   b) they feel that time passes quickly.
   c) they feel that they have a lot to do in a short time.
2. . . . . to get really *involved in* school activities. (l. 5)
   a) to do things they have never done.
   b) really to participate in school activities.
   c) to play a leading part in school activities.
3. . . . . that I struggle just to *get by.* (l. 9)
   a) to be popular with my classmates.
   b) to get past without being seen.
   c) to get passable results.

4. *Tedious tasks that further weigh down busy schedules.* (l. 13)
   a) uninteresting things that cause a lot of anxious feelings.
   b) uninteresting things that increase tensions.
   c) uninteresting things that increase the quantity of work to be done.

5 ***Show that the meaning of the following words and phrases can be guessed from the context:***

FROM THE CONTEXT

1. Applying to college. (l. 11) 2. My time in high school is getting short. (l. 22) 3. Feel a little bit let-down. (l. 24) 4. All this stress and tension can produce some physical side-effects. (l. 26)

LANGUAGE PRACTICE

6 ***Drawing on the text, make a few sentences beginning with:***

Seniors	don't know wonder aren't sure	how whether	....

7 ***Re-cast some of the above sentences, beginning with:***

INDIRECT QUESTIONS

What worries seniors (most) is (that) ....
As the end of the year approaches ....

8 ***Put into reported speech and use*** tell, order, ask ***as reporting verbs:***

AS

Voir p. 136

1. Make up your mind. 2. Don't panic. 3. Work harder. 4. Take more exercise. 5. Fill out this form. 6. Don't forget to apply for financial aid. 7. "I wonder if they'll like what I say", he said. 8. "Which college would you like to go to?", they asked him. 9. "Do you realize that you're going to be an adult soon?", they said to him. 10. "Why do you want to experience a lot of things before you go off to college?", I asked her.

REPORTED SPEECH

Voir p. 23

9 ***Imagine all that you could say to those seniors to help them (to) cool off, relax, unwind:***

.... and you will ....
Why don't you ...., it would help you (to) ....
You should ...., it would help you (to) ....
If you .... it would ....
I'm sure you could .... by ....
If I were you ....

HOW TO EXPRESS ADVICE

10 ***Using information from the text, make as many sentences as you can beginning with:***

They don't have time to ....

BY + GERUND

11 ***Then re-cast your sentences as follows:***

If they had more time, they could ....

12 ***Imagine what a senior could say to express the above ideas:***

I wish I could ....

13 ***Now in reported speech:***

He said he wished he could ....

WISH + PRET MODAL

Voir p. 25

14 ***Written work: drawing on the text, write statements consistent with the verbs given, then with the adverbs given:***

1. ". . . .", he complained.
2. ". . . .", they promised.
3. ". . . .", he explained.
4. ". . . .", he protested.
5. ". . . .", she suggested.
6. ". . . .", they objected.
7. ". . . .", he said accusingly.
8. ". . . .", they said sympathetically.
9. ". . . .", he commented derisively.
10. ". . . .", she answered sharply.

TOWARDS APPRECIATION

15 ***Recapitulate the major causes of senior-year stress, say if they are all of equal importance or if some of them strike you as more important.***

16 ***What should parents do or not do?***

They should (not) . . . .
Instead of . . . . they'd better . . . . It'd be better if they . . . . They'd do better to/not to . . . .

17 ***Creative oral work:***

a. What would you say to those seniors if you thought that they were dramatizing their problems a bit too much.
b. Imagine that you are polling your classmates about the kinds of senior-year events that cause stress and anxious feelings.

18 ***Paragraph writing.***

Expand into a paragraph of ten lines: *"After all, we live in a fast-paced society"*.

19 ***Creative written work.***

You are in your final year too. Do you experience the same anxious feelings, do you have to cope with the same problems? If so, say how you handle them? If not, say if you would like to be in an American high school.

20 ***Written or oral work:***

Translate from *"All this stress and tension"* down to the end.

FOR FURTHER INFORMATION

Growing squeeze

•Ph.D.s are not the only folks who have to do some calculating about career plans. Continuing a trend that began about ten years ago, college graduates will face fierce competition through the mid-1980s for jobs in fields ranging from anthropology and labor relations to sociology and political science.

According to a study by the U.S. Bureau of Labor Statistics, one out of every four students with bachelor's degrees will have to settle for a job that generally has not required a college education. In its *Occupational Outlook for College Graduates,* the bureau predicts that between 1976 and 1985, some 10.4 million people with undergraduate degrees will enter the job market with only 7.7 million finding the sorts of jobs that traditionally demand those degrees. The remaining 2.7 million will have to take jobs for which they are overeducated or go unemployed.

The terrain is rockiest in fields that are increasingly popular but are not expanding significantly, like journalism, and those that depend heavily on government funds, like oceanography. But the prospects are good to excellent in many careers. Health service administrators, engineers, registered nurses, accountants, bank officers, Catholic priests, computer programmers and systems analysts are among those expected to be in demand in the next decade. The BLS notes that while a bachelor's degree ensures a good chance at a job, a graduate degree in any of these fields would be an especially marketable asset.

TIME, August 14, 1978

• **Ph. D.s** [ˌpiːeitʃ'diːz] : Doctors of Philosophy.

Education

Now, $*30,000* Diplomas

College costs, up 77% in a decade, are still soaring

Long before the first dormitory opened to signal the start of a new academic year, tens of thousands of parents had received those familiar and depressing envelopes with word from the college of their offspring's choice: tuition, room and board. All due immediately.

Naturally college bills this year turned out to be the highest ever. The average cost of education at a four-year private college has increased 6.1% over last year and has soared 77% since 1968. And for the first time, at some of the most prestigious private institutions, tuitions alone have edged up past $5,000—not including the spiraling costs of food, housing, books, transportation, plus a little entertainment on the weekends. These necessities, on the average, add around $2,500 to the final tab, though prices vary wildly from school to school and from student to student.

The 1978-79 cost of the ten most expensive undergraduate schools in the U.S., including tuition, fees, room and board:

	$
M.I.T.	7,630
Bennington	7,540
Harvard	7,500
Yale	7,500
Sarah Lawrence	7,440
U. of Pennsylvania	7,300
Stanford	7,299
Brown	7,225
Princeton	7,217
Dartmouth	7,180

While the figures are staggering, there are still a few ways at least to soften the college tuition crunch. The College Board notes that almost any family, even one with a gross income in excess of $35,000 a year, might be eligible for some combination of grants or loans, depending on the number of children in college, among other financial considerations.

Families can also turn to state schools. Many public colleges offer splendid education for less money, but not all that much less. This year the University of Delaware actually cut its tuition for instate residents by $60 in order to attract more students. But overall costs at public four-year colleges have climbed almost as much as they have at private institutions during the past decade. Though tuition, room and board at public colleges average around $2,000, many run quite a bit higher. Samples: the University of Vermont ($3,192), the University of Wisconsin ($2,583), the College of William and Mary in Virginia ($2,804), and Southern Oregon State College ($2,411).

Relief of a sort may also be on the way from Washington. After months of debate, Senators and Representatives are now in the final stages of approving a tuition tax credit scheme. If it passes—and then survives threats of a presidential veto—parents could write off as much as $250 a year for each member of the family enrolled in college. By 1980, that credit could be as high as $500. And so it goes.

TIME, September 11, 1978

SPOTLIGHT ON...

school integration

Different Families, Different Worries

On the night before school began in Louisville, Elmer Woods, a •brewing company sales supervisor, took his sons, Byron, 13, and Kenneth, 12, aside. "Keep cool and watch yourselves," he told them. "No matter what they yell at you, just ignore it."

Next morning, the boys got up at 5:45 a.m. to have breakfast before their father drove them ten blocks to catch a school bus at 6:50 a.m. Then they rode for 40 minutes to cover 16 miles to their new school, Stuart High, in suburban Jefferson County. The bus was •pelted with rocks; passing motorists honked horns as a sign of antibusing protest and hurled racial insults. But there was no serious trouble at school, and the Woodses, a black middle-class family with an income of $20,000, felt the ordeal was well worthwhile.

That does not mean they enjoy busing. "I'm really not for it," says Woods. "I'd much rather have the boys closer to home." Last year Ken walked to Martin Luther King School, only two blocks from his trim red brick home in the city's predominantly black West End. Byron attended Shawnee Junior High School, ten blocks away. Says the boys' mother, Mary, a medical lab technician at Jewish Hospital: "If there was a better way of bringing about racial equality in the schools, we'd go for it, but there doesn't seem to be."

Mrs. Woods •frets, too, about the boys being so far from home. Both may want to stay after school for sports. To accommodate them, Woods says he is ready to drive out late every afternoon to pick them up.

But neither the parents nor the boys consider those disadvantages as too much.

On the day of school opening in Louisville, the three children of Al and Mildred McCauley —David, 15, Danny, 14, and Debbie, 10—remained in their brick home in Highview, a white middle-class suburb in Jefferson County. Debbie, who was not scheduled for busing and could have attended her old school a few blocks away, asked, "Mommy, when can I go? If I don't pretty soon, I'm going to be far behind." Mrs. McCauley shook her head and looked away.

McCauley, a dry-wall finisher from the Kentucky hill country, and his wife, an articulate spokeswoman for Save Our Community Schools, are keeping their children home to protest the busing plan. Their two boys would have had to get up at 6:35 a.m. and ride a bus for 50 minutes to reach Parkland Junior High, a black ghetto school 22 miles away in Louisville. "They won't go there—ever," •vows Mrs. McCauley.

The parents object primarily to what they consider the inferior education and disorderly conditions at Parkland. Mrs. McCauley visited it last year and claims that "it hadn't been painted in eight years. There was no maintenance." Moreover, they have heard rumors of •stabbings, rapes and other crimes in the Parkland neighborhood.

TIME, September 22, 1975

• **brewing company**: *brasserie (entreprise)* • **pelted with rocks** (U.S.), **stones** (G.B.) : *lapidé*
• **frets** : worries • **vows** : solemnly declares • **stabbings...** : *attaques à coups de couteau.*

TOWARDS COMPREHENSION

1 1st part. ***Right or wrong. Justify your answer.***

1. Mr. Woods expected busing to be an easy experience.
2. What he expected did indeed happen.
3. The Woodses regretted having gone through this painful experience.
4. The Woodses think that busing is the best solution.
5. Both parents and children think the advantages outweigh (are more important than) the disadvantages.

2 2nd part. ***Pick out the two verbs which best summarize what this part is all about.***

3 ***Right or wrong. Justify your answer.***

1. The McCauleys kept their children at home on the day of school opening.
2. The three children should have gone to a black ghetto school.
3. The parents objected to their going to that school because it had not been painted for eight years.

4 ***Fill in the gaps with words from the text without looking at it:***

1. For the Woodses, it was a difficult and painful experience, it was . . . .
2. Mr. Woods asked his children to . . . .
3. Motorists . . . . insults at the children on the bus.
4. The Woodses think busing is a means of . . . . racial equality in the schools.
5. Debbie McCauley could have gone to her old school because she was not . . . . for busing.
6. The white parents say that at Parkland High School the education is . . . . and the conditions . . . .

5 ***Justify the title.***

LANGUAGE PRACTICE

6 ***This text contains a great deal of information about the Louisville busing plan. Ask the corresponding questions.***

HOW TO SEEK INFORMATION

Example: Where did Mr. Woods have to drive his children to on the day of school opening?

7 ***Make as many sentences as you can on this pattern:***

Busing means that { the Woods children . . . . / the McCauley children . . . . / Mr. Woods . . . . / white parents . . . . } will . . . .

HOW TO EXPRESS OBLIGATION
have to

Voir p. 18

8 ***Drawing on the text, make a few sentences on this pattern:***

Instead of . . . . they'd much rather . . . .

HOW TO EXPRESS PREFERENCE

Voir p. 32

9 ***The McCauleys are speaking:***

We object to { sending . . . ./having to . . . . / our children going . . . . being sent . . . . }

HOW TO EXPRESS DISAGREEMENT

10 ***Compare the two families and their respective worries:***

What strikes one about the Woods is that . . . .
What's striking about the McCauleys . . . .

11 ***Connect the above sentences with*** whereas.

12 ***Express the above ideas differently:***

The McCauleys differ from the Woodses in that . . . .

IN THAT
=in the sense that

13 ***Creative oral work:***

"*But there was no serious trouble at school.*" Imagine what happened.

14 ***Creative written work.***

What is, in your opinion, the "philosophy" of busing?

FOR FURTHER DISCUSSION

L'intégration scolaire « à la carte » semble réussir à Los Angeles

Los Angeles. — Le jour de la rentrée des classes à Los Angeles, 1 200 autobus jaunes ont transporté les 86 600 élèves (soit 15 % des effectifs scolaires de la ville pour l'année 1978-1979) concernés par l'une des plus vastes opérations de déségrégation jamais tentées aux États-Unis.

Cette opération a pour but de rééquilibrer la composition raciale des classes allant de la huitième à la quatrième, dans deux cent soixante écoles primaires et secondaires de la ville afin qu'aucun groupe racial ne compose, à lui seul, plus de 70 % ni moins de 30 % des effectifs.

Ce programme de déségrégation, conçu par le Conseil d'éducation de la ville de Los Angeles (« Los Angeles Board of Education »), offre d'une part plusieurs formules d'intégration volontaire pour lesquelles ont opté 32 300 élèves : quarante-cinq « écoles-aimants » (« magnet-schools ») dont les programmes, particulièrement variés et intéressants, ont été conçus pour attirer des élèves de races diverses ; quatre écoles expérimentales, « intégrées » depuis déjà plusieurs années ; un système de « busing » (1) volontaire qui fonctionne depuis quelques années.

La décision de la Cour suprême

Cinquante-quatre mille trois cents autres élèves ont été répartis d'office entre des écoles et lycées auxquels le Conseil d'éducation a imposé les formes d'intégration suivantes : l'intégration par « accouplement » (« pairings ») qui oblige deux établissements voisins et de composition raciale différente à s'échanger leurs élèves jusqu'à ce que soit obtenue la combinaison requise par la déségrégation ; l'intégration par « regroupement » (« clusters ») où un groupe d'écoles voisines s'échangent entre elles des élèves de races diverses ; et enfin l'intégration « à mi-chemin » (« midsites ») où, pour leur éviter d'interminables trajets, on fait se rencontrer, dans des établissements situés à mi-chemin de leurs quartiers résidentiels respectifs, des élèves de races différentes.

L'application de ce programme est le couronnement de quinze années de disputes légales. En 1963, Mary Crawford, élève d'un lycée du ghetto noir de Watts à Los Angeles, ouvrait le débat et en déposait le dossier entre les mains de la justice. S'indignant de la composition presque exclusivement noire de son lycée, tandis que l'établissement immédiatement voisin était presque exclusivement fréquenté par des élèves blancs, Mary Crawford accusa le Conseil d'éducation de délimiter arbitrairement les « districts scolaires », afin de provoquer cette ségrégation.

(1) « Busing » : transport, par autobus, d'élèves issus de ghettos noirs ou des « barrios » latino-américains vers des écoles situées dans des quartiers habités presque exclusivement par des Blancs ou « anglos » et inversement, afin d'assurer la déségrégation scolaire.

En 1976, au terme d'une longue bataille livrée dans les tribunaux de l'État de Californie entre partisans et adversaires de l'intégration, la Cour suprême de Californie rendit son jugement : elle décréta que le Conseil d'éducation était directement responsable de la ségrégation dans les écoles de la ville et qu'il était de son devoir de remédier à cet état de choses. Les adversaires de l'intégration, par le biais de leur groupe le plus virulent Bustop, portèrent l'affaire jusqu'à la Cour suprême des États-Unis qui refusa, le 9 septembre 1978, de se saisir de l'affaire. Cette décision confirmait les mesures de déségrégation forcée qui devaient entrer en vigueur le 12 septembre.

A la veille de la rentrée, l'atmosphère était tendue à Los Angeles. Les forces de police avaient été massivement mobilisées. On craignait des violences. Il n'y en eut pas. Les premiers jours de classe furent calmes, plus calmes même que d'habitude.

Les arguments des adversaires

Car les adversaires de l'intégration ont riposté en silence : par le boycottage du « busing » obligatoire qui devait mener écoliers et lycéens à bon port — consigne d'ailleurs peu suivie, puisque environ 75 % des élèves étaient présents, — par la « fuite blanche », opposition ainsi surnommée parce qu'elle est presque toujours le fait de citoyens de peau blanche. Certains ont, en effet, protesté contre l'intégration raciale en retirant leurs enfants des écoles publiques et en les confiant à des établissements privés ou à des professeurs particuliers. D'autres ont préféré déménager pour habiter hors des limites de la ville de Los Angeles et échapper ainsi au mixage scolaire de la ville.

Les récalcitrants s'élèvent principalement contre le caractère obligatoire de cette mesure, contre les longs trajets imposés à leurs enfants (dont la durée, pour un aller simple, va de trente à quatre-vingt-dix minutes) et contre, disent-ils, la *« dégradation inévitable de la qualité de l'enseignement »*. Pourtant, le programme offre des avantages immédiatement perceptibles : aucune classe « intégrée » n'aura plus de 27 élèves et l'école recevra, pour chaque élève concerné, une bourse d'encouragement de 140 dollars.

Le processus de déségrégation dans les écoles de Los Angeles semble aujourd'hui bien enclenché, et ses adversaires seront sans doute impuissants à l'enrayer.

[...] En tout cas, l'opération « déségrégation » et les débats qu'elle a soulevés auront eu l'avantage de faire réfléchir la population de Los Angeles.

Sylvie GROSSMAN, *Le Monde*, 4 octobre 1978

1 ***The main points :***

The aims of the Los Angeles experiment are to . . . .
It all started when . . . .
Those who were against school integration first tried to . . . . by . . . ., then they . . . ., others went so far as to . . . .
They objected to . . . .
In spite of their opposition, there are some signs that the experiment will . . . .

2 ***Make a prècis of this text in English (in not more than 100 words).***

3 ***Expand the conclusion of the article into a paragraph of 15 lines***

4 ***Oral work :***

Explain what busing consists in. Sum up the pros and cons (the arguments in favour of busing and those against).
Does this article strike you as being unbiassed (objective). Justify your answer.

A photographer's model

Eileen ['aili:n], photographer [fə'tɔgrəfə], familiar [fə'miljə], magazine [,mægə'zi:n], commercials [kə'mə:ʃlz], products ['prɔdʌkts], effervescent [,efə'vesnt], agency ['eidʒənsi], photography [fə'tɔgrəfi], insecure [,insi'kjuə], hairdos ['hɛədu:z], subtle ['sʌtl], overt ['əuvə:t], automatic [,ɔ:tə'mætik], ridiculous [ri'dikjuləs], phony ['fəuni], catalogues ['kætəlɔgz], Bourbon ['bə:bən], advertising ['ædvətaiziŋ], vulnerable ['vʌlnərəbl], Ohio [əu'haiəu].

She is a photographer's model, high fashion. Her face is a familiar one in magazine ads as well as on television commercials. She has been engaged in this work for eight years. She earns the city's top rate: fifty dollars an hour.

I do whatever kind of products anyone wants. This week I had a job for some South American product. They said, "We want you to be sexy, •coy, •pert, but not too effervescent." It always means the same smile and open eyes. For forty-five minutes they tell you what they want. They explain and explain and •you sort of tune out and do the same thing.

There are a lot of people there: the person who has the product, the man from the ad agency, a couple of people from the photography studio, the stylist, who poses your dress to make sure it hangs right... suddenly there are a dozen people standing around. Each is telling you to do something else. You know they are even more insecure than you. You pretend you're listening and you do what you'd planned to do in the first place. When you've worked before a camera long enough, you know what they want even though they don't.

At first you work very hard to try to discover different looks and hairdos. After a while, you know them all. Someone once asked me, "Why do highfashion models pose with their mouths open? They look like they're catching flies." (Laughs.) This look has been accepted for a long time. They want everything to be sexy, subtle or •overt.

After a while, it's automatic.

Now the natural look is in. Jumping up and down or staring out there... What's natural about looking into space? They want you natural but posed. (Laughs.) How can you feel natural with three pounds of make-up, in some ridiculous costume, standing there and looking pretty? What they think of as being natural is very •phony.

I hadn't •set out to be a model. I worked as a receptionist in a beauty shop during high school. This was in South Dakota. A woman who had worked for Eileen Ford and had been in *Vogue* and *Harper's Bazaar* said to me, "Why don't you go to New York and be a model?" I didn't know what a model was. I thought they were •dummies in catalogues. I thought the people in the photographs were just •cutouts. I didn't think they were really people. I paid no attention to advertising.

I wanted to go to college, but I had saved only three hundred dollars. So I went to New York at eighteen. I had never put anything on but lipstick and had never worn high-heeled shoes. I walked up and down Lexington Avenue for three hours 'cause my room at the •Y wasn't ready. I didn't dare turn left or right. I just kept walking. A hamburger in South Dakota was twenty-five cents and in this drugstore suddenly it was a dollar and a quarter.

At Eileen Ford, they told me I was too long-waisted and that maybe I should think about something else, and it was too bad since I had come all the way from South Dakota. I was so •green.

I looked in the telephone book. Huntington Hartford had just bought this agency. So I went there, I was so bashful I couldn't even give my name to the receptionist. About a half an hour later, this •guy who had just •taken over the agency—he'd been a male model—came in. He was the first man I'd seen in New York, •close up. I was just staring at him. He said, "You! Come into my office!" I thought I had really been discovered. He probably called me because I was staring at him and he liked himself a lot. (Laughs.)

A week or two later there was a cocktail party. I'd never had a drink in my life. They said you should be there at five o'clock. At five I was the only person there. They asked me what I wanted to drink. I didn't know. I said, "Bourbon and water is really nice." It was awful. The party was for Sammy Kaye. I'd never heard of Sammy Kaye. The guy just wanted us to be there. He was having fifteen of his favorite models over. You just go. No pay. If there's an opening at a photography studio or whatever you go, because advertising people are there and you should be seen and you should make sure they remember your face. All the ridiculous things... That's what happens to a lot of girls who go into modeling. They're very vulnerable. They don't know what they're doing. Usually they come from very poor families. This seems •glamorous. Most of the girls I met were from Ohio or Indiana or some place like that.

• **coy** : (affectedly) shy or reserved • **pert** : coquettish • **you sort of tune out** : *et puis on coupe le son pour ainsi dire* • **overt** : undisguised, obvious • **phony, phoney** : unreal, artificial, not genuine, not authentic • **set out** : planned, my purpose was not to... • **dummies** : clothes are displayed on dummies in store windows • **cutouts** : *figurines* • **the Y** : the Y.W.C.A.=Young Women's Christian Association *(le foyer de la jeune fille)* • **green** : immature, inexperienced, naïve • **guy** (slang) man • **taken over** : *repris* • **close up** : *de près* ; **a close up** : *un gros plan* • **glamorous** : full of charm and prestige.

TOWARDS COMPREHENSION

1 ***Right or wrong. Justify your answer.***

1st part (down to : . . . . *is very phony*).

1. As a model, she is well-known.
2. Her salary is not very high.
3. She works only for American firms.
4. Her work is varied (full of variety).
5. There are lots of people standing around when she is posing.
6. They know exactly what they want her to do.
7. She doesn't listen to them.
8. It is not hard to get to know the tricks of the trade.
9. Ad people have a very strange idea of what looks natural.

2nd part.

1. She had always wanted to be a model.
2. She had always been interested in advertising.
3. She came to New York at the age of 18.
4. As they wouldn't give her a job at Eileen Ford, she went to a new agency run by Huntington Hartford.
5. She was sent to a cocktail party in honour of Sammy Kaye.
6. She was very happy because she had always wanted to meet Sammy Kaye.
7. She was there just to be seen and noticed by ad people.

LANGUAGE PRACTICE

2 ***Drawing on the text, or not, make up as many sentences as you can beginning with:***

A model is supposed to ....
A model is expected to ....
All they require of a model is that she should ....

SHOULD

se rencontre souvent dans les propositions complétives (prop. introduites par *that*, (that-clauses) après certains verbes (propose, recommend, suggest, require, decide ....) et certaines expressions (it's impossible/strange/natural/scandalous/imperative/indispensable/unthinkable/it's a pity/what worries me ....). *That* ne peut être omis.
It's strange that he should be so late. It's unthinkable that he should have done that. It's essential that he should be prepared.
On notera que toutes ces phrases permettent au locuteur d'exprimer son point de vue sur un fait. Lorsqu'il s'agit simplement de constater on peut rencontrer l'indicatif : she's surprised that your father objects.
En Américain, on rencontre le subjonctif : it's essential that he be prepared.

3 ***Drawing on the text, make as many sentences as you can beginning with:***

1. They wanted me to ....
2. Did they ask you to .... ?
3. You'll be asked to ....

LA PROPOSITION INFINITIVE

Voir p. 17

4 ***Compose 5 short dialogues like this:***

A. Did they make you work hard?
B. Oh yes, I was made to work hard.

THEY MADE ME...
but
I WAS MADE TO...
à la forme active :
make + bv
à la forme passive :
made + inf. comp.

5 ***React as follows:***

A. As a model, you'll have to work hard.
B. Well, I don't mind working hard.

A. As a model, you'll have to smile all the time/to stare at the camera all the time/to meet a lot of people/to get up early and go to bed late ....
B. ....

A. People will look at you in the street.
B. Well, I don't mind being looked at.

HOW TO EXPRESS INDIFFERENCE
I don't mind + gerund

Voir p. 143

A. People will recognize you in the street. B. . . . .
A. Men will stare at you on the bus. B. . . . .
A. You'll be invited to a lot of parties. B. . . . .
A. You'll receive letters from admirers. B. . . . .

Go on . . . .

HAVE TO

Voir p. 18

VOIX PASSIVE

On notera que les verbes suivis d'une préposition ou d'une postposition (particule adverbiale) peuvent se mettre au passif en anglais, alors qu'en français seuls les verbes transitifs admettent cette construction :
I don't mind being looked at in the street *(ça ne me dérange pas qu'on me regarde . . . .).*

6 ***Now she qualifies*** *(= nuance)* ***her indifference and lays down (stipulates) her conditions :***

Example : I don't mind working hard so long as it pays well/provided that it pays well = on condition that it pays well.
I don't mind being looked at in the street so long as men don't follow me . . . .

HOW TO EXPRESS CONDITION :
On condition that...
Provided that...
So long as...

7 ***Recast the following sentences, beginning with :***
It was the first time . . . .

1. I had never worn high-heeled shoes before.
2. I'd never had a drink in my life.
3. She'd never heard of Sammy Kaye before.
4. She'd never worked before a camera.
5. I'd never thought of becoming a model before.
6. She'd never dreamt of becoming a model before.

Ex. : It was the first time I had (ever) dreamt of becoming a model.

IT WAS THE FIRST TIME + PLUPERFECT

Voir p. 43

8 ***Complete the following sentences :***

1. She was so bashful that . . . .
2. I was so inexperienced that . . . .
3. I was so surprised when I saw him that . . . .
4. It was so unexpected that . . . .
5. I felt so ill-at-ease and awkward *(gauche)* that . . . .
6. When they told me I was too long-waisted, I was so disappointed that . . . .
7. Most girls are so eager to become models that . . . .
8. The job seems so glamorous that . . . .

SO + ADJ + THAT

9 ***Drawing on the text, answer the following questions as in the example :***

A. Do you have to be very intelligent to succeed as a model?
B. No, all you have to do is (to) watch the camera and smile.

A. Do you have to concentrate a lot? B. . . . .
A. Do you have to follow the instructions very carefully? B. . . . .
A. Do you have to be very original? B. . . . .
A. Do you have to invent new hairdos all the time? B. . . . .

10 ***Written work : complete the following in any way you like :***

All I want out of life is . . . .
All I'm interested in is . . . .
All I'm doing here is suggesting . . . .

ALL YOU HAVE TO DO IS (TO) ....

All you have to do is (to) watch the camera.
On notera que le sujet du verbe *be* est une proposition (all you have to do). On notera aussi que l'on peut avoir soit l'infinitif complet (to watch) soit l'infinitif incomplet (watch) avec do.
Autres exemples :
All I did was hit him on the head.
All he wanted was to move fast.
All she sought was to be loved.
All you've got to do is to run as fast as you can.
Mais : All I'm doing here is suggesting that .... (*parce que :* I'm suggesting).
All I'm interested in is finding a job (*parce que :* I'm interested in finding a job).

TOWARDS APPRECIATION

11 ***Explain to a model why she must go to cocktail parties :***

1. If there's an opening at a photography studio ....
2. If they need a model at a studio ....
3. If you manage to attract notice ....
4. If ....
5. There may be ....
6. They may need ....
7. You may ....

IF-CLAUSES

MAY

Voir p. 52

12 ***Pick out the details showing the model has a sense of humour.***

13 ***Paragraph-writing :***

Expand into a paragraph of ten lines : *"They're very vulnerable."*

14 ***Creative oral work :***

Two inexperienced models meet at the party for Sammy Kaye. Imagine their conversation. (It's the first time .... I'd never have thought .... Do you think I should .... Did you notice .... Perhaps we'd better .... I've been told that ....)

15 ***Creative written work :***

A friend of yours wants to go into modeling. You think it would be a mistake and you try to talk her out of her plan. (Lots of girls .... but only a few of them .... It may seem glamorous but .... Are you sure you could .... Don't you think you'd better .... That's what happens to .... If I were you ....)

Migrant people

Migrant ['maigrənt], perplexed [pə'plekst], worry ['wʌri], defeat [di'fi:t], pioneered [paiə'niəd], despair [dis'pεə], awestruck ['ɔ:-strʌk], guitar [gi'tɑ:], unwrapped ['ʌn'ræpt], tuned ['tju:nd], hummed ['hʌmd], braggarts ['brægəts], cowards ['kauədz], technique [tek'ni:k], privacy ['privəsi], adultery [ə'dʌltəri], unlawful ['ʌn'lɔ:ful], foul [faul], ostracism ['ɔstrəsizəm].

The cars of the migrant people crawled out of the side roads onto the great cross-country highway, and they took the migrant way to the West. In the daylight they •scuttled like bugs to the westward; and as the dark caught them, they •clustered like bugs near to shelter and to water. And because they were lonely and perplexed, because they had all come from a place of sadness and worry and defeat, and because they were all going to a new mysterious place, they •huddled together; they talked together; they shared their lives, their food, and the things they hoped for in the new country. Thus it might be that one family camped near a spring, and another camped for the spring and for company, and a third because two families had pioneered the place and found it good. And when the sun went down, perhaps twenty families and twenty cars were there.

In the evening a strange thing happened: the twenty families became one family, the children were the children of all. The loss of home became one loss, and the golden time in the West was one dream. And it might be that a sick child threw despair into the hearts of twenty families, of a hundred people; that a birth there in a tent kept a hundred people quiet and •awestruck through the night and filled a hundred people with the birth-joy in the morning. A family which the night before had been lost and fearful might search its goods to find a present for a new baby. In the evening, sitting about the fires, the twenty were one. They grew to be units of the camps, units of the evenings and the nights. A guitar unwrapped from a blanket and tuned—and the songs, which were all of the people, were sung in the nights. Men sang the words, and women •hummed the tunes.

Every night a world created, complete with furniture—friends made and enemies established; a world complete with •braggarts and with cowards, with quiet men, with humble men, with kindly men. Every night relationships that make a world, established; and every morning the world torn down like a circus.

At first the families were timid in the building and tumbling worlds, but gradually the technique of building worlds became their technique. Then leaders emerged, then laws were made, then codes came into being. And as the worlds moved westward they were more complete and better furnished, for their builders were more experienced in building them.

The families learned what rights must be observed—the right of privacy in the tent ; the right to keep the past black hidden in the heart ; the right to talk and to listen ; the right to refuse help or to accept, to offer help or to decline it ; the right of son to court and daughter to be courted ; the right of the hungry to be fed ; the rights of the •pregnant and the sick to transcend all other rights.

And the families learned, although no one told them, what rights are monstrous and must be destroyed: the right to intrude upon privacy, the right to be noisy while the camp slept, the right of seduction or •rape, the right of adultery and theft and murder. These rights were crushed, because the little worlds could not exist for even a night with such rights alive.

And as the worlds moved westward, rules became laws, although no one told the families. •It is unlawful to foul near the camp ; it is unlawful in any way to foul the drinking water ; it is unlawful to eat good rich food near one who is hungry, unless he is asked to share.

And with the laws, the punishments—and there were only two—a quick and murderous fight or ostracism ; and ostracism was the worst. For if one broke the laws his name and face went with him, and he had no place in any world, no matter where created.

John Steinbeck (1902-1968) was born in California and earned a living by doing all sorts of jobs while writing his first novels. His work reveals his sympathy for the poor and oppressed for whom the American dream has not come true. "The Grapes of Wrath" (1939) tells the story of the small farmers of Oklahoma in the 1930s and describes their losing battle against wind erosion and the big corporations (companies) that own the land. The "Okies" are driven away from their farms and set off on their long migration to California where they hope to earn their living by fruitpicking.

• **scuttled...** : hurried along like insects • **clustered** : formed close groups • **huddled** : crowded close together out of fear • **awestruck** : full of respect and wonder • **hummed** : *fredonnaient* • **braggarts** : *vantards* • **the pregnant** : the women expecting babies • **rape** : *viol* • **it is unlawful to foul...** : *défense de déposer des immondices.*

TOWARDS COMPREHENSION

WORD-BUILDING

Prefix	Roots (nouns)	Suffixes
Un-	home, law, event, sea, fear, use, pain, help, right, penny, success	-ful, -less, -ward

1 ***Using the above table, make adjectives corresponding in meaning to the definitions, explanations or equivalents given below:***

1. without a home. 2. causing pain. 3. that can be used. 4. permitted by law. 5. moving towards the west. 6. of no use. 7. without any money. 8. bold, brave. 9. towards the sea. 10. contrary to law. 11. obliging, kind, friendly. 12. full of incidents. 13. legitimate.

2 ***Using some of the adjectives thus made, fill in the gaps:***

1. *"Americans are always moving on"* is the opening line of Stephen Benét's poem about the .... migrations.
2. Such a journey to California must often have been ....
3. Poor people are often more .... than rich people.
4. Life on a migrant camp would have been impossible if it had not been codified. It was .... to steal, to be noisy, to commit adultery, etc.
5. Those people must have been .... Otherwise they would never have set out on such a long trek (journey).
6. If they decided to leave for California, it must have been because their lives had so far been ....

3 ***Find in the 1st paragraph words or phrases having the same or nearly the same meaning as:***

1. left slowly. 2. hurried. 3. stayed together. 4. solitary. 5. put in common. 6. had been the first to discover.

4 ***Test your memory: without looking at the text, say what the migrants were in the habit of doing:***

1. As soon as it was dark, they would . . . .
2. Every night, they would . . . .

WOULD

peut exprimer la répétition d'une action dans le passé, un comportement habituel, un trait de caractère.

5 ***Right or wrong? If the following statements are wrong, give the right answer:***

1. The migrants were moving towards the West.
2. They travelled night and day.
3. They hardly ever talked to each other.
4. In the evening all the migrants formed a kind of large family.
5. They helped each other.
6. Their world was completely lawless.
7. Their behaviour was very immoral.
8. There were various forms of punishment.
9. Those who broke the law could be excluded from the community.

LANGUAGE PRACTICE

6 ***Imagine all the questions a new-comer to the camp asked about his rights:***

Can we . . . .
Are we allowed to . . . .
Is it true we can't . . . .
Do I have the right to . . . .

7 ***Imagine the answers:***

No you can't . . . . it's forbidden . . . .
Well . . . . you'd better not . . . . or you'll . . . .
Well . . . . you can . . . . so long as you . . . .

HOW TO EXPRESS PROHIBITION

you oughn't to...
you shouldn't...
you'd better not...
I'm afraid you can't...
you may not...
you're not allowed to...
it's forbidden to...
you musn't...
no + gerund
(ex: no smoking)

On notera que les 3 premières formes sont plutôt un « conseil négatif » qu'une interdiction.

8 ***Imagine all the notices that could have been stuck up in the camp:***

Example: No fouling near the camp.

9 ***Drawing on the text, make as many sentences as you can on the following pattern:***

Those who were found guilty of . . . . were . . . .

HOW TO EXPRESS CONDITION

provided that...
so long as...
on condition that...

RECIPROCAL PRONOUNS

each other, one another

s'emploient pour exprimer la réciprocité. *Men should love one another.* On dit parfois que la seconde forme est préférable lorsqu'il y a plus de deux éléments, mais cette distinction n'est plus observée. Ces deux formes peuvent être précédées d'une préposition ; elles peuvent également s'employer avec un cas possessif. *They are not afraid of each other. They borrowed each other's car.*

10 ***Using the prompts given below, describe the life at the camp. Use as many reciprocal pronouns as you can.***

(help/understand/hate/dislike/talk/respect/one another's tools/one another's food ....)

11 ***React as follows :***

A. Where are they from?
B. I don't know where they are from/I wonder where they are from/I'd like to know where they are from/How should I know where they are from.
A. Who were their leaders? B. ....
A. How were laws made? B. ....
A. How did the system work? B. ....
A. Was the system satisfactory? B. ....
A. How did they learn what rights had to be observed? B. ....
Go on...

INDIRECT QUESTIONS

On notera que, dans l'interrogation indirecte, l'ordre des mots est celui d'une phrase affirmative. Comparez : *Where are you from?* et *He asked me where I was from.*

TOWARDS APPRECIATION

A. The Okies' past lives.

12 ***Pick out the words showing that their lives have so far been unsuccessful, then express the idea differently :***

So far they have experienced/met with ....
So far they have never experienced ....
If they have been compelled to migrate westward ....
Though we don't know much/we aren't given details about their past lives, we can guess that ....

IN OTHER WORDS

B. The Okies' present lives.

13 ***Pick out the two words best expressing what life at the camp is like. Express the idea differently :***

In the day-time .... at night ....
At the camp they were different/they felt they were different people in that they could ....
(= en ce sens qu'ils pouvaient ....)

14 ***Creative oral work: starting from the following prompts, make as many sentences as you can:***

At the camp they had to learn that . . . .
Life at the camp taught them that . . . ./how . . . ./why . . . .
Through community life they learned that . . . .
Of course, not everything was allowed at the camp . . . .

C. The Okies' future lives.

15 ***Pick out the two words referring to their future lives.***

16 ***Imagine what questions they could ask themselves about their future lives.***

(I wonder . . . . I'd like to know . . . . I can't help feeling . . . .)

17 ***Paragraph-writing.***

We can easily guess that all was not harmony in the camp. Imagine what happened *"if one broke the laws"*.

18 ***Essay:*** *"And the families learned, although no one told them, ..."*

What does the writer mean when he says (twice) "although no one told them/the families"? (He does not attempt to codify the rights . . . . as an artist he is concerned with depicting . . . . he does not explain how the system operates . . . . how can those people develop the proper attitude . . . . how can the education of the heart be achieved . . . . the idea of the brotherhood of all men . . . . become aware of a vast human family *beyond* the family . . . .)

SPOTLIGHT ON...

the new american farmer

The rule is : Get big or get out

For tall, burly Pat Benedict, 44, the day begins as early as it did for farmers in Mesopotamia in 8000 B.C. He rises before dawn to pull on boots, blue jeans and work shirt. By 6 a.m. he is breakfasting with some neighbors at the Double D •Diner off •Interstate 94 outside Sabin, Minn. (pop. 333). For an hour or so, he trades community gossip, argues about politics and drops casual remarks about crops and prices designed to feel out what his fellow farmers are doing without asking them a direct question, which is taboo. Then off to the fields—and into the computer age.

Benedict makes a quick trip by •pick-up truck around his 3,500 acres of wheat and sugar beets. At each of many stops he whips out a pocket calculator and does some rapid figuring before giving the hired hands orders on, say, exactly how much pesticide to spray on each field. By 8 a.m. he is heading home to start the most important part of his day : several hours spent at a roll-top desk in his small study. There Benedict goes over computer •print-outs analyzing his plantings acre by acre : inputs of seed, fertilizer, irrigation water, machine time ; output in •bushels and dollars. [...]

Sometimes he pauses to reflect •wistfully that the demands of managing a business with $3.5 million in •assets keep him from doing as much of the actual planting and harvesting as he would like. Says Benedict : "I miss it, because spending eight hours in a tractor cab is a therapeutic kind of work. But I can't assign myself an all-day task running a machine any more. I have to be able to move about to make sure that it all comes together."

For a farmer to complain that he does not get to spend enough time in the fields must be something new in the 10,000-year history of agriculture. But in the U.S. of 1978, Pat Benedict is archetypal of the farmers who make U.S. agriculture the nation's most efficient and productive industry and by far the biggest force holding down the trade deficit. Revolutionary changes are sweeping the croplands, making agriculture an increasingly capital-intensive, high-technology, mass-production business. As a result, U.S. farmers are dividing into two distinct classes. Small farmers, who do not have the technical expertise, are rapidly leaving the land. Large farmers, like Benedict, who know how to use credit and the latest in agricultural science, are gaining an ever greater share of the market. They produce most of the food that the U.S. eats and almost all that it sells to the world.

To succeed in this fast-changing business, a fellow has to be •nimble. Says Jack Neuman, 45, who raises corn, soybeans and hogs in Sangamon County, Ill.: "It used to be that if you had a child who wasn't too bright, you'd say, "Son, you're going to be a farmer." Nowadays, if that dumb kid comes along volunteering to farm, you've got to say, "Oh, a man in hell would love to drink a glass of ice water, but it just can't be done.'"

Time, *November 6, 1978*

● **diner** : small restaurant ● **Interstate** : Intersate highway ● **pick-up truck** : small open truck for transporting things ● **print-outs** : *listages (ordinateur)* ● **bushels** : one bushel=about 35 liters ● **wistfully** : regretfully ● **assets** : capital ● **has to be nimble** : *doit avoir l'esprit vif*

TOWARDS COMPREHENSION

1 ***The life of Pat Benedict. True or false? (In some cases, it may be partly true or partly false.)***

1. Pat Benedict gets up very early.
2. He breakfasts at home.
3. He spends whole mornings talking with the other farmers.
4. He never "talks shop" with the other farmers.
5. He spends his mornings in the fields and his afternoons at his desk.
6. He seldom (rarely) uses his pocket calculator.
7. It is he who assigns to the hands the work to be done in the fields.
8. He wishes he could spend more time in the fields.
9. He leads a businessman's life.
10. He is representative of American farmers today.

2 ***U.S. agriculture. True or false?***

1. Small farmers are more and more numerous.
2. Agriculture is the best asset *(le meilleur atout)* in the American balance of payments.
3. The U.S. has to import most of the food it needs.
4. The gap between large farmers and small farmers is getting wider and wider.
5. U.S. agriculture keeps on changing. (continues to change)

3 ***Make a list of the problems Pat Benedict has to solve nearly every day.***

4 ***Pick out the sentence which, in your opinion, best explains what U.S. agriculture is like to-day.***

5 ***Make a prècis of this text in not more than 50 words.***

LANGUAGE PRACTICE

6 ***Using information from the text, make as many sentences as you can beginning with:***

1. To succeed, the American farmer has to . . . .
2. To survive . . . .
3. If he is to succeed/survive . . . .
4. He can't survive/succeed unless . . . .

UNLESS
= if not

7 ***Now, the required qualities to succeed:***

It takes . . . . to be a farmer . . . .
Those who can't . . . . are doomed to disappear (condemned).

8 ***Agriculture as an increasingly capital-intensive, high-technology, mass-production business. The pros and cons.***

(On the one hand . . . . on the other. It can't be denied that . . . . but we can't help thinking . . . . the survival of the fittest, of the wealthiest . . . .)

9 ***Creative oral or written work:*** *"Get big or get out".*

Imagine how a politician defending the small farmer could make capital of (exploit) this slogan.

FOR FURTHER INFORMATION

Agriculture

A few figures

1. One farmer in the U.S. now feeds 59 people. (Western Europe: 19.2, Japan: 13.7, Soviet Union: 10).

2. Food accounts for only 23% of all private spending by Americans. (25.8% in France, 27% in West Germany, 33.1% in Japan, 42% in Brazil, 52% in the U.S.S.R.)

3. Farm-product exports tripled in the past 6 years to almost 27 million dollars. The U.S. exports more wheat, corn and other coarse grains (barley, oats, sorghum) than all the rest of the world combined.

4. By April 1977, only 1 of every 28 Americans lived on a farm, vs 1 in 21 in 1970 and 1 in 3 early in the century. There are 2.7 million farms in the U.S. to-day.

Modern times

Flaunting [ˈflɔːntiŋ], bowler [ˈbəulə], machinery [məˈʃiːnəri], experiment [iksˈperimənt], automatic [ˌɔːtəˈmætik], enable [iˈneibl], amok [əˈmɔk], hygienic [haiˈdʒiːnik], human refuse [ˈhjuːmənˈrefjuːs], maternal optimism [məˈtəːnl ˈɔptimizəm], cowards [ˈkauədz], propagandist [ˌprɔpəˈgaendist], fantasy [ˈfæntəsi], Black Maria [ˌblæk məˈraiə], mechanic [miˈkænik], pursuing [pəˈsjuiŋ], nihilistic [ˌnaiəˈlistik], amply sufficient [ˈæmpli səˈfiʃənt].

For the first time the little man does not go off alone, flaunting his cane and battered bowler along the endless road out of the screen. He goes in •company looking for what may turn up.

What *had* turned up was first a job in a huge factory twisting screws tighter as little pieces of nameless machinery passed him on a moving belt, under the televised eye of the manager, an eye that followed him even into the lavatory where he snatched an illicit smoke. The experiment of an automatic feeding machine, which will enable a man to be fed while he works, drives him crazy (the •running amok of this machine, with its hygienic mouth-wiper, at the moment when it has reached the •Indian corn course, is horrifyingly funny ; it is the best scene, I think, that Mr. Chaplin has ever invented). When he leaves hospital he is arrested as a Communist leader (he has picked up a red street flag which has fallen off a lorry) and released again after •foiling a prison hold-up. Unemployment and prison punctuate his life, starvation and lucky breaks, and somewhere in its course he attaches to himself the other piece of human •refuse.

The Marxists, I suppose, will claim this as *their* film, but it is a good deal less and a good deal more than Socialist in intention. No real political passion has gone to it: the police batter the little man at one moment and feed him with buns the next: and there is no warm maternal optimism... about the character of the workers: when the police are brutes, the men are cowards ; the little man is always left •in the lurch. Nor do we find him wondering "what a Socialist man should do", but dreaming of a steady job and the most bourgeois home. Mr. Chaplin, whatever his political convictions may be, is an artist and not a propagandist. He doesn't try to explain, but presents with vivid fantasy what seems to him a crazy comic tragic world without a plan, but his sketch of the inhuman factory does not lead us to suppose that his little man would be more at home at Dneipostroi. He presents, he doesn't offer political solutions.

The little man politely giving up his seat to the girl in the crowded •Black Maria: the little man when the dinner-bell sounds tenderly sticking a spray of celery into the mouth of the old mechanic whose head has been caught between the cog-wheels: the little man littering the path of the pursuing detectives with overturned chairs to save his girl: Mr. Chaplin has, like •Conrad, "a few simple ideas"; they could be expressed in much the same phrases: courage, loyalty, labour: against the same nihilistic background of purposeless suffering... These ideas are not enough for a reformer, but they have proved amply sufficient for an artist.

GRAHAM GREENE, *The Spectator*,
in THE PLEASURE DOME, published by Martin Secker and warburg Ltd
Reprinted with the permission of Laurence Pollinger Limited

For five years in the 1930s, Graham Greene, the writer, reviewed films for "The Spectator", a weekly newspaper.

● **in company** : that is, with his girlfriend, played by Paulette Goddard ● **running amok** : *le détraquement* ● **Indian corn** : maize ● **foiling** : frustrating ● **refuse** : *rebut* ● **left in the lurch** : abandoned at the critical moment ● **Black Maria** : police car *(panier à salade)* ● **Conrad (Joseph)** : the novelist (1857-1924).

TOWARDS COMPREHENSION

1 ***The little man's tribulations. Right or wrong?***

1. He gets a job in a big factory.
2. He works on the assembly line.
3. The manager keeps a constant watch over him.
4. The only place where he can be free is the lavatory.
5. The automatic feeding machine enables a man to be fed while he sleeps.
6. This machine makes him sick.
7. When he leaves hospital he is arrested as a dangerous gangster.
8. He has been seen reading a Communist newspaper.
9. He is set free after helping the police to arrest a Communist leader.

2 ***Pick out the words or phrases referring to Chaplin's purpose.***

LANGUAGE PRACTICE

3 ***Using the passive voice, make a few sentences describing all that happened to the little man:***

Example: He was engaged in a big factory/ as a factory hand . . . .
there he . . . .
On leaving hospital, he . . . .

THE PASSIVE VOICE

Voir p. 52

4 ***Drawing on the text, make as many sentences as you can beginning with:***

If this film had been Socialist in intention, Chaplin would have . . . .
If Mr. Chaplin had been out to reform society (=had been trying to), he would have . . . .

IF-CLAUSES

Whatever his political convictions may be . . . .
Mr. Chaplin may be a man of the left . . . .
Nothing allows the Marxists to claim . . . .
Nothing allows us to suppose . . . .
Mr. Chaplin's main purpose is . . . .

5 ***Written work: make a few sentences on this pattern:***

A propagandist . . . . whereas an artist . . . .

HOW TO EXPRESS CONTRAST
whereas

TOWARDS APPRECIATION

6 ***According to Greene, Chaplin is content with presenting society, but isn't his presentation slightly tendentious?***

Although Chaplin is not a propagandist, we can wonder . . . . in so far as . . . .

7 ***Now imagine the counter-arguments:***

He never . . . . it's up to the audience to . . . .

8 ***Creative oral work***

How do you react to Chaplin's films? Do they make you laugh? Do they make you want to cry? Do they give you the impression that the world is absurd? Do you like them?

9 ***Creative written work***

What is the cinema in your opinion? An art, a business or a means of propaganda? Can a film be both good and committed *(engagé)?*

10 ***Oral or written translation***

From the beginning down to "*the other piece of human refuse*".

The sailor's sweetheart

O •if love were had for asking
  In the markets of the town,
Hardly a •lass would think to wear
  A fine •silken gown:
But love is had by •grieving
By choosing and by leaving,
And there's no one now to ask me
If heavy lies my heart.

O if love were had for a deep wish
  In the deadness of the night,
There'd be a •truce to •longing
  Between the •dusk and the light:
But love is had for sighing,
For living and for dying,
And there's no one now to ask me
If heavy lies my heart.

O if love were had for taking
  Like •honey from the hive,
The bees that made the tender stuff
  Could hardly keep alive:
But love it is a •wounded thing,
A •tremor and a •smart,
And there's no one left to kiss me now
Over my heavy heart.

DUNCAN CAMPBELL SCOTT

Duncan Campbell Scott (1862-1947) was a Canadian poet. He was born in Ottawa.

● **if love...** : if you could get love by asking for it ● **lass** : girl ● **silken gown** : *robe de soie* ● **grieving** : feeling sad *(s'affligeant)* ● **truce** : *trêve* ● **longing** : ardently desiring, ardent desires ● **dusk** : *crépuscule* ● **honey** : *miel* ● **wounded** : *blessé* ● **tremor** : trembling ● **smart** : sharp pain.

1 ***From her remarks about love, what must have happened to the sailor's sweetheart?***

2 ***Is love seen as a pleasant, romantic passion here? How is it seen? Do you think that the verse form, the rhymes and so on are well-chosen?***

(In verse 2, for instance, why is there a repetition of the [ai] sound? Why does the poet end so many lines with gerunds *(longing, sighing, dying...)*?

A. Choose the right answer :

1. Come next week . . . . you hear to the contrary.
   a) because. *b)* while. *c)* unless. *d)* after.
2. . . . . the end of the term approaches, they are getting more and more anxious.
   a) while. *b)* as. *c)* unless. *d)* before.
3. According to Greene, a true artist never uses his art as a means of propaganda . . . . a bad one does not hesitate to do so.
   a) because. *b)* whereas. *c)* if. *d)* in so far as.
4. I wish I . . . . as much money as you do.
   a) could make. *b)* will make. *c)* should make. *d)* can make.
5. They will . . . . you work hard, whether you like it or not.
   a) let. *b)* make. *c)* order. *d)* ask.
6. It is natural that they . . . . expect you to be present at the cocktail party.
   a) will. *b)* may. *c)* should. *d)* must.
7. It was the first time she . . . . a camera.
   a) saw. *b)* will see. *c)* had seen. *d)* would have seen.

B. Fill in the gaps with verbs from the following list : apply for, apply to, cope with, make up one's mind, remind, object to, succeed, wonder.

1. I . . . . what he would have done if I hadn't helped him. 2. Of course, it's a serious problem, but you'll have to . . . . it. 3. To whom should I . . . . further information? 4. I'm still hesitating, I haven't yet . . . . 5. Do you think I could . . . . that firm for a job? 6. You should . . . . him to answer that letter, he is apt to forget. 7. I don't . . . . your going out to-night so long as you are back by midnight. 8. I . . . . if he'll . . . . in getting the post, there are so many applicants.

C. Dans l'exercice suivant, vous proposerez le plus de solutions possible :

1. Vous vous demandez comment l'un de vos amis a réussi à obtenir un poste aussi important.
2. Un de vos amis est nerveux avant un examen, vous essayez de le calmer et vous lui donnez des conseils.
3. Vous racontez ce que vous lui avez conseillé de faire.
4. On vous propose de partir pour la Grande-Bretagne, mais vous préféreriez aller aux États-Unis. Que dites-vous?
5. On vous informe que vous allez devoir travailler dur, vous répondez que cela vous est égal si le salaire est élevé.
6. Vous dites que vous détestez que l'on vous regarde dans la rue.

TEST YOUR ENGLISH - TEST YOUR ENGLISH – TEST YOUR ENGLISH

Extract from: The women's room

Women's suffrage ['wiminz 'sʌfridʒ], inequality [,ini'kwɔliti], constitutionally [,kɔnsti'tju:ʃənli], continually approached [kən'tinjuəli ə'prəutʃt], hauteur [əu'tə:], elevator ['eliveitə], aged ['eidʒid], crooked ['krukid], beloved [bi'lʌvd], erased [i'reizd], injustice [in'dʒʌstis], protest (verb) [prə'test], protest (noun) ['prəutest].

She was a woman and that alone was enough to deprive her of freedom no matter how much the history books pretended that women's suffrage had ended inequality, or that women's feet had been bound only in an ancient and outmoded and foreign place like China. She was constitutionally unfree. She could not go out alone at night. She could not in a moment of loneliness go out to a local tavern to have a drink in company. The twice she had taken the train during the daytime, to make excursions to museums in New York, she had been continually approached. She could not even appear to be lacking an escort ; if that escort decided to abandon her, she was helpless. And she couldn't defend herself ; she had to depend on a male for that. Even frail, limping •Biff could handle such a situation better than she. Had those guys gotten to her, all the rage and hauteur and fighting in the world wouldn't have helped her.

And she would never be free, never. Never. It would always be like this. She thought about her mother's friends and suddenly understood them. No matter where she went or what she did, she would always have to worry about what men were thinking, how they looked at her, what they might do. One day some months before, in an elevator on her way to the dentist's office, she had overheard an ugly aged woman with dyed red hair and a •crooked back talking to another woman, fiftyish and fat, about rape. Both of them were clucking their tongues, talking about locks on doors and windows, and they looked to her as if to include her in conversation, as if she were one of them. She had looked away, full of •contempt for them. Who would want to rape them? It was •wishful thinking, she thought. Yet a few nights later there was an item in the newspaper about an eighty-year-old woman, raped and killed in her own apartment.

She thought about what would have happened had Biff not been there [...]

Horrible, horrible it would have been, and her beloved Lanny would no doubt have called her •slut and said she had gotten what she deserved. He would simply have erased her from his list of women one is required to treat with respect. That was the way things were. And no matter how high she held her head, no matter how alone she walked, that is the way things would stay. It was ridiculous to talk about injustice ; it was useless to protest. She knew from her few experiences of talking about women and freedom that such protests were always taken by men as invitations to their taking greater freedoms with her.

MARILYN FRENCH, 1977, The Women's Room
Reprinted with the permission of André Deutsch Limited

Marilyn French was born in New York City and studied at Harvard, where she has also taught. She is the author of several scholarly works but "The Women's Room" is her first novel.

• **Biff** : Biff, who is physically handicapped, saved the heroine from being raped • **crooked** : deformed • **contempt**≠ esteem • **wishful thinking** : *elles prennent leurs désirs pour la réalité* • **slut** : *traînée.*

TOWARDS COMPREHENSION

1 **1st part** (down to: *"raped and killed in her own apartment"*).

The passage is mainly about:

a. women's life at night. b. women's fight for equality. c. women's lack of freedom.

2 ***Pick out the sentence which best justifies your answer.***

3 ***Right or wrong. Justify your answer.***

1. According to history books, the right to vote put an end to women's inequality.
2. According to the author, women are not completely free yet.
3. The author has never personally suffered from this lack of freedom.
4. She thinks that things are looking up (getting better).
5. She felt pity for the two women in the elevator.

4 ***Test your memory: after reading or listening to the text again, finish the sentences without looking at the text:***

1. She could not in a moment of loneliness ....
2. She couldn't defend herself: she ....
3. No matter where she went or what she did ....

5 **2nd part.**

The dominant tone is one of:

a. horror. b. revolt. c. resignation. d. hatred.

6 ***Justify your answer.***

7 ***Right or wrong. Justify your answer.***

1. She is horrified at the thought of what would have happened if Biff had not arrived.
2. The boy she is in love with would have pitied and comforted her.
3. She excites women to revolt.

8 ***What is, in your opinion, the sentence which best sums up the central idea of the passage?***

LANGUAGE PRACTICE

9 ***React as follows:***

A. She says she isn't free.
B. But she is, isn't she?
A. She says it will always be like this.
B. But it won't, will it?

A. She says she can't go out alone. B. .....
A. She says Lanny would have called her slut. B. ....
A. She says she couldn't defend herself. B. ....
A. Men say they have changed. B. ....
A. Men say they are in favour of equality. B. ....
Go on

10 ***Using the verbs given below—and others of your own—compose dialogues like this:***

HOW TO EXPRESS RESIGNATION

A. You could protest, couldn't you?
B. Of course I could, but I know it isn't much use protesting/or: but is it any use protesting?/or: but you know perfectly well it's no use protesting, don't you?
(rebel, revolt, fight for equality, expain all this to Lanny ....)

HOW TO ASK FOR CONFIRMATION
TAGS (généralités)

Ce sont des reprises interrogatives correspondant à peu près à notre « n'est-ce pas? ».

a. Il peut s'agir d'une affirmation déguisée. Le locuteur est sûr de ce qu'il avance et il n'attend pas de réponse. Le schéma intonatif du « tag » est alors généralement descendant.

b. Il peut s'agir d'une véritable question. Le locuteur attend une réponse. Le schéma intonatif est alors ascendant.

c. Le sujet du « tag » est toujours le pronom personnel correspondant au sujet de l'énoncé auquel le « tag » fait suite.

d. L'énoncé auquel le « tag » fait suite est affirmatif : reprise interro-négative :
It's true, isn't it?
The man looked up, didn't he?
Men are clinging desperately to their prerogatives, aren't they?

e. L'énoncé auquel le « tag » fait suite est négatif : reprise interrogative :
It isn't true, is it?
He can't know, can he?
He won't change his mind, will he?

COULD

1. **A la forme affirmative :** est de maniement délicat. Le point essentiel à retenir est que **could** ne dit pas si un acte a été accompli. Il informe sur l'aptitude du sujet à accomplir cet acte. Cette possibilité peut porter sur le passé ou sur l'avenir. Si l'on veut marquer qu'une action a été accomplie, il faut employer : **be able to, manage to, succeed in.**

a) passé : when I was younger, I could work ten hours on end *(...je pouvais travailler dix heures de suite)* mais : yesterday I succeeded in working four hours on end without smoking. I was able to understand this letter without using a dictionary.

b) avenir : **could** prend alors un sens conditionnel. I could do it if I wanted to *(je pourrais le faire si je voulais).*

2. **A la forme interrogative :** fréquent comme formule de politesse. Could you please tell me who this man is. On trouve souvent également la forme interro-négative : "So I'll come next Tuesday." "Couldn't you come on Monday instead?"

3. **A la forme négative :** marque qu'une action n'a pas pu être accomplie. She could not get him to change his mind *(elle n'a pas pu...).* Le contraire serait : She managed to get him to change his mind.

Could not peut également avoir un sens conditionnel :
even if you asked him, he could not come, he is too busy.

11 ***Fill in the gaps with :*** still ***or*** always

1. Although things have changed, too many men . . . . look upon women as sex objects.
2. No matter what we may say, we women are . . . . in the wrong.
3. "I . . . . don't understand what you were doing in that pub", he said to her.
4. Men have . . . . been convinced they are superior to us, how could they change?

12 ***Make a few more similar sentences.***

ALWAYS, STILL, NOT... ANY MORE, STILL NOT, NOT YET :

Ne pas confondre **still** et **always. Always** marque qu'un événement, une situation, ou un état ont un caractère invariable ou se répètent : it has always been so *(il en a toujours été ainsi).* You always say that. Notez la place de **always** dans : he always *is* here *(il est toujours fourré ici).* C'est **is** qui porte l'accent d'intensité.
A ne pas confondre avec : he is still here *(il est toujours, c'est-à-dire, encore, ici).* Le contraire serait : he isn't here any more.
On notera que **always,** comme tous les adverbes de fréquence, se place entre le sujet et le verbe, si celui-ci est au présent ou au passé, et, dans les autres cas, entre l'auxiliaire (modal, have, be, will...) et le verbe.
Notez la place de la négation dans **still not :** I still don't understand why he did that *(je ne comprends toujours pas...).* He still hasn't answered my question *(il n'a toujours pas).*
Comparez avec : he hasn't answered my letter yet *(il n'a pas encore).* **Still not** est plus fort et a, en quelque sorte, une valeur modale, il exprime un point de vue, une prise de position tandis que **not... yet** exprime le plus souvent une simple constatation. Still no answer *(toujours pas de réponse).*
Still s'emploie souvent devant ou après un comparatif : He is still taller ou he is taller still (=even taller ; *encore plus grand*).

13 ***Complete the following sentences, drawing on the text or not :***

1. No matter what history books pretend, women are . . . .
2. No matter how much she feels like going out alone, she knows . . . .
3. No matter how old they are, they still . . . .
4. . . . . men keep approaching her.
5. . . . . Lanny will blame her.
6. . . . . things won't change.

NO MATTER WHAT/WHO/ WHEN/WHERE/HOW
= whatever, whoever, however...

14 ***Written work : make up 4 or 5 sentences expressing how useless it is to fight. Use :*** unless no matter, it's no use...
Example : It's no use arguing with him, no matter what you say he won't believe you unless you can prove to him he was wrong.

TOWARDS APPRECIATION

15 ***Does this woman strike you as being a liberated woman? If so, why? If not, say how a liberated woman would react.***

16 ***Analyze the attitude of some men to rape.***

They still believe that . . . . they are still of the opinion that . . . . they still contend that . . . . they haven't yet understood . . . .

17 ***Creative written work :***

Draw the portrait of the modern male chauvinist.

18 ***Find a suitable title for this passage.***

19 ***Written translation :***

Translate the first paragraph.

FOR FURTHER DISCUSSION

Au pays des femmes

Marilyn French fait un malheur aux États-Unis avec son premier livre : un monument.

Notez bien le titre : *Toilettes pour femmes*. Un graffiti dans les toilettes de Harvard. On a biffé « Dames » (Ladies'Room) sur la porte. On a écrit à la place « Femmes » (Women's Room). Il n'y a plus de « dames » face aux « gentlemen », mais des femmes face aux hommes. Femme, entre femelle et dame, à part entière. Ça signifie quoi, au juste ?

Au début, on se dit « Encore cinq cents pages à avaler ! » Grand format, en plus ! Le gros machin américain, bien ficelé, mais sans le souffle d'Erica, c'est sûr. Erica, c'est Erica Jong. Celle-là est exceptionnelle. Elle dit la femme qu'elle est, drôle, virulente, affamée. [...] Bon, sûrement pas de l'Erica. Mais quoi ? Alors, on y va. Courageusement. C'est un peu comme entrer dans la mer à la Pentecôte. Pas à pas au début, dix pages pour se mettre en forme, et puis, ça y est. On s'immerge. On n'en sort plus. On lit d'une traite. On arrive au bout, K.O., ravie, changée.

L'art de survivre

Marylin French vous a prise par la main pour vous entraîner au pays des femmes. Avant elle, je me disais « le féminisme, la barbe ! » A chacune de se débrouiller comme elle peut, comme elle sait. A chacune ses tourments, ses défenses, à chacune ses constructions pour s'en sortir. Le militantisme acharné ? La barbe aussi. Mieux vaut cultiver ses géraniums — ou ses lauriers roses, — en attendant autre chose. Autre chose pas tellement pour soi — quand on a à peu près ce qu'il faut. Autre chose pour les autres, moins armées, moins indépendantes, moins fatalistes, ou moins rouées. Bref, Marilyn French a réussi à me donner mauvaise conscience. Parce que ce qu'elle dit, à quarante-cinq ans passés, c'est la solidarité féminine.

Être femme, c'est être seule. Être seule, c'est la déprime. La folie, même. Être femme, comme sa Mira qui lui ressemble comme une sœur, c'est grandir dans un monde bardé d'interdits, et ne rien comprendre avant d'en avoir tellement bavé que la vie n'est plus qu'une survie. Être femme, c'est ça, c'est survivre.

Et ce qu'il y a d'inouï, c'est que c'est pareil pour les autres femmes que vous connaissez. Mais tant qu'elles n'en disent rien, vous croyez aux apparences. Vous l'ignorez. Jusqu'au jour où vous vous parlez... Alors, comme Woolf — que Marilyn French vénère, que nous vénérons — vous traversez les apparences. Et au-delà, vous trouvez toutes les femmes, la femme. [...]

Mira, donc, il faut bien vous en parler, c'est un bon produit des années 30-40. Une petite fille qui n'avait pas le droit de jouer à chat dans la rue, une jeune fille à qui on a appris à ne pas porter plus de trois bijoux à la fois, qui lisait *Seventeen* et, accessoirement, Frédéric Nietzsche. Elle a peur des garçons, commence des études, se conduit sagement et apprend très vite qu'il est impossible de vivre au pays des fées. Au pays des hommes alors ? Dans sa famille, elle ne bronche pas, et pourtant, dit-elle, elle se sent « *comme un champ de bataille vociférant* ». Elle se marie jeune : « *bardée du titre de Madame* », le monde lui fait moins peur. Pour ce qu'elle en connaît !...

Un mari gentil et fade, l'*homo americanus* typique, étudiant en médecine. Des enfants. Peu d'argent. Beaucoup de travail. Plus aucune autonomie. [...]

Mira, dans sa banlieue stéréotypée du New-Jersey, lave les couches-culottes. Elle se rapproche des jeunes femmes qui l'entourent et qui, comme elle, lavent les couches-culottes. Les voix, les destins des unes et des autres, pas bien reluisants, mais si justes, témoignent d'une époque, d'une société : la « middle class » américaine. Monsieur de Balzac, s'il lisait ce livre aujourd'hui, aimerait, je vous le garantis.

Que veut l'homme ?

Mira, son mari, leur marmaille, deviennent plus riches avec les années. On change de banlieue. On change d'amis. La médiocrité est moins médiocre. Un beau jour, alors qu'elle commence à souffler un peu, Mira s'entend dire par son mari — les hommes, c'est comme ça — qu'il la quitte. Net et sans bavure. Ou plutôt si, pas mal de bavures pour elle, pas mal de larmes et de verres de brandy. « *Il n'y avait pas de justice. Il n'y avait que la vie. Et elle était en vie.* » Mira, la trentaine, était en train d'acquérir, au-delà de son insatisfaction, une sorte de sérénité, de calme. De sagesse. Que faire ?

Elle reprend ses études. La voilà à Harvard, Cambridge comme on dit, « *un abri pour les sans-abri* ». Un endroit où l'élitisme intellectuel est insupportable. Le temps passe. Les temps changent : 1968 ; la guerre au Vietnam ; les grandes marches pour la paix ; les mouvements de libération des femmes ; les communautés. Pudique, un peu déphasée, mais très sagace, Mira vit entourée de filles plus jeunes — la génération d'Erica, justement, trente-cinq ans aujourd'hui — qu'elle écoute. Leurs vies traversent le livre, elles aussi, plus violentes, plus brutales.

Un jour, elle rencontrera un homme qui, enfin, lui apprendra l'intimité et la spontanéité vraies. Vous savez, ce genre d'homme qui se penche sur vous en cherchant sur votre visage quelque chose qui n'est pas sur les visages... Et ça ne collera pas. Pas très longtemps. Elle, et ses amies — très anti-hommes pour la plupart — s'interrogent sur ce que veut l'homme, ce qu'il est.

Françoise WAGENER, *Le Monde,* 21 juillet 1978

1 ***Read this review of* The Women's Room *carefully once or twice, then shut your book and make a precis of it :***

(*The Women's Room,* Mrs. French's first novel, is a big hit . . . . At the beginning you are a bit apprehensive, but once . . . . you can't . . . . It is the story of . . . . we learn that . . . . As a child . . . . she got married . . . . Marriage means . . . . She had to go back to college . . . . and in the end . . . .)

2 ***Judging from this review, what are the main themes touched upon in the novel? How did the reading of this novel make the writer of the review change her views on feminism?***

(Before reading the novel, she thought: "It's up to every woman to shift for herself/to manage as best she can/to get out of her own mess. Relentless militancy. How boring ! . . . .

3 ***A critic has written about the novel:*** *"A classic .... the kind of book that changes lives."* ***Can a book really change lives?***

4 ***Two types of men are alluded to. Can you imagine what they were like?***

5 ***Would you say that the extract from the novel which you have studied gives you a balanced impression of the whole novel? Do you see why it was chosen?***

6 ***Debate: "Male chauvinism." What is meant by these two words so often used these days? Isn't it to be feared that a certain form of feminism should lead to "female chauvinism"? Isn't it possible to find a middle course?***

(What men want ..../women's liberationists ..../the male chauvinist makes it quite clear that ..../he emphasizes ..../It is fashionable to pretend that ..../What has led women to revolt is ..../What every man fears is that .... may ..../Needless to say ..../Now that I think of it ..../I get frightened at the thought that ..../The truth is that ..../to play the dominant role in public ..../The power of the media to promote meaningless ideas ..../Male chauvinism reminds me of war. Everybody is against it, but nobody can stop it.)

"Suffer women once to arrive at equality with you, and they will from that moment on become your superiors."

—Cato the Elder, 195 B.C.

Witch hunt

Jordache ['dʒɔ:dɑ:ʃ], abortionist [ə'bɔ:ʃənist], Coed ['kəu'ed], Socrates ['sɔkrəti:z], academic [,ækə'demik], lamentable ['læməntəbl], dossier ['dɔsiei], sacrifice ['sækrifais], specifically [spi'sifikəli], reference ['refrəns], economic theories [,i:kə'nɔmik 'θiəriz], moron ['mɔ:rɔn], legislator ['ledʒisleitə], committee [kə'miti], patriot ['peitriət .Am:pæ], politics ['pɔlitiks], independently [,indi'pendəntli], Registered Republican ['redʒistəd ri'pʌblikən], vouch [vautʃ], testimony ['testiməni].

The action takes place in 1954, at the time of the McCarthy witch hunts. Denton, a history professor at Whitby college in the State of New York, has asked Rudolph Jordache, one his former students, to meet him in a bar because he wants to ask him a favour.

Denton dropped his voice and leaned forward over the table. "I'm in trouble, Jordache." He's going to ask me for the name of an •abortionist, Rudolph thought wildly. *Love on the Campus.* He saw the headlines. *History Professor Makes History by Moonlight with Coed. Doctor in Jail.* Rudolph tried to keep his face noncommittal and went on eating.

The hamburger was gray and •soggy and the potatoes were oily.

"You heard what I said?" Denton whispered.

"You're in trouble, you said."

"Exactly." There was a professorial tone of approval—the student had been paying attention. "*Bad* trouble." Denton sipped at his coffee, Socrates and •hemlock.

•"They're out to get me."

"Who's out to get you?"

"My enemies." Denton's eyes scanned the bar, searching out enemies, disguised as workmen drinking beer.

"When I was in school," Rudolph said, "you seemed to be well liked everywhere."

"There are currents, currents," Denton said, •"eddies and whirlpools that the undergraduate never has an •inkling of. In the faculty rooms, in the offices of power. In the office of the President himself. I am too outspoken, it is a failing of mine. I am naive, I have believed in the myth of academic freedom. My enemies have •bided their time. The vice-chairman of the department, I should have •fired him years ago, a hopeless scholar; I restrained myself only out of pity, lamentable weakness. As I said, the vice-chairman, yearning for my job, has prepared a dossier, scraps of gossip over a drink, lines out of context, insinuations. They are preparing to offer me up as a sacrifice, Jordache."

"I think you'd better tell me specifically what's happening," Rudolph said. "Then perhaps I'd be able to judge if I could help."

"Oh, you could help, all right, no doubt about that." Denton pushed the half-eaten hamburger away from him. "They have found their witch," he said. "Me."

"I don't quite understand..."

"The witch hunt," Denton said. "You read the papers like everybody else. Throw the Reds out of our schools."

Rudolph laughed. "You're no Red, Professor, you know that," he said.

"Keep your voice low, boy." Denton looked around worriedly. "One does not broadcast on this subject."

"I'm sure you have nothing to worry about, Professor." Rudolph said. He decided to make it seem like a joke. "I was afraid it was something serious. I thought maybe you'd got a girl pregnant."

"You can laugh," Denton said. "At your age. Nobody laughs in a college or a university anymore. The wildest charges. A five-dollar contribution to an obscure charity in 1938, a reference to Karl Marx in a class, for God's sake, how is a man to teach the economic theories of the nineteenth century without mentioning Karl Marx! An ironic joke about prevalent economic practices, picked up by some stone-age •moron in a class in American History and repeated to the moron's father, who is the Commander of the local •American Legion Post. Ah, you don't know, boy, you don't know. And Whiby gets a yearly grant from the •State. For the School of Agriculture. So some windbag of an •upstate legislator makes a speech, forms a committee, demands an investigation, gets his name in the newspaper. Patriot, Defender of the Faith. A special •board has been set up within the university, Jordache, don't mention it to a soul, headed by the President, to investigate charges against various members of the faculty. They hope to •head off the State, throw them a few bodies, mine chief among them, not imperil the grant from the State. Does the picture grow clearer, Jordache?"

"Oh, Christ," Rudolph said.

"Exactly. Oh, Christ. I don't know what your politics are..."

"I don't have any politics," Rudolph said. "I vote independently."

"Excellent, excellent," Denton said. "Although it would have been better if you were a registered Republican. And to think that I voted for Eisenhower." He laughed hollowly. "My son was in Korea and he promised to end the war. But how to prove it. There is much to be said for public balloting."

"What do you want me to do, Professor?" Rudolph asked. "Specifically?"

"Now we come to it," Denton said. He finished his coffee. "The board meets to consider my case one week from today. Tuesday at two P.M. Mark the hour. I have only been allowed to see a general outline of the charges against me; contributions to Communist front organizations in the thirties, atheistic and radical utterances in the classroom, the recommendation of certain books for outside reading of a doubtful character. The usual academic •hatchet job, Jordache, all too usual. With the temper of the country what it is, with that man Dulles roaring up and down the world, preaching nuclear destruction, with the most eminent men •traduced and dismissed like errand boys in Washington, a poor teacher can be ruined by a whisper, the merest whisper. Luckily, they still have a sense of shame at the university, although I doubt it will last the year, and I am to have a chance to defend myself, bring in witnesses to •vouch for me..."

"What do you want me to say?"

"Whatever you will, boy," Denton said, his voice broken. "I do not plan to coach you. Say what you think of me. You were in three of my classes, we had many instructive hours outside the courses, you have been to my house. You're a clever young man, you are not to be fooled. You know me as well as any man in this town. Say what you will. Your reputation is high, your record at the university was impeccable, not a blot on it, you are a rising young businessman, •untainted, your testimony will be of the utmost value."

IRWIN SHAW, *Rich Man, Poor Man*
Published by Dell Publishing Co. Inc.

Irwin Shaw was born in New York City in 1913, and educated at Brooklyn College. His first novel, The Young Lions *was published in 1949. Since then, he has written several novels and many stories, film-scripts and plays.*

● **abortionist** : *avorteur* ● **soggy** : full of water ● **hemlock** : *ciguë* ● **they're out to get me** : *ils veulent ma peau* ● **eddies and whirlpools** : *des remous et des tourbillons* ● **an inkling** : the least idea ● **bided their time** : waited for the right moment ● **fired** : *flanquer à la porte* ● **moron** : imbecile ● **American Legion** : conservative association of men who fought in the two world wars, etc. ● **State** : from the State of New York ● **upstate** : from somewhere in the north of the State of New York ● **board** : committee ● **head off** : *prendre les devants* ● **hatchet job** : *exécution en règle* ● **traduced** : *diffamé* ● **vouch for me** : guarantee my innocence ● **untainted** : uncontaminated.

TOWARDS COMPREHENSION

1st part (down to . . . . *"you'd got a girl pregnant"*).

1 ***Right or wrong. Justify your answer.***

1. Denton has got a girl pregnant.
2. Denton has enemies.
3. His enemies accuse him of being a Communist.
4. He is a member of the Communist Party.
5. It is the vice-chairman who has master-minded (planned) the whole affair.
6. It is for political reasons that the vice-chairman opposes Denton.
7. Jordache takes all this very seriously.

2 ***Pick out the two sentences which best explain the kind of trouble Denton is in.***

2nd part

3 ***Understanding some key-words and sentences.***

1. The *wildest charges* (l. 37)
   a) the best jokes. *b)* the highest prices. *c)* the most ridiculous accusations.
2. A *charity* (l. 37) is:
   a) a political party. *b)* an organization for helping the poor. *c)* a group of extremists.
3. A *moron* (l. 40) is:
   a) an extremist. *b)* a very stupid person. *c)* a foreigner.
4. A *wind-bag* (l. 43) is:
   a) a Fascist. *b)* a policeman. *c)* a man who talks a lot but has nothing to say.
5. A special *board has been set up* (l. 45)
   a) a special committee has been formed. *b)* a special tribunal has been formed.
   c) special investigators have been nominated.
6. There *is much to be said* for public balloting. (l. 56)
   a) Lots of people are in favour of voting openly, in public.
   b) More and more people say that the vote should not be secret.
   c) Voting openly, and not in secret, would have many advantages.
7. I am to have a chance *to bring in witnesses to vouch for me.* (l. 68)
   a) he will be allowed to produce documents.
   b) some of his friends will have to say what they know about him.
   c) the people who know him will be allowed to speak in his favour.
8. I do not plan to *coach* you (l. 71)
   a) to give you some money. *b)* to tell you what to say. *c)* to appeal to your pity.
9. Your *testimony* will be of the *utmost value.* (l. 76)
   a) your presence will comfort me. *b)* your presence will impress the members of the board.
   c) what you will say will have a great effect on the members of the board.

4 ***Show that the meaning of the following words and sentences can be guessed from the context.***

1. The *wildest* charges. (l. 37)
2. Not imperil the grant from the State. (l. 48)

FROM THE CONTEXT

3. There is much to be said for public balloting. (l. 56)
4. With the temper of the country what it is . . . . (l. 63)
5. I do not plan to coach you. (l. 71)
6. You are not to be fooled. (l. 74)
7. Your record at the university was impeccable. (l. 75)

(If we look a little further down, we can understand . . . . the meaning of this word is clarified by another coming before . . . .)

5 ***Right or wrong. Justify your answer.***

1. Denton is the only member of the faculty to be in trouble.
2. He knows exactly what he is accused of.
3. The members of the board are afraid of losing the money given by the State.
4. The political climate is one of suspicion.
5. Jordache has the same political views as Denton.

6 ***Say which sentences are essential to the understanding of the passage :***

1. He's going to ask me for the name of an abortionist.
2. Rudolph tried to keep his face noncommittal.
3. Denton's eyes scanned the bar, searching out enemies.
4. "When I was in school", Rudolph said, "you seemed to be well liked everywhere."
5. I am too outspoken.
6. I have believed in the myth of academic freedom.
7. The vice-chairman, yearning for my job, has prepared a dossier.
8. They have found their witch.

7 ***Sum up the passage.***

LANGUAGE PRACTICE

8 **2nd part**

HOW TO EXPRESS HELPLESSNESS IRRITATION

Compare :

A. How is a businessman like Jordache to understand intrigues of that sort?
B. How can you expect a businessman like Jordache to understand intrigues of that sort?
C. How can a businessman like Jordache be expected to understand intrigues of that sort?

Give the other two forms :

A. What is Jordache to do about it all?
A. How can you expect an outspoken man like Denton to hold his tongue?
A. How can Jordache be expected to guess what Denton is driving at? *(où Denton veut en venir)*
A. What can a naive man like him be expected to know about witch hunts?
A. What is Jordache to conclude from Denton's remarks?
A. How can you expect a University to exist without freedom of speech?
A. What is a moron like him to know about economics?
A. How can Jordache be expected to judge the situation if Denton keeps beating about the bush? *(tourner autour du pot)*
A. What can you expect him to say in a situation like that?
A. How am I to vouch for him? I don't even know him!

WHAT AM I TO ....? HOW AM I TO ....?

Ces questions, de style oratoire, peuvent exprimer le désarroi du locuteur, ou son irritation, voire son agressivité. L'intonation en détermine souvent le sens.
How am I to prove (that) I'm not guilty *(= comment est-ce que je peux, comment voulez-vous que je prouve, comment prouver...?).*

9 ***"What do you want me to do?"***
Using the prompts given below, make as many sentences as you can on the following patterns:

HOW TO EXPRESS A WISH
Voir p. 25

I want you to . . . .
I'd like you to . . . .
I don't expect you to . . . .
(say I am an honest man/give evidence in favour of . . . ./bear witness to my honesty/praise me/tell lies/. . . . never been a Communist/try to influence students/what you really think of me/etc. . . . .)

10 ***Imagine what other questions Jordache could ask:***

What am I supposed to . . . . ?
What am I expected to . . . . ?
Am I supposed to . . . . ?
What am I supposed to . . . . if they . . . . ?

11 ***Imagine how Denton could defend himself:***

A. You mentioned Karl Marx.
B. How is a teacher/man to teach the economic theories of the 19th century without mentioning Karl Marx.
A. You referred to Marxism. B. . . . .
A. You recommended books about Marxism. B. . . . .
A. You spoke of the flaws of capitalism (faults, defects). B. . . . .
A. You drew your students' attention to the faults of our economic system. B. . . . .

WITHOUT + GERUND

TOWARDS APPRECIATION

12 ***Analyse Denton's feelings. Is he angry, indignant, frightened, indifferent?***

(He is . . . . and that's quite understandable. His . . . . is understandable. It is not surprising that he should be . . . . If I were in his place . . . . I'd . . . . too.)

13 ***Drawing on the text, describe the atmosphere of suspicion and collective hysteria of the time.***

a. *Denton is speaking.* (If you . . . . you're sure to . . . . Anyone can be suspected of/accused of/No one is safe from . . . . You can't . . . . without . . . . People don't dare to . . . . for fear of . . . . and you career is ruined.)
b. *You are speaking.* People must have stood/in fear of . . . . We can easily picture to ourselves/imagine what life was like in the States . . . . I wonder how . . . .

14 ***Imagine what Denton and Jordache could have said if they had given vent to their indignation:***

It's a shame that a nation should . . . .
Isn't it a scandal that a man should be . . . .
It's unthinkable that . . . . should.

SHOULD
Voir p. 97

15 ***Creative oral work: Denton is before the special board. Imagine the scene:***

(You will understand that we have to ask you some questions . . . . have you ever been a member . . . . interested in politics . . . . In those days . . . . far out on the left . . . . a man of the left . . . . a Radical . . . . you mixed with persons of extreme political views . . . . you have been intimate with . . . . you are reported as having said that . . . . it is reported that you said . . . .)

16 ***Creative written work:*** (15 lines)

Though the hearing was secret, the news has leaked out *(il y a eu une fuite)* and articles appear in the press.
a. Write one for a newspaper defending Denton.
b. Write another for a paper dead against Denton.

Freedom is a habit

Freedom is a habit
and a coat worn
some born to wear it
some never to know it.
Freedom is cheap
or again as a •garment
is so costly
men pay their lives
rather than not have it.
Freedom is •baffling:
men having it often
know not they have it
till it is gone and
they no longer have it.
What does this mean?
Is it a •riddle?
Yes, it is first of all
in the •primers of riddles.
To be free is •so-so:
you can and you can't:
walkers can have freedom
only by never walking
away their freedom:
runners too have freedom
unless they overrun:
eaters have often outeaten
their freedom to eat
and drinkers overdrank
their fine drinking freedom.

CARL SANDBURG, *Complete Poems*
"Freedom is a habit"

Carl Sandburg (1878-1967) was born in Illinois. He was a writer of extraordinary vitality. His career as a poet really began when he moved to Chicago at the age of thirty-five and wrote a series of poems inspired by that city. He is the poet of American democracy and of ordinary American people whose speech rhythms he captures in his poems.

• **a garment**: a piece of clothing • **baffling**: puzzling, hard to understand • **riddle**: *devinette*
• **primers**: elementary books • **so-so**: *comme ci comme ça*, passable.

1 ***What does Sandburg tell us about people's attitude to freedom?***
What does he tell us about the nature of freedom? Do you agree with him? (for example, is he right when he says *'some born to wear it—some never to know it'?*)

2 ***Freedom is usually spoken of in a more grandiloquent style.***
Why did Sandburg choose to write in this everyday style?

How I got there

Texas House of Representatives [ˈteksəs ˈhausəv ˌrepriˈzentətivz], political experts [pəˈlitikəl ˈekspəːts], naivete [nɑːˈiːvtei], articulate [ɑːˈtikjulit], opponent [əˈpəunənt], confronted [kənˈfrʌntid], politicians [ˌpɔliˈtiʃənz], the moneyed and politically influential interests [ðə ˈmʌnidən pəˈlitikəli ˌinfluˈenʃəl ˈintrists], acknowledged [əkˈnɔlidʒd], editorially [ˌediˈtɔːriəli], identifiable [aiˈdentifaiəbl], precincts [ˈpriːsiŋkts], senatorial [ˌsenəˈtɔːriəl], unsuccessful [ˈʌn-səkˈsesful].

In 1962, I, a black woman, ran for election to the Texas House of Representatives (in Harris County, which includes Houston). The political experts gave me no chance of winning, but in my political naivete I believed that I was more articulate than my opponent, and sensitive to people's needs and aspirations. These qualities, I felt, would help me overcome the •odds against my election to the Texas House.

I rarely saw my opponent in person, but was confronted by his face on many billboards and on the television screen. He was obviously well financed. I had borrowed my •filing fee of $500. I felt that if politicians were believable, and •pressed the flesh to the maximum extent possible, the people would overlook race, sex and poverty—and elect me. They did not.

My name on the ballot brought out a heavy black vote ; every other "liberal" candidate running for the House in 1962 won. The black vote helped them win, but it didn't help me. It was clear then that to win a seat in the Texas House of Representatives, it was necessary to be backed by money, power and influence. If I was to win the right to represent some of the people of Texas, I had to persuade the moneyed and politically influential interests either to support me or to remain neutral.

In 1964, I tried again for the same position in the Texas House. I went to the newspaper publishers and acknowledged their probable difficulty in supporting me •editorially, but urged them not to support my opponent—just to take a chance on the people making the best choice. One of the major papers in Houston made no endorsement ; the other endorsed my opponent. A half-victory of sorts. But I lost the election. This time there was identifiable support in traditionally white, conservative •precincts. I was "on the move," according to my supporters, but I was dispirited.

I considered abandoning the dream of a political career in Texas and moving to some section of the country where a black woman candidate was less likely to be considered a novelty. I didn't *want* to do this. I am a Texan ; my roots are in Texas. To leave would be a •cop-out. So I stayed.

In 1966 I lived in a newly created Texas senatorial district which contained more than 70 percent of the precincts which I had carried in my two previous unsuccessful races. I would run for the Senate. It was a different kind of race from the one I had run before, because my opponent was a liberal who had served in the Texas House for several terms.

He called me before the filing •deadline and asked if I was planning to run for the Senate. I said I was. He said he was going to run no matter what I did. It was a friendly and candid conversation.

The new district was 38 percent black; the balance was comprised of Chicanos and whites. Many laborers affiliated with the •AFL-CIO lived in the district. My opponent asked, "Can a white man win?" My supporters were angered by the seeming intrusion of racism, and answered the question with "No, not this time." I was elected to the Texas Senate by a margin of two to one.

On the day I was sworn in to the Senate, the gallery was filled with proud supporters. Although demonstrations are not permitted, my supporters cheered when I walked onto the floor. They didn't know about the rules. I looked up at them and covered my lips with my index finger. They became quiet instantly, but continued to communicate their support by simply smiling. Finally I had won the right to represent a portion of the people of Texas. What next?

BARBARA JORDAN, *New Woman*, July-August 1975

● **odds**: chances ● **filing fee** (U.S.), **deposit** (G.B.) : *cautionnement : somme versée par le candidat pour faire acte de candidature* ● **pressed the flesh**: *prenaient un bain de foule* ● **supporting me editorially**: giving me the official support of the paper ● **precincts** : election districts ● **a cop-out** : *une dérobade* ● **deadline** : *date limite* ● **AFL-CIO** : see A.B.C.

TOWARDS COMPREHENSION

1 ***The facts. Right or wrong? Justify your answers.***

1. Barbara Jordan ran for election to the United States House of Representatives.
2. She ran three times.
3. She ran three times for election to the Texas House of Representatives.
4. She was finally elected to the Texas Senate.

2 ***The causes. Multiple Choice Questions***

1. She lost the election in 1962 because:
   a) she was black.
   b) she was a black woman.
   c) she was poor.
   d) she was not supported by the people having money and influence.
2. In 1964, she asked the neswpaper publishers:
   a) to attack her opponent.
   b) to remain neutral.
   c) to allow her to write in their papers.
   d) to support her.
3. In 1966, she was elected because:
   a) it is easier to be elected to the Senate.
   b) her opponent was white.
   c) the district in which she ran was different from the one in which she had run before.
   d) she conducted her campaign differently.

3 ***Show that the meaning of the following words and phrases can be guessed from the context.***

FROM THE CONTEXT

(If we look a little further down .... the meaning of .... is clarified by another word coming before ....)
1. Billboards (l. 6). 2. My name on the ballot brought out a heavy black vote (l. 11). 3. One of the major papers .... made no endorsement (l. 20). 4. Precincts (l. 22). 5. I was dispirited (l. 23). 6. a cop-out (l. 27).

IMPROVE YOUR VOCABULARY
How to express probability

It is likely that he will win.
He is likely to win. ≠ he is not likely .... he is unlikely to win.
It is most unlikely that he will win.
The chances are that he will win.
He stands a good/fair chance of winning.
He has no chance of winning, he has little chance ....
The odds are that he will win.
What are the odds of his getting the post?
There is every sign that ....
There are signs that ....
All the signs are that .... *(tout indique, tout permet de penser que...).*

4 ***Using some of the above phrases and patterns, express differently, in as many ways as you can:***

1. She will probably be defeated. 2. It seems probable that this big paper will remain neutral. 3. There is every sign that she will have the support of the minorities in the election. 4. It is most unlikely that she will succeed in persuading the papers to endorse her. 5. All the signs are that she will lose the election.

5 ***Make up a few sentences beginning with:***

Do you think there is any likelihood of his/her/their .... *(+ gerund)*
In all likelihood, ...

6 ***React as in the example:***

A. She didn't win.
B. How could she have won? I don't see how she could have won. I wonder how she could have won.
A. She didn't have the money to pay her filing fee. B. ....
A. She wasn't backed by the people having money and influence. B. ....
A. She didn't succeed in persuading the paper not to endorse her opponent. B. ....
A. She couldn't make them remain neutral. B. ....
Go on

COULD + HAVE + PART. PASSÉ

Voir p. 40

7 ***Drawing on the text, make as many sentences as you can:***

No wonder she was defeated/she lost the election the first two times: in the first place .... in the second place/to begin with .... secondly .... and to conclude ....

8 ***Re-cast the above sentences:***

That she should have been defeated is not surprising if we bear in mind that ....
It's not to be wondered at that she should have been ....
How could she have won ....

IN THAT
=in the sense that

9 ***The third time, things were different in that ....***

10 ***Using information from the text, make a few sentences beginning with:***

You can't expect to win an election unless ....

UNLESS

A black woman can't expect . . . . unless . . . .
She was naive enough to believe . . . .
She was too naive to realize . . . .

ENOUGH + ADJ. + TO-INF

TOO + ADJ. + TO-INF

TOWARDS APPRECIATION

11 ***The qualities required to win against such odds (in such unfavourable circumstances).***

It takes . . . . to . . . .
If you are to win . . . . you've got to . . . .
She must have needed . . . .
Other women might have . . . . but she . . . .

BE TO

Voir p. 151

12 ***Creative oral work:***

A white woman, a member of the League of Women Voters, has decided to canvas for Barbara Jordan (to go from person to person and ask for votes). Follow her.

13 ***Creative written work:***

"*What next?*". In 1972 she was elected to the United States House of Representatives. Imagine how the Texas papers covered the event.

14 ***Translation.***

Translate from "*My name on the ballot vote* . . . ." to " . . . . *making the best choice.*"

FOR FURTHER INFORMATION

Join the league if you want to:

- participate in the political process,
- learn more about your local government,
- help protect the voting rights of all citizens,
- work for a more equitable tax system,
- promote more effective and efficient government structures,
- provide citizens with non-partisan information about candidates and issues,
- study and act on issues of current concern such as equal opportunity in housing, employment, and education; a sound judicial system; a clean environment,
- be part of an effective citizen's lobby,
- meet and work with others who share your concerns,

The Purpose of the League of Women Voters is to Promote Political Responsibility Through Informed and Active Participation of Citizens in Government.

As a league member you will:

- help choose items for study,
- find out the facts,
- discuss the problems,
- reach agreement on solutions and goals,
- take action to implement these goals,
- educate and inform others,
- help get out the vote.

League membership is open to:

- all citizens 18 years and older,
- noncitizens may become associate (nonvoting) members.

About the LWV:

The League is a nonpartisan organization established in 1920.
The League studies and acts on the local, state, and national levels.
The League is a grassroots association of members who control the destiny of the organization.
Local League members belong to the League of Women Voters of Massachusetts and the League of Women Voters of the United States.
There are approximately 12,000 members in 110 local Leagues in the League of Women Voters of Massachusetts.
There are 160,000 members in more than 1,300 local Leagues in all 50 states, the District of Columbia, the Commonwealth of Puerto Rico, and the Virgin Islands in the League of Women Voters of the United States.

When he says he can cut taxes
Buckley, you can believe

Almost every candidate for public office this year is promising to cut taxes. As Sheriff of Middlesex County, John J. Buckley proved that he could cut taxes by saving the taxpayers $800,000 a year by refusing to open the unneeded new jail in Cambridge.

When he says he can cut unemployment
Buckley, you can believe

As Sheriff of Middlesex County, John J. Buckley created a work release program . . . keeping.inmates' families off welfare. Over 750 participated in this program, earning more than a million in salaries and paying $330,000 in taxes and another $114,000 to the County for room and board.

When he says he can cut crime
Buckley, you can believe

Since assuming the office of Sheriff in 1970, Buckley has stopped forever the Massachusetts practice of jailing juveniles with hardened, older criminals; established a restitution program to have offenders pay back their victims for losses of property crime cases and established a work program to ease inmates re-entry into the community after release as productive citizens.

When he says he can restore faith in elected officials
Buckley, you can believe

For the past eight years, as Middlesex County Sheriff, John J. Buckley has served the people in 21 out of the 24 cities and towns of the 5th district. And he has demonstrated 3 basic qualities urgently needed in public service today . . . character, competence and creativity.

As sheriff, Buckley turned down an official residence, thus saving the taxpayers an estimated $180,000. He passed up the chauffered car along with refusal of $3,000 a year credited toward a pension.

John J. Buckley says, "The word 'apathetic' has been used to,describe the public mood. Apathetic, no. Angry, yes. And, justifiably so. Angry about empty pledges. Angry about meaningless promises. And angry about the inadequate performance of all too many politicians. I believe that personal sacrifice is a small price to pay to restore public confidence in elected officials." Buckley you can believe.

Paid for by the Buckley for Congress Committee
A copy of our report is filed with and available for purchase from the Federal Election Commission, Washington, D.C.

Elect John J. Buckley to Congress

• **work release program** : system by which prisoners are allowed out of jail to work in the normal way so as to be able to support their families, etc.

The fourth estate or the power of the press

Issue [ˈiʃu:], designed [diˈzaind], occurrences [əˈkʌrənsiz], inculcate [ˈinkʌlkeit], literature [ˈlitəritʃə], advertising [ˈædvətaiziŋ], competed [kəmˈpi:tid], pseudo-events [ˈsju:dəu iˈvents], Bly [blai], Phineas [ˈfiniæs], product [ˈprɔdʌkt], citizenry [ˈsitiznri], areas [ˈɛəriəz], descendants [diˈsendənts], alerting [əˈlə:tiŋ], knowledge [ˈnɔlidʒ], technology [tekˈnɔlədʒi], indispensable [ˌindisˈpensəbl].

The Exploring Press. The traditional role of the daily press was well stated by the first American journalist in the first issue of the first newspaper printed in British North America. "It is designed," Benjamin Harris explained in his *Publick Occurrences Both Forreign and Domestick*, which appeared in Boston on September 25, 1690, "that the Countrey shall be furnished once a moneth (or, if any Glut of Occurrences happen, oftener), with an Account of •such considerable things as have arrived unto our Notice." [...] A century later, the New York *Evening Post* in its opening issue of November 15, 1801, showed that the newspaper function had hardly changed. "The design of this paper is to diffuse among the people correct information on all interesting subjects, to inculcate just principles in religion, morals, and politics, and to cultivate a taste for •sound literature." Newspapers, then, set themselves the task of "reporting," of bringing information to the public.

During the nineteenth century, as weeklies became dailies, as the size of papers increased, as advertising expanded, as readership enlarged into a mass circulation, and as papers competed with one another for the hundreds of thousands of readers, newspapers found it hard to fill their columns only with "such considerable things as have arrived unto our Notice." They had to make news [...] and to create pseudo-events. Enterprising newspapermen personally financed the staging of news—for example, James Gordon Bennett sent Stanley on the African journey to find Livingstone, Joseph Pulitzer sponsored the round-the-world trip of Nellie Bly to beat the eighty-day record of Jules Verne's Phineas Fogg. Newspapers had to make things happen so that they could be reported.

Toward the end of the nineteenth century, a new tradition emerged in the American press. Compounded of conscience, imagination, ambition, and original sin, it was the product of the •"Muckrakers." [...] The best of them were explorers. Their service was perhaps less in bringing reliable new information than in awakening the citizenry to vast areas of national life that were still unexplored. While the muckraking journalists made their money and their reputations as discoverers, turning up what they knew in advance must be there, their enduring place in American life would be as explorers. They, too, pointed to dark continents.

Their descendants in our time are the so-called "investigative reporters." These helped awaken the nation to the Watergate Scandals, and since then have opened the way to many obscure islands of national life. Their service, too, is less as messengers of fact than as watchmen in the night, alerting us to the limits of our knowledge. As our government becomes bigger and more powerful, armed with a technology against which the individual citizen feels powerless, the exploring press has become more than ever indispensable to a free society.

DANIEL J. BOORSTIN, *The Exploring Spirit : America then and the World.*

• **such ... as** : any ... that • **sound** : *saine* • **muckrakers** : people who are always looking for scandals and corruption, generally in the hope of bringing about reforms.

TOWARDS COMPREHENSION

1 *Choose the nearest equivalent :*

1. The traditional role of the daily press was *well stated* by . . . . (l. 1)
   a) formulated. *b)* criticized. *c)* summarized.

2. If *any glut of occurrences* happen. (l. 5)
   a) if very important events happen. *b)* if lots of events happen. *c)* if scandals break out.

3. *The design* of the press is to diffuse . . . . (l. 9)
   a) the ambition. *b)* the aim/purpose/object. *c)* the conception.

4. Joseph Pulitzer *sponsored* the round-the-world trip . . . . (l. 19)
   a) organized. *b)* financed. *c)* planned.

5. *Reliable* new information. (l. 26)
   a) sensational.
   b) in which you can have confidence.
   c) connected with information already received.

6. *Turning up* what they knew in advance must be there. (l. 28)
   a) denouncing. *b)* rushing to. *c)* revealing.

2 *Right or wrong :*

1. The Muckrakers appeared at the end of the 19th century.
2. Their purpose was to expose scandals.
3. They took pleasure in exposing scandals.
4. To-day's muckrakers are called "investigative reporters".
5. Their function is to bring to light some obscure aspects of our national life.
6. They are not really necessary in a free society.

3 *Pick out the word or phrase which best expresses the kind of role they play in our society.*

4 ***Compare :***

Newspapers found it hard to fill their columns . . . .
It was hard for newspapers to fill their columns . . . .

Give the other construction.

1. It was hard for them to increase their readership.
2. It must have been hard for newspapers to fill their columns with noteworthy events.
3. It is not hard for a newspaper to increase its circulation.
4. He found it hard not to distort the facts.
5. It must have been very hard for them to awaken the nation to the Watergate cover-up.

Make a few more sentences on the same patterns.

5 ***Drawing on the text, make a few sentences on the following pattern :***

In America, a journalist is { expected / supposed } to . . . .

AS

Ce petit mot peut avoir de nombreux sens.

- Il peut être conjonction et avoir les sens suivants : *since* au sens de *because, seeing that, when, while.* Il correspond alors à : comme, vu que, étant donné que, au moment où, à mesure que, en + part. présent.
  As you are tired, you'd better go to bed *(comme, étant donné que... vous feriez mieux de...).*
  As time went on, things got worse and worse *(à mesure que le temps passait...).*
  As we grow old, ... *(en vieillissant).*
- AS peut également avoir une fonction qui l'apparente à une préposition et signifier : *considered as, in the role of, in the capacity of :* he was famous as a journalist *(comme, en tant que)* As President, his powers were limitless.
- AS s'emploie encore après un adjectif et exprime une idée de concession qui peut également être rendue par **though** ou **however** : Powerful as he is/may be, he'll have to resign. Though he is powerful, ...however powerful he may be... *(si puissant qu'il soit il devra démissionner).*

6 ***Compare :***

As we grow old, we become more tolerant.
The older we grow, the more tolerant we become.

Give the other form :

1. As journalists get more confident they probe further into the dark areas of public life.
2. The worse a scandal gets, the more curious the public grows.
3. As governments become less liberal citizens are allowed less freedom.
4. As the workings of the administration become obscure the journalist's responsibility becomes greater.
5. The more popular television becomes, the harder it is to increase the circulation of newspapers.
6. As a paper grows less subservient it enjoys more prestige.
7. As a journalist becomes well-known he becomes self-assured.
8. As a newspaper acquires financial independence it is more likely to tell the truth.
9. The more the circulation of a paper decreases, the more publicity it is obliged to print.
10. As the cover-up became apparent the president's statements became less credible.

7 ***Compare what the newspapers did in the 19th century, when they*** *"found it hard to fill their columns . . . ."* ***and what they do to-day.***

(pander to the public interest in crime, scandals, sensational events . . . . make heroes of . . . . hunt for scoops . . . . give prominence to unimportant events . . . .)

8 *". . . . to awaken the nation".* ***Show that it is not always easy for a journalist to know where to draw the line.***

He may let himself be carried away by . . . .
He may take his role too seriously . . . .
He may ruin reputations . . . .
Go on . . . .

9 ***Paragraph-writing***

"The best of them were explorers." What about the worst of them?

10 ***Creative oral work:***

The press as a safeguard against increasingly powerful governments.
(. . . . the protector of the public interest/the journalist's responsibility goes beyond reporting . . . ./he goes so far as to produce evidence of . . . ./he exposes . . . ./he makes known . . . ./he defends the underdog, the oppressed . . . ./the press is the fourth estate = *le 4e pouvoir*)

11 ***Creative written work:***

Do you feel that television has taken over the role of the press, or are there some needs that only a newspaper can satisfy?

FOR
FURTHER DISCUSSION

La liberté de la presse en question

Aux États-Unis

Un journaliste, grâce à une longue et minutieuse enquête, contribue à faire rouvrir un vieux dossier criminel, ce qui entraîne l'inculpation d'un homme soupçonné de cinq meurtres. Doit-il révéler pour autant ses sources au tribunal chargé de l'affaire? Ou peut-il au contraire invoquer le premier amendement à la Constitution américaine qui garantit la liberté de la presse, et taire le nom de ses informateurs, comme il le leur avait promis?

Telle est la grave question qui risque de se poser bientôt à la Cour suprême, la plus haute instance judiciaire des États-Unis. Cette question est loin d'être théorique : à court terme, elle concerne le *New York Times* et l'un de ses journalistes; à plus long terme, c'est la liberté de la presse américaine qui pourrait être visée.

L'affaire à l'origine de cette querelle constitutionnelle relève du meilleur « thriller » : entre 1965 et 1966, treize pensionnaires d'un hôpital du New-Jersey meurent dans des conditions mystérieuses. Dix ans plus tard le *New York Times* publie l'enquête de l'un de ses reporters, Myron Farber. Le journaliste met en cause un chirurgien de l'hôpital, qu'il n'identifie que comme le « Dr X », et révèle que des flacons de curare ont été découverts dans son placard. La police rouvre le dossier et arrête finalement un chirurgien, le Dr Mario Jascalevich. Au cours du procès du médecin, qui s'est ouvert voilà cinq mois, les avocats de la défense citent comme témoin le journaliste du *New York Times* et exigent qu'il produise devant le tribunal toutes ses notes sur son enquête. A l'appui de leur requête, ils invoquent le sixième amendement à la Constitution, qui garantit à chacun un procès juste. Leur demande est approuvée par le juge du tribunal, mais Myron Farber refuse d'obtempérer et se réclame, lui, du premier amendement. Le *New York Times* soutient son collaborateur, qui fait en outre remarquer que tout le monde est capable de refaire l'enquête qu'il a effectuée.

Condamné à rester indéfiniment en prison

Inculpé d'offense à la Cour, Myron Farber est alors condamné à six mois de prison et à 2 000 dollars d'amende; il est également condamné à rester indéfiniment en prison, jusqu'à ce qu'il accepte de livrer ses notes. Le *New York Times,* toujours solidaire de son collaborateur, se voit infliger une astreinte de 5 000 dollars par jour jusqu'à ce que les fameuses notes soient remises au juge, qui décidera de leur publication.

Farber et le quotidien new-yorkais ont tout de suite demandé à un juge de la Cour suprême, comme ils en avaient le droit, de suspendre ces peines, pour avoir le temps d'entreprendre la procédure d'appel. Le premier juge de la Cour saisi, M. Byron White, a refusé, et Myron Farber aurait dû entrer en prison le mercredi 2 août. Le même jour, cependant, un autre juge de la Cour suprême, M. Thurgood Marshall, le seul noir de la Cour, a accordé aux accusés un délai supplémentaire. Ce délai expire le vendredi 4 août. Passée cette date, Myron Farber devra aller en prison et le *New York Times* commencer à payer 5 000 dollars par jour, à moins que la cour du New-Jersey n'accepte de revoir l'affaire ou que quatre des neuf juges de la Cour suprême ne décident de se saisir du dossier pour trancher ce conflit constitutionnel.

En attendant, le *New York Times* se dit prêt à ne pas céder et son journaliste à aller en prison. L'influent quotidien de New York a bien sûr les moyens de payer 5 000 dollars par jour. Il n'empêche que, s'il avait visé une publication aux reins moins solides, le jugement du New-Jersey aurait tout simplement pu la contraindre à s'incliner ou à déposer son bilan. Une affaire à suivre, donc.

Jacques AMALRIC, *Le Monde,* 4 août 1978

1 ***Sum up the facts.***

2 ***What problems does this affair raise?***

3 ***Is the life of the New York Times in jeopardy?*** (or ***in danger***)
(a solid financial backing)

4 ***Why is this a matter worth keeping an eye on?***

5 ***What is your impression of the American press after studying*** *The Exploring Press* ***and reading this article?***

Father's folly

Greenwich ['griniðʒ,], delivered [di'livəd], curtailed [kə:'teild], disobediently [,disə'bi:djəntli], featured ['fi:tʃəd], pioneer [,paiə'niə], sophisticated [sə'fistikeitid], clandestine [klæn'destin], occasionally [ə'keiʒənəli], brusquely ['bruskli], Bahamas [bə'hɑ:məz], apologize [ə'pɔlədʒaiz], balmy ['bɑ:mi], blithely ['blaiðli], vampire movie ['væmpaiə 'mu:vi], crucifixes ['kru:sifiksiz], events of consequence [i'vents əv 'kɔnsikwəns], current events ['kʌrənt i'vents], mandatory ['maendətəri], Academy [ə'kædəmi], devotee [,devə'ti:], televised presidential campaign ['telivaizd ,prezi'denʃl kæm'pein], Adlai Stevenson ['ædlei 'sti:vnsn], imaginatively [i'mædʒinətivli], images ['imidʒiz].

Shortly after we moved to Greenwich, a heavy •crate was delivered to our house with a lot of •hoopla. In it was a gift from Father: one of the first television sets on the market. From the moment of its arrival, Mother treated it like an unwelcome intruder and strictly curtailed our watching to no more than three programs a week, one for each of us. We began to look forward to the evenings when she went out to dinner ; the minute she left the house we'd disobediently race for the set and, feeling •giddy and light-headed, stay up way past bedtime watching the black-and-white cowboy movies that were •heavily featured in the pioneer days of TV. As time went by, programming became more sophisticated and •Elizabeth joined our clandestine nocturnal •huddle. Occasionally, thinking she heard car wheels on the •gravel driveway, she'd spring up and look out the window. "Just another five minutes," she'd say brusquely, and settle down for another hour. Best of all were the two weeks every spring when Mother went down to the Bahamas or the Virgin Islands to get some sun. She never understood why we didn't mind her being away. "My darlings," she'd apologize, "I hate leaving you like this—like a rat deserting a sinking ship. Will you be able to manage without me?" We'd extend her our sweetest long-suffering smiles and assure her that we'd make do somehow ; off she'd go, down to the •balmy •coral-flecked beaches where she loved to sunbathe nude, and we, left behind, would •blithely •plump up our pillows in front of the television set. One night, Elizabeth, Bridget, and I stayed up until two o'clock watching *The Dead Don't Die*, a vampire movie that so profoundly terrified all of us that we went to bed in my room with crucifixes around our necks, our arms crossed over our chests as we lay rigidly staring up at the ceiling.

•For all its •shortcomings, television did link us to the rest of the world. When it came to covering events of consequence (Current Events, as the biweekly •mandatory course at the •Academy was called), television became a kind of animated newspaper. Although Mother herself was not a devotee of baseball, she tolerated—from a distance—our annual involvement with the •World Series, then dominated by the New York Yankees and the great Joe DiMaggio. And even she had to admit, when it came to the first televised presidential campaign—Dwight D. Eisenhower versus Adlai Stevenson—that television wasn't all bad. I never thought I'd see Mother firmly entrenched in front of Father's "folly," as it was referred to, but all during the McCarthy hearings, she ordered lunch and dinner served in the playroom, to which she'd banned the •accursed television set. That was quite a time. We children were treated to the privilege of observing Mother's rage, at its most imaginatively expressed, directed not at us but at the •flickering images of •Senator Joseph McCarthy, Vice-President Richard Nixon, and •counsel Roy Cohn.

BROOKE HAYWARD. •*Haywire*

Brooke Hayward is the daughter of Margaret Sullavan, one of the most famous actresses of the 1940s. This passage is taken from Brooke's autobiography; her parents are divorced and the children are living with their mother at Greenwich, Connecticut.

● **crate** : *caisse* ● **hoopla** : *" mise en scène "* ● **giddy and light-headed** : *nous étions comme grisés* ● **heavily-featured** : very often shown; given a prominent place ● **Elizabeth** : the black cook ● **huddle** : group ● **gravel driveway** : *allée de gravier* ● **balmy** : warm ● **coral-flecked** : *parsemée de corail* ● **blithely** : gaily ● **plump up** : shook up our pillows to make them comfortable ● **for all** : despite; in spite of ● **shortcomings** : defects ● **mandatory** : obligatory ● **Academy** : private school ● **World Series** : games played between the two winning teams of the big American base-ball leagues ● **accursed** : *maudit* ● **flickering** : *tremblotantes* ● **Senator Joseph McCarthy** : see A.B.C. ● **counsel** : legal adviser ● **haywire** : crazy.

TOWARDS COMPREHENSION

1st part.

1 ***Choose the best equivalent, explanation or definition:***

1. Shortly after we *moved* to Greenwich. (l. 1)
   a) left. *b)* went and lived in. *c)* arrived at. *d)* bought.
2. *curtailed* (l. 4)
   a) allowed. *b)* changed. *c)* reduced. *d)* watched.
3. *look forward to* the evenings .... (l. 5)
   a) envisage with pleasure. *b)* think of. *c)* be afraid of. *d)* hate.
4. we'd *race for* the set. (l. 6)
   a) switch on. *b)* turn on. *c)* rush to. *d)* watch.
5. She never understood *why we didn't mind her being away.* (l. 13)
   a) why we were so unhappy.
   b) why we were always complaining.
   c) why we would have liked to have gone with her.
   d) why we were perfectly happy when she wasn't at home.
6. Will you be able *to manage* without me? (l. 15)
   a) to repair the television set. *b)* to survive. *c)* to do the shopping. *d)* to do the cooking.
7. We'd .... assure her that *we'd make do somehow.* (l. 16)
   a) we'd manage to survive in some way or other.
   b) we'd be happy in some way or other.
   c) we'd keep the house clean somehow.
   d) we'd lack for nothing.

2 ***After reading the text once—or listening to a recording of it—, give details showing that:***

1. the family is wealthy.
2. the mother disapproved of TV.
3. the children were fascinated by TV.
4. the mother had some reason to be against TV.

3 ***Test your memory. Make as many sentences as you can beginning with:***

The minute she left the house we'd . . . .
As soon as she left . . . .
Every spring, while she was . . . ., we'd . . . .

WOULD

Voir p. 102

2nd part.

4 ***Pick out the words showing that the mother's attitude to TV is changing.***

5 ***Pick out the words expressing the children's surprise.***

6 ***Express their surprise:***

To my/our surprise, she . . . .
Great was our surprise when she . . . .
Much to my/our surprise, she . . . .
We were surprised to see that . . . .

LANGUAGE PRACTICE

THE GERUND

- **Il peut avoir les fonctions du nom et celles du verbe :**

Do you mind my watching this program?
Watching a la fonction d'un nom puisqu'il est complément de *mind*, mais il a également la fonction d'un verbe, puisqu'il a un complément : *this program*.
Le gérondif a toutes les fonctions du groupe nominal :
Watching television every night isn't good for children. (sujet)
Her being away didn't prevent us from getting by (sujet précédé d'un adj. poss., comp. prépos.). *(Son absence ne nous empêchait pas de nous débrouiller.)*
The most surprising thing was his presenting us with a T.V. set. (attribut)
She was angry at the children('s) staying up late. (génitif)

- **Emplois importants :**

a. *Après les prépositions :* after reading his newspaper, he went to bed without eating *(après avoir lu son journal, il alla se coucher sans manger).* He must be tired of doing the same thing over and over again *(il doit être fatigué de toujours faire la même chose).* He is very good at telling funny stories *(il sait très bien raconter les histoires drôles).* I don't feel like going to the cinema to-day *(je n'ai pas envie d'aller...).* This M.P. has made a name for himself by exposing several scandals *(ce député s'est fait un nom en dénonçant plusieurs scandales).*

Cas particulier de "to" : il convient de distinguer **to** particule marquant l'infinitif de **to** préposition. Cette dernière doit être suivie du gérondif. Lorsque la distinction paraît difficile, on peut découvrir la fonction de **to** en essayant d'employer un nom au lieu d'un verbe. Si cette opération est possible, c'est le gérondif qu'il faut :
I am looking forward to hearing from you *(j'espère avoir bientôt le plaisir de vous lire.* On pourrait dire : I am looking forward to the holidays*).* He is accustomed to driving in Britain. I object to being treated like a child *(je ne veux pas être traité comme un enfant).*

N.B. Ne pas confondre "**used to**" + **infinitif,** qui marque la répétition d'une action dans le passé ou l'opposition entre le passé et le présent (I used to work more when I was young *(je travaillais davantage quand j'étais jeune)* et "**be used to**" + **gérondif,** qui signifie *être habitué à :* he is used to working ten hours a day.

b. **Après certains verbes et expressions :** admit, anticipate, avoid, consider, deny, enjoy, envisage, finish, keep (on) (= persist in), mind, postpone, prevent, risk, can't help, can't stand, stop, it's no good, it's no use, it's (not) worth. (Cette liste n'est pas exhaustive.) Exemples : we anticipate spending a pleasant evening *(nous nous promettons de passer une agréable soirée),* we are considering buying a new car *(nous envisageons de...),* he kept on singing all through the morning *(il n'arrêta pas de chanter de toute la matinée),* would you mind moving your chair back a little? *(est-ce que cela vous ennuierait de reculer un peu votre chaise?),* she couldn't help jumping for joy when she heard the news *(elle ne put s'empêcher de sauter de joie...),* he can't stand being kept waiting *(il ne supporte pas qu'on le fasse attendre),* it's no good trying to make him change his mind *(ça ne sert à rien d'essayer de lui faire changer d'avis),* this book is worth reading *(ce livre mérite d'être lu).*

Remarque : dans ce dernier exemple, le gérondif a un sens passif. Il en est de même après *want* et *need.* My car wants repairing (=needs to be repaired, or needs repairing).
Les verbes *begin, start, continue* peuvent être suivis du gérondif ou de l'infinitif + **to.**

Ne pas confondre : he stopped talking when he saw her *(il s'arrêta de parler)* ; et he stopped to talk to her *(il s'arrêta pour lui parler).*

MIND THE VERB MIND :

Compare :

- I don't mind watching this program. (Le sujet de *mind* est le même que celui de *watching* = *je veux bien regarder... ça ne me dérange pas de regarder...*)
- Do you mind my/me/your mother('s) going away? (il y a deux sujets différents).

On notera encore que *do you mind?/would you mind?* sont souvent suivis de *if :* do you mind if I go out to-night?

7 ***Make up a few sentences beginning with :***

"Do you mind if . . . .", said the mother.
"Do you mind me . . . .", asked the mother.
"Would you mind your mother . . . . ?"
"We don't mind her . . . ."

8 ***Drawing on the text—or not—complete the sentences :***

1. She apologized for . . . .
2. "Don't bother, we'll succeed in . . . ."
3. "Don't worry, we're used to . . . ."
4. We were very fond of . . . .
5. We were severely reprimanded for . . . .
6. She didn't approve of our . . . .
7. "You ought to be ashamed of . . . ."
8. She accused us of . . . .
9. "Television doesn't prevent us from . . . ."
10. "I see no reason for not . . . ."
11. "You ought to think about . . . . instead of . . . ."
12. "Far from . . . . television links us to the rest of the world."

9 ***Make up as many dialogues as you can on the following pattern:***

Instead of . . . . you'd better . . . .
Instead of . . . . we'd rather . . . .

YOU'D BETTER = YOU HAD BETTER
YOU'D BETTER NOT = YOU HAD BETTER NOT

sont suivis de BV, expriment un conseil.
You'd better go now (= *vous feriez mieux de partir maintenant*).
You'd better not tell him about it (= *vous feriez mieux de ne pas lui en parler*).

TOWARDS APPRECIATION

10 ***Someone against television could find a lot of arguments in the first paragraph. What are they?***

(. . . . prevent from . . . ./glued to their sets/television-addicts/their taste for violence/ . . . .)

11 ***Now qualify** (nuancez) **the above statements:***

It's easy to put all the blame on television . . . . Isn't the mother to blame too?
She could be blamed for . . . .
She could be reproached for . . . .
Don't you think she'd better . . . . instead of . . . .

12 ***Someone in favour of television could find arguments in the second paragraph.***

Pick them out, showing that television can be a source of information and entertainment. What details make us feel that the children had a sense of humour.

13 ***Creative oral work:***

The children are mimicking their mother in front of television during the McCarthy hearings.

14 ***Creative written work:***

They moved to Greenwich in 1949. Re-write the first paragraph supposing the scene is set in 1979.

SPOTLIGHT ON...

T.V.
Did T.V. make him do it?

Miami [mai'æmi], fatal ['feitl], accomplice [ə'kɔmplis], Defense Attorney [di'fens ə'tə:ni], involuntary [in'vɔləntəri], subliminal [sʌb'liminl], testimony ['testiməni], psychiatrists [sai'kaiətrists], client ['klaiənt] episodes ['episəudz], therapist ['θerəpist], psychologists [sai'kɔlədʒists], argue ['ɑ:gju:], vicarious release [vai'kεəriəs ri'li:s].

A young killer—and television—go on trial for murder

On June 4 Elinor Haggart, 82, a Miami Beach widow, discovered two teen-agers burglarizing her home. It was a fatal incident: the intruders abruptly shot the old woman to death with a gun they had found in the house, grabbed $415 in cash and made their getaway in the victim's 1972 Buick. Four days later Ronald Zamora, 15, confessed to police that he had killed Mrs. Haggart, who also happened to be his next-door neighbor. This week Zamora is facing a Miami jury—his accomplice will be tried separately—charged with first-degree murder, burglary, robbery and possession of a firearm while committing a •felony.

Another desperate young drug addict •plundering to maintain his habit? Not at all. Defense Attorney Ellis Rubin, 52, claims Ronald Zamora is •hooked on something far less exotic. Rubin's unusual trial strategy: to prove that Zamora is innocent because he "was suffering from and acted under the influence of prolonged, intense, involuntary, •subliminal television intoxication."

To persuade the jury that Zamora has been electronically "brainwashed," Rubin plans to introduce testimony from several psychiatrists that his client appears to be living in a "television fantasy world," diminishing his sense of right and wrong. For Zamora, says Rubin, "the tube became his parents and his school and his church." Adds the defense attorney: "Pulling the trigger became as common to him as killing a fly." Zamora did not realize he was committing cold-blooded murder, contends Rubin, but "was just acting out a television script." The defense has claimed that circumstances of the crime were •eerily similar to two recent episodes of *Kojak* and a Dracula movie Zamora watched the night before the murder. For its part, the prosecution disputes the •plea of insanity, pointing out, for instance, that after the murder, Zamora treated four friends to a long week-end of fun at Disney World, •compliments, he told them, of his father.

But Zamora's parents believe their son has been mentally disturbed since he witnessed a close friend drown two years ago; they even sent him to a therapist ten days before the crime. The Zamoras will also testify Ronald was a confirmed TV addict who spent at least six hours a day staring at the screen; he refused to eat unless the television was on and sometimes sneaked out of bed to catch a late movie. His favorite shows: such cops-and-robbers series as *Kojak, Baretta* and *Starsky and Hutch*. According to Mrs. Zamora, Ronald is such a Kojak fan, "he even asked his father to shave his head because he wanted my husband to look like him."

[...] Though Rubin has given an unprecedented twist to the standard insanity plea, it is hardly the first time television has been accused of a lethal influence. In Hartford City, Ind., an accused murderer testified last month that he and a friend were involved in killing four brothers in a trailer camp shortly after viewing a television dramatization of the Manson murders. While some psychologists argue that for the vast majority of viewers TV violence •provides a vicarious release of aggression, most leading researchers have found that violence on television tends to reduce a child's inhibitions against behaving aggressively. Studies indicate TV teaches the young that violence often succeeds and that problems can be solved by aggressive behavior. Moreover, kids are likely to copy what they see. And they see plenty: according to the Nielsen Index figures for TV viewing, Americans will have watched 18,000 TV murders by age 18—•*v.* having spent only 11,000 hours in school. In response to pressure from parents and Congress, the networks now seem to be trying to tone down •the thud and blunder.

TIME, october 10, 1977

● **felony** : major serious crime (murder, armed robbery) ● **plunder** : pillage ● **hooked on** : addicted to (TV was his drug) ● **subliminal** : acting on the subconscious mind ● **eerily** : *à vous donner froid dans le dos* ● **plea** : reason, excuse ● **compliments** : he means that this week-end of fun has been paid for by his father ● **provides a vicarious release of aggression** : *constitue une sorte de purgation de l'agressivité* ● **v.** = versus = as against ● **the thud and blunder** : a spoonerism *(contrepéterie)* = blood and thunder.

TOWARDS COMPREHENSION

1 ***After reading the text, find in it the words and phrases corresponding to the equivalents given in italics:***

1. They *had broken into the house and were stealing things.*
2. The *burglars escaped* in a stolen car.
3. When *will they appear before a court?*
4. What are they *accused of?*
5. They *declare* that he is insane.

2 ***Say which sentences are essential to the understanding of the article:***

Elinor Haggart was 82.
She discovered two teen-agers burglarizing her home.
They shot the old woman to death.
They shot her with a gun they had found in the house.
They made their getaway in the victim's car.
Mrs. Haggart was Zamora's next-door neighbour.
This week Zamora is facing a Miami jury.
His accomplice will be tried separately.
His Defense Attorney wants to prove that Zamora is innocent because he was under the influence of television intoxication.

He wants to persuade the jury that Zamora has been electronically "brainwashed".
He plans to introduce testimony from psychiatrists.
He wants to prove that his client is living in a "television fantasy world".
He says that for Zamora the tube became his parents and his school and his church.

3 ***In your opinion, which sentence best expresses:***

a. the Defense Attorney's position.
b. the position of the prosecution.
c. the parents' position.

4 ***Express each point of view in your own words.***

5 ***Sum up the article in 4 sentences.***

6 ***Present the facts as if you were a TV journalist.***

LANGUAGE PRACTICE

7 ***Supply the missing prepositions, without looking at the text:***

1. They broke . . . . Mrs. Haggart's house.
2. They shot her . . . . death.
3. He is charged . . . . first-degree murder.
4. According . . . . Rubin, Zamora is innocent.
5. Zamora suffered . . . . TV intoxication.
6. He had been brainwashed . . . . TV.
7. The murder is similar . . . . two recent episodes of *Kojak*.
8. He usually sneaked . . . . bed to catch a late movie.
9. He wanted his father to look . . . . Kojak.
10. Americans will have watched 18,000 TV murders . . . . the age . . . . 18.

TOWARDS APPRECIATION

8 ***Debate: in your opinion, did TV make him do it?***

(It's easy to make TV responsible for . . . ./to put the blame on TV for . . . ./aren't the parents to blame?/shouldn't the educational system . . . .?/It can't be denied that TV glamorizes/encourages/the question is whether . . . ./what is needed is . . . ./censorship/freedom of expression.)

9 ***Written work:***

Mother loses her case against TV violence

Write the article.

What makes a nation fight well

Preoccupied [pri:ˋɔkjupaid], imagine [iˋmædʒin], identity [aiˋdentiti], a liberal historian's attitude [əˋlibərəl hisˋtɔ:riənzˋætitju:d], dramatically [drəˋmætikəli], materials [məˋtiəriəlz], individual [,indiˋvidjuəl], complicated [ˋkɔmplikeitid], morale [mɔˋrɑ:l], undependable [ˋʌndiˋpendəbl], Southerners [ˋsʌðənəz], judiciously [dʒuˋdiʃəsli], comparatively [kəmˋpærətivli], democracy [diˋmɔkrəsi], exaggerated idea [igˋzædʒəreitid aiˋdiə], peasant [ˋpezənt], injustice [inˋdʒʌstis], inferiority [in,fiəriˋɔriti], depot [ˋdepəu. U.S.:ˋdi:pəu], Colonel [ˋkə:nl], proportionately [prəˋpɔ:ʃnitli], contemptuous [kənˋtemptjuəs] subordinates [səˋbɔ:dnits].

This war novel is partly about the capture of the island of Anopopei from the Japanese. General Cummings is one af the major characters. Hearn is a middle-class liberal lieutenant.

"When I was your age, a little older, the type of thing that preoccupied me was what makes a nation fight well."

"I imagine it would be a kind of identity between the people and the country whether it's for good reasons or bad."

The General shook his head. "That's a liberal historian's attitude. You'd be surprised what a tiny factor that is." [...] "There are just two main elements. A nation fights well in proportion to the amount of men and materials it has. And the other equation is that the individual soldier in that army is a more effective soldier the poorer his standard of living has been in the past."

"That's •the whole works, huh?"

"There's one other big factor I've played with for a time. If you're fighting in defense of your own soil, then perhaps you're a little more effective."

"Then you come back to my point."

"I wonder if you know how complicated that is. If a man fights on his own soil, it's also a great deal easier for him to desert. That's one problem I never have to consider on Anopopei. It's true the other thing •overweighs it, but stop and think about it. Fondness for a country is all very lovely, it is a morale factor at the beginning of a war. But fighting emotions •are very undependable, and the longer a war lasts the less value they have. After a couple of years of war, there are only two considerations that make a good army: a superior material force and a poor standard of living. Why do you think a regiment of Southerners is worth two regiments of Easterners?"

"I don't think they are."

"Well, it happens to be true."

The General placed his fingertips together •judiciously and looked at Hearn. •"I'm not peddling theories. This is observation. And the conclusions leave me, as a general officer, in a poor position. We have the highest standard of living in the world and, as one would expect, the worst individual fighting soldiers of any big power. Or at least in their natural state they are. They're comparatively wealthy, they're spoiled, and as Americans they share most of them the peculiar manifestation of our democracy. They have an exaggerated idea of the rights due to themselves as individuals and no idea at all of the rights due to others. It's the reverse of the peasant, and I'll tell you right now it's the peasant who makes the soldier."

"So what you've got to do is break them down." Hearn said.

"Exactly. Break them down. Every time an enlisted man sees an officer get an extra privilege, it breaks him down a little more."

"I don't see that. It seems to me they'd hate you more."

"They do. But they also fear us more. I don't care what kind of man you give me, if I have him long enough I'll make him afraid. Every time there's what you call an Army injustice, the •enlisted man involved is confirmed a little more in the idea of his own inferiority." He smoothed the hair over his temple. "I happen to know of an American prison camp in England which'll be a terror once we invade Europe. The methods used will be brutal, and it's going to cause a •stink •eventually, but it happens to be necessary. In our own back yard we have a particular •replacement depot where an attempt was actually made to kill the Colonel in command. You aren't capable of understanding it, but I can tell you, Robert, that to make an Army work you have to have every man in it •fitted into a fear ladder. Men in prison camps, deserters, or men in replacement camps are in the back-waters of the Army and the discipline has to be proportionately more powerful. The Army functions best when you're frightened of the man above you, and contemptuous of your subordinates."

Norman Mailer, *The Naked and the Dead*, 1948

Norman Mailer was born in 1923 in New York and studied at Harvard. "The Naked and the Dead" *is based on his own experiences in the Philippines during World War II.*

● **That's the whole works, huh?** : *c'est à ça que ça se ramène* ● **overweighs** : has more influence ● **are very undependable** : are things you really can't count on ● **judiciously** : with an air of sagacity ● **I'm not peddling...** : *je ne cherche pas à vendre...* ● **enlisted man** : *simple soldat* ● **a stink** : a scandal ● **eventually** : in the end ● **replacement depot** : *centre de réserve* ● **fitted into a fear ladder** : placed somewhere in a hierarchy based on fear.

TOWARDS COMPREHENSION

1 ***Find in the text phrases or sentences having the same, or nearly the same meaning as:***

1. He said "no".
2. . . . . how unimportant it is.
3. Patriotism.
4. It is the contrary of . . . .
5. You can give me any kind of man.

2 ***Find in the text words or phrases having the opposite meaning:***

1. There's another minor element.
2. It's much less easy.
3. Hatred.
4. They don't attach much importance to their own rights.

5. They pay great attention to the rights of others.
6. They'll love you.
7. You must be respectful of the people working under you.

3 ***We can say that this text is a long answer to a short question. What is the question?***

4 ***Pick out some of the most significant elements of the answer.***

LANGUAGE PRACTICE

5 ***Complete the sentences from the table:***

Fear Hatred Discipline	can	make	a soldier . . . . a nation . . . . an army . . . .

MAKE + BV
(voix active)
MADE + TO-INF
(voix passive)
I'll make him obey.
He'll be made to obey.
Voir p. 97

6 ***Use the above pattern:***

According to Cummings, a good officer is the one who is capable of . . . .

7 ***Drawing on the text, make a few sentences beginning with:***

He claims he can make any soldier . . . .

8 ***Now in the passive:***

Any soldier can . . . .

ANY

WHAT

=the thing(s) which . . . ., something which . . . .

Peut être sujet ou complément :
What he is doing is very dangerous *(ce qu'il...)*. I don't understand what he means. I'm very grateful to you for what you've done *(je vous suis très reconnaissant de ce que vous avez fait)*.
Remarque : on ne peut pas employer **what** après **all.** Il faut employer **that.** Dans ce cas **that** est souvent omis : I have told you all (that) I know.

9 ***Make up a few sentences after this pattern:***

Fear is what makes a soldier fight well.
Hatred . . . .
Contempt . . . .
Discipline . . . .

10 ***Re-cast the above sentences as follows:***

Do you know what makes a soldier fight well? It's fear.
Or: I'm going to tell you what makes a soldier fight well, it's fear.

11 ***Make up 5 sentences on this pattern:***

To make an Army work, what you have to do is . . . ./all you have to do is . . . .
To make . . . .

12 ***Drawing on the text, make as many sentences as you can on the following patterns:***

The poorer a soldier's standard of living is . . . .
The more a soldier hates you, ...
The less you respect them . . . .
Go on.

PLUS . . . . PLUS . . . .
MOINS . . . .
MOINS . . . .
the + comp. . . . .,
the + comp.
The more he works, the better he feels.
The less he drinks, the better it is for him.

FOR + { NOM / PRON. PERS. COMP. } + TO-INF

exprime **le but, la condition.**
For a nation to survive, its citizens must work hard *(= pour qu'une nation).*
For the army to recover its morale . . . .
For discipline to be maintained, we must take strong measures against trouble-makers.

13 ***Drawing on the next, make up a few sentences beginning with :***

For a nation to fight well, it must have . . . .
For a soldier to fight well, he must . . . .
For a man to become an effective soldier, ...

14 ***Re-cast some of the above sentences, using the*** unless-***pattern :***

Example : A nation can't survive unless its citizens work hard.

UNLESS = IF... NOT

15 ***Complete the following :***

If we are to win this war, ...
If you are to become a good officer, ...
If they are to become effective soldiers, ...
If we were to lose this war . . . .

IF + BE TO
peut exprimer

1. Une idée de but, de volonté, d'intention, de condition :
if we are to win, we had better start training now *(si nous voulons gagner, nous ferions mieux de . . . .).*

2. Une hypothèse :
if it were (ou : *was* dans un style moins soutenu) to rain to-morrow, they would stay at home *(s'il devait pleuvoir demain).*

TOWARDS APPRECIATION

16 ***Using the following patterns, say what you think of the General's views :***

What strikes me about his views is . . . .
What worries me . . . .
We can easily see what such views could lead to . . . .
What surprises me most . . . ./What irritates me . . . ./What makes me angry . . . .
What must be borne in mind is that . . . .
What must not be forgotten is that . . . .
What makes him feel so superior . . . .
For him, war is a means of . . . ./Through war he can . . . .

17 ***Creative oral work :***

Imagine what Lieutenant Hearn could say to show he disagrees with the views expressed in the last sentence.

18 ***Creative written work :***

a. At another moment, Cummings says to Hearn : *"You can consider the Army as a preview of the future".* Expand this statement into a paragraph of 15 lines.

b. Describe what a soldier's life would be like if the General's views were carried out (put into practice). (Perhaps you have seen the film : *From Here to Eternity.* In French : *Tant qu'il y aura des Hommes.*)

IMPROVE YOUR VOCABULARY

In my opinion/to my mind ....
Opinions are divided on this question *(avis... partagés).*
My view is that ....
What are your views on the subject?
I'm sorry but I don't share your views (=I disagree with you).
I take a different view of the question.
In support of this view, I'd like to say/to suggest that ....
One gets a better view of this question if one considers ....
His contempt of soldiers ....
He has/feels nothing but contempt for ....
He despises soldiers=he considers them worthless.

A fellow in the Army lost his rifle. The Sergeant said, "You'll have to pay for it."

He said, "What! Pay for it? That's ridiculous. What would you do if I lost a tank?"

The Sergeant said, "You'd have to pay for it, just the same."

He said, "Blimey! No wonder, in the Navy, the Captains go down with their ships."

SPOTLIGHT ON...

jogging

Psychiatrist [sai'kai-ətrist], psychotherapy ['saikəu'θerəpi], social barrier ['səuʃl 'bæriə], therapist ['θerəpist], marathoner ['mærəθənə], schizophrenia [,skitsəu'fri:njə], psychiatry [sai'kai-ətri], chemical ['kemikl], neurotics [njuə'rɔtiks], psychologists [sai'kɔlədʒists], sedentary ['sedntəri], enthusiastic [in,θju:zi'æstik], evaluated [i'væljueitid], agony ['ægəni].

Jogging for the mind

The mystique of jogging, with its claims to work wonders for body and soul, has begun to invade American psychiatry. Some psychiatrists now routinely prescribe jogging instead of pills for moderate depression. Others use it to break down patients' defenses in talk therapy, and a few believe running produces chemical changes that help cure serious disorders. [...]

Several studies report that jogging works well for moderately depressed neurotics. In one test of 28 depressed patients, a team of psychiatrists and psychologists at the University of Wisconsin Medical School found that for most of them, 30 to 45 minutes of jogging three times a week was at least as effective as talk therapy. Psychiatrist Robert S. Brown of the University of Virginia at Charlottesville, who says it •dawned on him one day that "nobody jogging down at the •track ever appeared depressed," finds that the exercise works better than pills in •controlling depression. [...]

Psychiatrist Ronald M. Lawrence is founder and president of the American Medical Joggers Association, a group of 3,000 jogger-doctors. This •fall he plans to start a Jungian talk-and-job therapy with neurotic patients on Malibu Beach, charging $75 an hour. "Jogging is a way of reaching the unconscious rapidly," he says. "Man was meant to be a moving animal, but he's become sedentary. Distance running can bring us back to the basics of what we're here for." Lawrence has noticed that after 14 to 18 miles of a marathon, people often break down and cry, or •babble to strangers about their childhood memories and problems—exactly the kind of•breakthrough that conventional talk therapists look for.

Though there is no hard •evidence, some jogger-doctors believe that running cures mental problems by changing the chemical composition of the body. A.H. Ismail, professor of physical education at Purdue University, reports "significant relationships" between changes in certain hormone levels of joggers and improvements in emotional stability. Some critics think the joggers he studied, a group of out-of-shape professors, could have felt better simply because they were getting away from their desks for a change, but Ismail doubts that theory. Psychiatrist Brown thinks running fights depression by inducing chemical changes in the brain, and he is now working with researchers at the National Institute of Mental Health to test the theory.

But even convinced jogger-doctors are reserving final judgment on the running cure. Psychiatrist Jerome Katz of the Menninger Foundation says jogging makes patients more talkative and helps a bit with depression, but cautions that "the enthusiastic claims of instant cures of depression have to be evaluated •with a great deal of salt." In the common-sense view, all exercise is likely to bring a temporary feeling of well-being and a distraction from personal •woes. Clinton Cox, a reporter for the New York *Daily News*, thinks he knows the real secret of the jogging cure. Says he: "It's almost impossible to worry about your job or other such •mundane pursuits when your body is in total •agony."

Time, July 24, 1978

• **dawned on him** : he suddenly realized • **track** : *piste* • **controlling** : mastering • **fall** : autumn • **babble** : talk incoherently • **breakthrough** : important progress • **evidence** : proof • **with a great deal of salt** : very skeptically • **woes** : *malheurs* • **mundane** : insignificant • **agony** : terrible pain.

TOWARDS COMPREHENSION

1 1. ***Enthusiasts*** [in'θju:ziæsts] ***claim that jogging*** . . . .
2. Those who are more moderate in their enthusiasm [in'θju:ziæzəm] say that jogging . . . .
3. Skeptics doubt if jogging can . . . . and say that . . . .

2 ***Sum up this article in 3 sentences, then in 2, then in one.***

LANGUAGE PRACTICE

3 ***The benefits of jogging. Make as many sentences as you can beginning with:***

1. Jogging makes people . . . .
2. Jogging helps people . . . .
3. Jogging is a means of . . . .
4. Through jogging doctors can . . . .
5. While jogging, people . . . .
6. Jogging cures mental problems by . . . .

TOWARDS APPRECIATION

4 ***Talking point:***
Jogging can't do any good, it can't do any harm either.

5 ***Creative oral work: imagine a conversation between a jogger-doctor and a jogger-patient.***

Tell me about . . . . when did you first . . . . your anxieties . . . . out of breath. I've got a stitch in the side . . . . I've got cramp . . . . I feel as if I've burst a blood vessel . . . .

IMPROVE YOUR VOCABULARY

He claims that ....
There isn't enough evidence to prove that ....
They'll have to produce evidence in support of ....
We lack evidence ....
We can't .... until your theory has been tested.
I doubt your theory.
Nobody can possibly doubt what he said.
I have my doubts/serious doubts about ....

A. *Choose the right answer:*

1. In some circles, women are .... looked upon as second-class citizens.
   a) ever. *b)* always. *c)* still. *d)* already.
2. .... what you may say, you won't get him to change his mind.
   a) whatever. *b)* however. *c)* no matter. *d)* wherever.
3. There is something to be said on both sides, ... ?
   a) isn't? *b)* is there? *c)* is it? *d)* isn't there?
4. .... I can't understand is why so many men behave so foolishly.
   a) which. *b)* that. *c)* what. *d)* whom.
5. She wanted her mother to look .... a film star.
   a) as. *b)* for. *c)* into. *d)* like.
6. The question is .... television can be held responsible .... all muggings.
   a) how .... of. *b)* if .... in. *c)* whether .... for. *d)* why .... before.

B. *Re-write the sentences as instructed:*

1. *Connect the pairs of sentences with:* without
   a) Don't begin. Ask for advice.
   b) He can speak English. He does not make mistakes.
   c) They do what they are told to do. They don't try to understand.
   d) He left the room. He did not even apologize.
2. *Connect the pairs of sentences using either* too *or* enough:
   a) This man won't admit he was mistaken. He is proud.
   b) I don't believe things will change quickly. I am not naïve.
   c) What he is suffering from is serious. It can't be cured by jogging.
3. *React to the following sentences, beginning with:* "I don't see how .... could":
   a) She didn't defend herself.
   b) They didn't refuse to obey.
   c) Didn't she suspect what you were doing when she was away?
4. ***Re-write the following sentences, beginning with:*** it
   a) He found it hard to keep such a secret.
   b) She will find it hard not to express her resentment.
   c) Didn't she find it hard to calm (down) her supporters?

C. *Dans l'exercice suivant, vous proposerez le plus de solutions possible :*

1. Vos parents s'inquiètent parce que :
   a) vous allez conduire ;
   b) vous allez rester seule à la maison ;
   c) vous allez devoir travailler dur.
   Vous les rassurez et vous dites que vous avez l'habitude.

2. Vous faites des pronostics pour les prochaines élections. Vous estimez que Mr. Smith a de grandes chances d'être élu, que tout indique que les femmes voteront pour lui.

3. Vous êtes dans une situation difficile et vous expliquez à un ami ce que vous attendez de lui.

That moment on the lawn

Encroaching [in'krəutʃiŋ], passionately ['pæʃənitli], embarrassment [im'bærəsmənt], homage ['hɔmidʒ], awkwardly ['ɔ:kwədli], giggled ['gigld], spraddle-legged ['sprædl'legd], wicked ['wikid], abstractedly [æb'stræktidli], obediently [ə'bi:diəntli], debonair [,debə'nεə], languor ['læŋgə], Democrat ['deməkraet], paradox ['pærədɔks], legislative career ['ledʒislətiv kə'riə], Southern ['sʌðən], Southerner ['sʌðənə], paradoxically [,pærə'dɔksikəli], Virginians [və'dʒiniənz].

Milton Loftis, whose life has been one long failure, and whose favorite daughter, Peyton, has just committed suicide, looks back on happier times.

On a spring morning years before, when the •dew had nearly melted on the grass and Loftis, deep in the lawn chair and full of coffee, •wavered mildly between the Port Warwick *Sunday Tribune* and contemplation of the early sunlight •encroaching upon his private beach, he was aroused by a •tumble of feet on the grass behind him, a small voice announcing passionately: "Daddy, Daddy, I'm beautiful!" So he had turned and with the attentive respect given young daughters by their fathers he had watched Peyton—standing in the grass beside him, age nine—while she gazed into a little mirror and said again, "I'm beautiful, Daddy!"

For a moment all this crushed his heart. She *was* beautiful. Perhaps it was the first cigarette of the morning, or the coffee, but he •felt quite giddy. Anyway, he would always remember that moment on the lawn: picking Peyton up with a sudden, almost savage •upwelling of love, pressing her against him as he murmured in a voice slightly •choked, "*Yes*, my baby's beautiful," with wonder and vague embarrassment paying homage to this beautiful part of him, in which life would continue limitlessly.

"... beautiful," he was saying; he held her •awkwardly against his chest. Her long brown hair was in his face, blinding him. She •giggled, •pounded his back, and the mirror which she held fell silently to the grass.

"But you mustn't be so •vain," he said.

"No," she said.

"Come on, get up."

"No."

"No what?" he said.

"No, thank you, stupid."

"Is that nice? Come on, get up."

"O.K.," she said.

Now she was off his lap, •spraddle-legged and barefoot on the grass, making faces at him.

"Don't," he said. "You'll freeze that way, you know. All your life you'll look like the wicked witch."

"I don't care," she said. "Let me see the funnies." [...]

"Chances are it'll rain," he said •abstractedly.

"Yes," said Peyton. "Chances are. Gimme the funnies."

"Don't say 'gimme'."

"Let me, then."

"That's better, baby," he said. "I'll give you the funnies on one condition. See that rosebush over there? Go and pick a rose and bring it to me. Careful, don't get stuck on the thorns."

Peyton ran off obediently and in a moment came back with a big red rose, trembling with dew. "Thank you, baby," he said. There was something •mildly debonair, he thought pleasantly, in presenting your wife with a rose on a sunny morning.

"Let me have the funnies," Peyton said. She took the funnies without a word and sprawled out on the lawn beside him, reading Jiggs, plucking grass with her toes. In a lazy voice, as if in after-thought, she said, "Thank you very much."

He looked down at her. "Children," he murmured, "should respect their parents."

Peyton said nothing, with infinite languor turning the pages, while Loftis, legs outspread, leaned back and read the news—mayor admits, woman denies, something about the •N.R.A.; *Roosevelt*, he thought—well, he'd voted for him, but Christ knows what he'd end up doing. The •blue eagle fluttering everywhere. A good man, most likely, a Democrat, but watch him. Paradox: youngish, •well-to-do barrister Milton Stuart Loftis plans maybe legislative career, could be maybe junior senator •(D-Va.), President (Nation Hails First Southern Chief Since •Wilson). *Question :* Senator, what is your attitude toward the Common Man? *Answer :* Ah, since I'm a Democrat... *Question :* Thank you. What is your attitude, Mr. President, toward the Common Negro? *Answer :* Ah, since I'm a Southerner... *Question :* Thank you. Social Security? *Answer :* Ah, well... Thank you, thank you. •*(My son, paradoxically enough... being a Southerner and a Virginian and of course a Democrat you will find yourself in the unique position of choosing between (a) those ideals implanted as right and proper in every man since Jesus Christ and no doubt before and especially in Virginians and (b) ideals inherent in you through a socio-economic culture over which you have no power to prevail; consequently I strongly urge you my son always to be a good Democrat but to be a good man too if you possibly can...*

William Styron, *Lie Down in Darkness*, 1951

William Styron is a Southern writer and in his novel "Lie down in darkness" (1951) he describes the charm and the complications of life in the South. His characters are shown with all their aspirations and fatal weaknesses.

• **dew** : *rosée* • **wavered** : hesitated • **encroaching upon** : (here) advancing little by little upon • **tumble of feet** : the sound of hurrying footsteps • **he felt quite giddy** : *il se sentit tout étourdi* • **upwelling of love** : *un brusque élan d'amour* • **choked** : strangled (with emotion) • **awkwardly** : *maladroitement* • **giggled** : *eut le fou rire* • **pounded...** : hit him hard on the back • **vain** : pleased with your own appearance • **spraddle-legged** : with her legs wide apart • **abstractedly** : in an absent-minded way • **mildly debonair** : quite courteous ; *assez galant* • **The N.R.A.** : the National Recovery Administration (see A.B.C.) • **the blue eagle** : emblem of the National Industrial Recovery Act, 1933 • **well-to-do** ≠ poor • **D-Va** : Democrat Virginia • **Wilson** : Woodrow Wilson (President of the U.S. from 1913-1921) • **My son...** : Milton Loftis imagines the comments that his dead father would have made.

TOWARDS COMPREHENSION

1 First part. ***Drawing on the text, complete the following sentences:***

1. Loftis didn't really feel like . . . .
2. On the contrary, he felt like enjoying . . . .
3. He was interrupted by . . . .
4. Instead of scolding her, he responded by . . . .
5. But he didn't approve of her . . . .
6. He asked her to pick a rose so that he could . . . .
7. Then she started reading . . . .

2 2nd part. ***Fill in the gaps with words taken from the text:***

1. Loftis wondered whether he had been right to . . . .
2. Though Roosevelt was a good Democrat, Loftis thought . . . .
3. Loftis, who was a . . . . barrister, was considering going in for . . . .
4. He might even end up . . . .
5. The most important issues at the time were . . . .

3 ***Test your comprehension. Right or wrong. Justify your answers.***

Examples: The action takes place on a spring morning.
Right. The first words of the passage are: *"On a spring morning"*.
There are 3 characters: the father, the mother and the daughter.
Wrong. There are only 2 characters: the father and the daughter. The mother is mentioned, but not seen.

1. The events the father was re-living had happened twenty years before.
2. He was asleep in a lawn chair.
3. The daughter, Peyton, was ten years old at the time.
4. She was beautiful and she knew she was beautiful.
5. The father experienced something unusual, exceptional.
6. She wanted to read the comic strips in the paper he was reading.
7. He let her read them.
8. The reading of the paper reminded the father of the election of Roosevelt.
9. He had no confidence in Roosevelt.
10. Then he imagined himself as a Senator.
11. He even went so far as imagining himself as President.
12. The last part of the text is what he imagined his father could have told him.

LANGUAGE PRACTICE

THE ARTICLE

Voir p. 61

4 ***Supply the article*** (∅, a(n), the) ***without looking at the text, and justify your choice (in French):***

1. On . . . . spring morning . . . . years before, when . . . . dew had nearly melted on . . . . grass and Loftis, deep in . . . . lawn chair and full of . . . . coffee, wavered mildly between . . . . Port Warwick *Sunday Tribune* and . . . . contemplation of . . . . early sunlight encroaching upon his private beach, he was aroused by . . . . tumble of . . . . feet on . . . . grass behind him, ... small voice announcing passionately: "Daddy, Daddy; I'm beautiful!" So he had turned and with . . . . attentive respect given . . . . young daughters by their fathers he had watched Peyton—standing in . . . . grass beside him.

2. . . . . people often say that . . . . racialism is more widespread in . . . . South than in . . . . North. . . . . Southerners are supposed to be . . . . racists.
. . . . Southern element in . . . . Styron's novel is one of . . . . major points of interest. . . . . novel seems to be presented as . . . . rendering of . . . . situation that is specifically of . . . . South. If you had read . . . . novel, you would know that Milton Loftis is . . . . failed lawyer and . . . . failed father.
. . . . novel is looked upon as . . . . tragedy of . . . . love.

THE PERFECT INFINITIVE
have + past participle

On peut l'employer avec les verbes *seem, appear,* ainsi qu'avec la forme passive des verbes tels que : *think, know, consider.* On emploie cette construction lorsque le locuteur fait, dans le moment présent, référence à un fait passé. (On trouve fréquemment cette valeur de l'infinitif passé avec les modaux : he could/should/must have done it). The murder appears to have been committed by a foreigner. They seem to have enjoyed the show. He is thought to have been the first to protest.

On notera toutefois que ces formes ont un caractère littéraire et qu'il est plus courant de dire : it appears that the murder was committed by a foreigner. It seems that they enjoyed the show. It is thought that he was the first to protest.

Autres emplois de l'infinitif passé :

1. L'infinitif passé peut également signifier qu'une action doit être achevée avant une certaine date : I want to have finished the job by next Monday. They expect me to have made out my report by the time they leave for New York. *(Ils espèrent que j'aurai/ils s'attendent à ce que j'aie achevé mon rapport avant qu'ils ne partent pour N. Y.)*

2. Il s'emploie également pour marquer qu'un événement qui devait se produire (en vertu d'un projet, d'un plan, d'un arrangement) ne s'est pas produit. (Unrealised past). I was to have met him last week, but I didn't *(je devais le rencontrer).*

5 ***Compare :***

— They seem to have loved each other passionately.
— It seems that they loved each other passionately.

Give the other form :

1. It seems that Peyton was a spoilt child.
2. Milton Loftis seems to have been very proud of his daughter.
3. They seem to have understood each other perfectly.
4. Milton Loftis seems to have been a very fond father.
5. It is thought that Roosevelt was a great President.

6 ***Compare :***

Southerners are supposed to be racialists.
A Southerner is supposed to be a racialist.
As a Southerner, he is supposed to be a racialist.
Being a Southerner, he is supposed to be a racialist.
As he is a Southerner, he is supposed to be a racialist.
Since he is a Southerner, he is supposed to be a racialist.

HOW TO EXPRESS REASON and CONSEQUENCE

Voir p. 18

Build similar sentences with the following prompts :

1. Virginians/Democrats.
2. Democrats/believe in equality.
3. Democrats/fight for liberal ideals.
4. Southerners/believe in the superiority of the white man over the Common Negro.

TOWARDS APPRECIATION

7 ***Right or wrong? Justify your answer in either case.***

1. The main interest of the passage lies in the conflict between a father and his daughter.
2. The main interest of the passage lies in the fact that Milton Loftis is a representation of the Southern man.

3. The main interest of the passage lies in Milton's sudden realization that his love for his daughter is akin to passion (akin to = like).

4. The main interest of the passage lies in Milton's dreams of success as a politician.

5. The main interest of the passage lies in the fact that the action is set in the South.

6. The main interest of the passage lies in its poetic quality.

8 ***Pick out all the words or phrases suggesting:***

a. passion. b. languor, the idyllic quality of life in the South (for the happy few).

9 ***Compare:***

A. The scene is pathetic, Peyton is dead now.
B. The scene is all the more pathetic as Peyton is dead now.
A. Her father is sad, he blames himself for her suicide.
B. Her father is all the sadder as he blames himself for her suicide.

ALL THE + COMPARATIVE +
{ AS
SINCE
BECAUSE
= *(d'autant plus que)*

Give the B-pattern:

1. He is unhappy, he feels guilty.
2. Peyton's death is horrible, she was beautiful and intelligent.
3. His grief must have been deep, he loved his daughter passionately.
4. He must have been miserable, he had no one to turn to for comfort.
5. He is much to be pitied, his life is a complete failure.

10 ***Oral work: Milton Loftis seems to have found himself in a paradoxical position. Explain how.***

As a Southerner . . . . as a Democrat . . . .
He is divided between . . . . and . . . .
Perhaps we can go so far as to say that he is torn between . . . . and . . . .
How can . . . . be reconciled with . . . .
I wonder how . . . . can be reconciled with . . . .
It can't have been easy for him to . . . .
He seems to have been a man of divided loyalties in so far as . . . .

11 ***Written work:***

What does the text reveal about:
a. life in the South. b. the social, political and racial attitudes of Southerners?

12 ***Written translation:***

From the beginning down to: *"fell silently to the grass"*.

Extract from: Haywire

Priority [prai'ɔriti], Greenwich ['grenitʃ], slew [slu:], exclusive [iks'klu:siv], reprehensible [,repri'hensəbl], bigotry ['bigətri], idly ['aidli], irresistible [,iri'zistəbl], supposedly [sə'pəuzidli], whereupon [,wεərə'pɔn], particularly [pə'tikjuləli], anti-semitism ['ænti'semitizm], emphasis ['emfəsis], superstitiously [,sju:pə'stiʃəsli], oratory ['ɔrətəri], prejudice ['predʒudis], vehemently ['vi:iməntli], dramatize ['dræmətaiz], Genesis ['dʒenisis], agitatedly ['ædʒiteitidli].

We moved •there in the •fall of 1948. Mother had decided to civilize us. The time had come to give priority to the serious matters of education, culture, and social structure, none of which was provided by Brookfield or California. But Greenwich had a •slew of excellent private schools [...] It also had a multitude of exclusive clubs (the Greenwich Country Club, the Round Hill Club, the Field Club, the Indian Harbor Yacht Club, the Belle Haven Beach Club), which was one aspect of life there that Mother found reprehensible. Despite our eventual importunings for her to join one (like the parents of all our friends), she drew the line and •steadfastly refused. "I'm not a joiner," she'd say, "and anyway, I don't believe in that kind of *nouveau-riche* snobbism."

She also had grave •misgivings about the •bigotry in Greenwich; there were no Jews. I'd never heard the word "Jew" until we moved to Greenwich. One afternoon we were all drinking iced tea on the •flagstone terrace when a friend of mine idly quoted *her* mother as being greatly relieved that the owners of such-and-such a house had held out against the irresistible •bid of a rich New York Jewish couple who'd driven out *three* times to look at it—supposedly *very* prominent, too, but you know how that is: let one in, then another, and suddenly property values—• Whereupon Mother exploded. It was one of the only two times I ever saw her really lose her temper (the other was when I punched Bridget in the nose for breaking one of my •china horses), and I was extremely impressed. She sprang to her feet, her face purple with emotion. "There is one thing I will *not tolerate*—not in my house, not from anyone, not ever!—and that is discrimination of any kind, particularly anti-Semitism." She pounded one fist in the other hand for •emphasis. "The finest, most brilliant people I know are Jews, my closest friends are Jews!" She paced agitatedly back and forth, superstitiously avoiding the cracks in the flagstone, delivering herself of a long •impassioned lecture that not only detailed the entire history of the Jewish race, its accomplishments and persecutions, but also lamented the incalculable loss—cultural, intellectual, and scientific—that the rest of civilization would have suffered without it. Inflamed by her oratory, we felt a terrible collective shame at not being Jewish ourselves. "I find the only •prejudice worth having," she concluded vehemently, "is against people who are prejudiced." •Further to dramatize her point and to remedy what she saw as her personal neglect of our religious training, she thereafter, instead of sending us each Sunday morning to Sunday School, read the Old Testament to us, starting with Genesis (and ending halfway through Ezra, when her interest in the sessions •lagged as much as ours).

BROOKE HAYWARD, *Haywire*
Reprinted with the permission of Random House, Inc.

● **there** : Greenwich, Connecticut ● **fall** : autumn ● **slew** : a lot of ● **steadfastly** : firmly ● **grave misgivings** : serious doubts ● **bigotry** : intolerance ● **flagstone** : *dallage* ● **bid** : offer ● **whereupon** : at this point ● **china** : porcelain ● **for emphasis** : to underline her words ● **impassioned** : revealing deep feelings ● **prejudice** : *préjugé* ● **further to dramatize...** : *pour donner plus de relief à...* ● **lagged** : *tomba.*

'What's he charged with?' asked the judge,
'Bigotry, Your Honour. He married three women.'
'Don't be absurd, Guard. That's not bigotry that's trigonometry.'

TOWARDS COMPREHENSION

1 ***After listening to a recording of the text, or reading it, bring out the two points of interest.***

In this text, the narrator tells us that her mother was against . . . . and . . . . , but she tells us much more about . . . . than . . . .

2 ***Pick out the two sentences which, in your opinion, best illustrate or sum up these two points.***

3 ***Are you sure you understand some of the key-words?***

1. A joiner (l. 8)
   a) is a good democrat.
   b) likes clubs, organizations etc.
   c) a craftsman who makes tables, chairs, doors, etc.
2. A bigot (l. 10)
   a) is an old woman always praying to God.
   b) spends most of his time at church.
   c) is intolerant and narrow-minded.
3. She had misgivings . . . . (l. 10)
   a) because she hated narrow-mindedness.
   b) because her best friends were Jews.
   c) because she hated snobbism.
4. The owners of the house *held out* . . . . (l. 13)
   a) they were impolite.
   b) they resisted.
   c) they were hesitant.
5. The mother of the narrator's friend was *relieved* because:
   a) she wanted Jews to come and live in the neighbourhood.
   b) she did nor want Jews to come and live in the neighbourhood.
   c) she did not want her children to play with Jewish children.

4 ***Complete the sentences with verbs from the following list:*** have a prejudice against/lose one's temper/let somebody in/draw the line/believe in/relieve/hold out/join.

1. I'm quite willing to let you do lots of things, but we've got to . . . . somewhere.
2. If you . . . . our club, I don't think you'd still . . . . such organizations.
3. I don't . . . . letting children have their own way (=do what they want).
4. I wanted to enter but they refused to . . . . me . . . .
5. The soldiers . . . . for a week, then they surrendered.
6. His self-control is tremendous, I have never seen him . . . . *(careful!)*
7. This treatment will soon . . . . you.

5 ***Right or wrong? Justify your answers.***

1. There were good private schools in Greenwich.
2. There were a lot of expensive clubs in Greenwich.
3. Anyone could join those clubs.
4. The children were against their mother joining a club.
5. The mother didn't know which club to join.
6. She hated snobs.
7. There were bigots in Greenwich.
8. The story about the rich New York Jewish couple proves that the narrator's friend was an anti-Semite.
9. This story caused the narrator's mother to lose her temper.
10. She would fly into a rage (become very angry) at the least thing.
11. She had a very high opinion of Jews.
12. She decided to devote herself to the religious training of her children.
13. Both the mother and the children took a great interest in that religious training.

LANGUAGE PRACTICE

6 ***Add the article*** (the) ***where necessary, and say why (in French):***

THE ARTICLE

Voir p. 61

1. . . . . priority should be given to . . . . education, ... culture, ... social structure.

2. . . . . snobbism is widespread in . . . . fashionable circles.

3. . . . . narrow-mindedness is also widespread among . . . . actors and . . . . writers.

4. . . . . education you have received so far is insufficient as regards . . . . religious training.

5. . . . . bigotry in Greenwich was something that worried her.

6. Until . . . . turn of . . . . century . . . . problem of . . . . anti-Jewish feeling was little different from that of . . . . anti-immigrant feeling in general.

7. There was little outcry against . . . . Jews from . . . . Eastern Europe as long as they stayed as . . . . proletarians in . . . . needle trades, but when they moved into . . . . middle classes and made a bid (=tried to gain) for . . . . higher living standards . . . . better schools and . . . . residences, ... anti-Jewish movement mounted (Max Lerner).

8. It was not until . . . . era of . . . . Depression and . . . . Nazism that . . . . anti-Semitism took its place, after . . . . anti-Negro racism, as . . . . most serious movement of . . . . ethnic hatreds in . . . . America.

7 ***Written work: connect the following pairs of sentences with a relative pronoun, as in the example:***

RELATIVE PRONOUNS

(all of which, none of which, all of whom, none of whom, too many of whom . . . .)

Example: The time had come to give priority to the serious matters of education, culture, and social structure. None of them was provided by Brookfield or California. The time had come . . . . and social structure, none of which was provided by Brookfield or California.

1. Greenwich had a lot of private schools. All of them were excellent.

2. Greenwich had a lot of exclusive clubs. None of them attracted mother.

3. Their mother was a movie-star, with several films to her credit. Several of them had received rather flattering reviews.

4. The persecutions of the Jewish race should have put an end to anti-Semitism. All of them are very well-known *(Careful!)*

5. The attitude of our friends' parents was a source of misgiving to Mother. Too many of them were bigoted.

8 ***Now translate the above sentences.***

9 ***Imagine what the children said to their mother to persuade her to join a club:***

You should ....
Why don't you ....
We'd like you to ....
If I were you, ...

HOW TO EXPRESS ADVICE

Voir p. 32

HOW TO EXPRESS VOLITION

- **How to assert one's will, how to make one's will felt.**
  (Comment affirmer, faire sentir sa volonté.)
  Compare :

  I'll have my children show respect for their elders.
  =I insist upon my children showing respect ....
  (= je veux que, je tiens absolument à ce que ....)
  — *I'll have* + comp. + inf. sans *to*

  In the negative = refusal.
  I won't have them answer me back rudely.
  =I won't allow them to answer me back rudely.
  — *I won't have* + comp. + inf. sans *to*

- **Other ways of expressing refusal:**
  I'm not going to ....
  I won't ....
  Don't expect me to ....

10 ***Using some of the above patterns, express the following ideas differently:***

1. I won't allow my children to become racists.
2. I won't allow them to join racist organizations.
3. I won't allow you to forget what the Jews did for us.
4. I won't allow my children to develop a prejudice against anyone.
5. I won't tolerate discrimination of any kind in my house.

Go on ....

11 ***Drawing on the text, make a few sentences beginning with:***

But for the Jewish race, ...

BUT FOR
=without

12 ***Then re-cast your sentences beginning with:***

Thanks to the Jewish race ....

13 ***Pick out all the words and phrases expressing the mother's anger and indignation.***

14 **"She had grave misgivings . . . ."**
Make up as many sentences as you can beginning with:

1. She is afraid . . . . may . . . .
2. She was afraid . . . . might . . . .
3. She was afraid . . . . would . . . .

(*Example:* she is afraid her children may develop a prejudice against . . . .)

15 ***Sum up her views about anti-Semitism:***

She is against . . . . she says she won't . . . . because we mustn't forget . . . . thanks to . . . .

16 ***The narrator's point of view. Is she taking her mother's indignation very seriously?***

We are made to feel that . . . . We can wonder if . . . .

17 ***Creative oral work:***

One of the children tries to bring home to his/her mother (to make her realize) the fact that her hatred of clubs is a form of prejudice. Imagine the dialogue:
a. the mother loses her temper and explodes.
b. the mother keeps her temper.

18 ***Précis writing:***

Make a précis of this text in not more than 50 words.

Extract from: In dubious battle

Dynamite [ˋdainəmait], slaughter-house [ˋslɔ:təhaus], reputation [ˌrepjuˋteiʃn], riot [ˋraiət], covered with blood [ˋkʌvəd wið ˋblʌd], stove [stəuv], vagrancy [ˋveigrənsi], Catholic [ˋkæθəlik], wrapping [ˋræpiŋ], squad [skɔd], perplexity [pəˋpleksiti].

"Why do you want to join the Party?"

Jim stirred his coffee. His face •wrinkled up in concentration. He looked down into his •lap. "Well I could give you a lot of little reasons. Mainly, it's this: My whole family has been ruined by this system. My old man, my father, was •slugged so much in labor trouble that he went •punchdrunk. He got an idea that he'd like to dynamite a •slaughter-house where he used to work. Well, he caught a •charge of buckshot in the chest from a •riot gun."

Harry interrupted, "Was your father Roy Nolan?"

"Yeah. Killed three years ago."

"Jesus!" Harry said. "He had a reputation for being the •toughest mug in the country. I've heard he could lick five cops with his bare hands."

Jim •grinned. "I guess he could, but every time he went out he met six. He always got •the hell beat out of him. He used to come home all covered with blood. He'd sit beside the cook stove. We had to let him alone then. Couldn't even speak to him or he'd cry. When my mother washed him later, he'd whine like a dog." He paused. "You know he was a •sticker in the slaughter-house. Used to drink warm blood to keep up his strength."

Nilson looked quickly at him, and then away. He bent the corner of the application card and creased it down with his thumb nail. "Your mother is alive?" he asked softly.

Jim's eyes narrowed. "She died a month ago," he said. "I was in jail. Thirty days for •vagrancy. Word came in she was dying. They let me go home with a cop. There wasn't anything the matter with her. She wouldn't talk at all. She was a Catholic, only my old man wouldn't let her go to church. He hated churches. She just stared at me. I asked her if she wanted a priest, but she didn't answer me, just stared. 'Bout four o'clock in the morning she died. Didn't seem like dying at all. I didn't go to the funeral. I guess they would've let me. I didn't want to. I guess she just didn't want to live. I guess she didn't care if she went to •hell, either." Harry •started nervously. "Drink your coffee and have some more. You act half asleep. You don't take anything, do you?"

"You mean •dope? No, I don't even drink."

Nilson pulled out a piece of paper and made a few notes on it. "How'd you happen to get •vagged?"

Jim said fiercely, "I worked in Tulman's Department Store. Head of the wrapping department. I was out to a picture show one night, and coming home I saw a crowd in Lincoln Square. I stopped to see what it was all about. There was a •guy in the middle of the park talking. I climbed up on the pedestal of that statue of Senator Morgan so I could see better. And then I heard the sirens. I was watching the riot squad come in from the other side. Well, a squad came up from behind, too. Cop slugged me from behind, right in the back of the neck. When I •came to I was already booked for vagrancy. I was •rumdum for a long time. Got hit right here." Jim put his fingers on the back of his neck at the base of his skull. "Well, I told 'em I wasn't a vagrant and had a job, and told 'em to call up Mr. Webb, he's manager at Tulman's. So they did. Webb asked where I was picked up, and the sergeant said "at a radical meeting," and then Webb said he never heard of me. So I •got the rap."

Nilson plugged in the hot plate again. The coffee started rumbling in the pot. "You look half drunk, Jim. What's the matter with you?"

"I don't know. I feel dead. Everything in the past is gone. I •checked out of my rooming house before I came here. I still had a week paid for. I don't want to go back to any of it again. I want to be finished with it."

Nilson poured the coffee cups full. "Look, Jim, I want to give you a picture of what it's like to be a Party member. You'll get a chance to vote on every decision, but once the vote's in, you'll have to obey. When we have money we try to give field workers twenty dollars a month to eat on. I don't remember a time when we ever had the money. Now listen to the work: In the field you'll have to work alongside the men, and you'll have to do the Party work after that, sometimes sixteen, eighteen hours a day. You'll have to get your food where you can. Do you think you could do that?"

"Yes."

Nilson touched the desk here and there with his fingertips. "Even the people you're trying to help will hate you most of the time. Do you know that?"

"Yes."

"Well, why do you want to join, then?"

Jim's grey eyes half closed in perplexity. At last he said, "In the jail there were some Party men. They talked to me. Everything's been a •mess, all my life. Their lives weren't messes. They were working toward something. I want to work toward something. I feel dead. I thought I might get alive again."

JOHN STEINBECK, *In Dubious Battle*, 1936

• **wrinkled up in concentration** : *il se concentra et ses traits se crispèrent* • **lap** : *genoux* • **slugged** : hit • **punch-drunk** : *hébété* • **slaughter-house** : *abattoirs* • **a charge of buckshot** : *une décharge de chevrotine* • **riot gun** : gun used by the police to disperse rather than hurt rioters *(émeutiers)* • **the toughest mug** : *le type le plus costaud* • **grinned** : smiled broadly (from ear to ear) • **the hell beat out of him** : *se faisait ratatiner* • **sticker** : *tueur de porcs* • **vagrant, vagrancy** : a vagrant is a vagabond • **hell** ≠ paradise • **started** : made a sudden movement • **dope** : (colloq) harmful (dangerous) drug • **vagged** : arrested on a charge of vagrancy • **guy** : (colloq) man • **came to** : recovered consciousness • **rumdum** : *abruti* • **I got the rap** : I was condemned • **checked out of my rooming house** : left • **everything's been a mess** : *ma vie jusqu'à maintenant a été un gâchis.*

TOWARDS COMPREHENSION

1 ***Complete the following sentences without looking at the text.***

1. Jim worked in Tulman's Department Store as . . . .
2. One night, as he was coming out of a cinema he saw . . . .
3. Jim did not stay long on the pedestal of the statue because . . . .
4. Jim was arrested for . . . .
5. The only man who could have testified that Jim was not a . . . . was . . . . but he . . . . because . . . .
6. Nilson explained to him what . . . .
7. Jim hates the capitalist system because . . . .

2 ***How many parts are there in this text? Sum up each of them in one or two sentences.***

3 ***Select essential information: say which sentences are essential to the understanding of the passage.***

1. My whole family has been ruined by the system.
2. My father was slugged so much in labor trouble that he went punch-drunk.
3. He caught a charge of buckshot in the chest from a riot gun.
4. He was killed three years ago.
5. He had a reputation for being the toughest mug in the country.
6. He used to come home all covered with blood.
7. When my mother washed him later, he'd whine like a dog.
8. He used to drink warm blood to keep up his strength.
9. My mother died a month ago.
10. I was in jail. Thirty days for vagrancy.
11. They let me go home with a cop.
12. I didn't go to the funeral.
13. I worked in Tulman's Department Store.
14. I was out to a picture show one night, and coming home I saw a crowd in Lincoln Square.
15. I climbed up on the pedestal of that statue of Senator Morgan so I could see better.
16. Cop slugged me from behind, right in the back of the neck.
17. When I came to I was already booked for vagrancy.
18. I told them to call up Mr. Webb.
19. He asked where I was picked up and then said he never heard of me.
20. In the jail there were some Party men.

LANGUAGE PRACTICE

4 ***Pick out all the*** would-***forms from the text and say which meaning they convey (express).***

WOULD

peut s'employer pour marquer qu'un comportement était prévisible, il peut également indiquer la répétition d'une action, d'un comportement dans le passé : "I've lost my wallet." "You would." *(C'est bien de vous! Ça ne m'étonne pas de vous!)* At such times he would behave like a child. *(Il se comportait en enfant.)*
A la forme négative **would** exprime une volonté, un refus. I wanted to go out, but she wouldn't let me *(mais elle ne voulait pas)*.

5 ***Fill in the blanks with*** as if/as though, even if/even though, ***or*** (al)though :

1. His father cried . . . . he were a child.
2. His mother didn't want a priest . . . . she was a catholic.
3. Jim looked . . . . he had taken dope.
4. Jim wanted to join the Party . . . . he'd have to work very hard.
5. Mr. Webb pretended he didn't know him . . . . Jim had been working in his store for some time.
6. Jim was arrested on a vagrancy charge . . . . he was not a vagrant.
7. The cops used to treat the reds . . . . they were criminals.

NE PAS CONFONDRE :

• **as if/as though** qui introduisent une comparaison hypothétique. It isn't as if he were poor *(ce n'est pas comme s'il était pauvre)*

• **(al) though, even though** qui expriment le contraste et introduisent une prop. concessive : *bien que, même si.*

6 ***Replace*** allow ***by*** let, ***and vice versa, where possible :***

1. They won't allow me to go to the funeral.
2. Do you think they would allow me to go to the funeral if I asked them to?
3. Prisoners aren't allowed to go out.
4. I don't think the cops will let you stand there.
5. Did your father allow her to go to church?
6. Cops shouldn't be allowed to slug people.
7. They wouldn't let me say what I had to say.
8. Perhaps they would have allowed me to go if I had wanted to.

7 ***Paragraph writing : imagine what*** *"the guy in the middle of the park was saying"* (about 10 lines).

If we let the boss . . . . don't let yourselves be . . . . don't let them . . . . if you allow them . . . . I won't let it be said that . . . .

TO ALLOW
TO LET

Ces deux verbes expriment une idée de permission :
He allowed us to smoke.
He let us smoke.
Noter la différence de construction : **let + bv** (inf. sans to).
A noter également la fréquence de **wouldn't let :**
She wouldn't let us do it. *(Elle n'a pas voulu nous laisser le faire.)*
He wanted to go but his wife wouldn't let him.
Au passif, **let** est très rare, c'est **allowed to** qui est employé.
You won't be allowed to go abroad. *(On ne vous permettra pas . . . .)*
abroad. *(On ne vous permettra pas . . . .)*
Noter l'expression : I won't let it be said that . . . . *(je ne laisserai pas dire que).*

8 ***Imagine all that Jim asked when he was in jail, then you will imagine the answers.***

Prisoners aren't allowed . . . .
As a prisoner, you can't/you aren't allowed to . . . .

9 ***Make up as many sentences as you can on this pattern :***

He wanted to . . . . but they wouldn't let him.

HOW TO ASK, GIVE, REFUSE PERMISSION

Can I smoke in here? { Yes, you can.
No, I'm afraid you can't.

On trouve également : May I .... yes, you may, no you may not. Mais ces formes, moins fréquentes que les précédentes appartiennent à la langue recherchée, ou officielle.

A l'interrogation on trouve aussi :
Are we allowed to ...?
Is it all right if we ...? *(plus familier).*
Do you mind if I smoke? Would you mind if I smoked? Do/would you mind my smoking *(plus recherché).*
On trouve également : **could** et **might.**
Could I use your phone? I wonder if I could/might ....

Remarque : Might a rarement le sens de permission. C'est **could** ou **was/were allowed to** que l'on emploie. Mais au style indirect on trouve **might :** When I was your age, I was allowed to smoke a cigarette every Sunday. He said you might smoke.

10 *Ask and say in as many ways as you can what a Party member has to do :*

A Party member has to ....
Party members have got to ....
As a Party member you'll have to ....
Joining the Party means that you'll have to ....
If you join the Party, you'll have to ....
When/once you have joined the Party, you'll have to ....

HOW TO EXPRESS OBLIGATION

have to ou **have got to** (au prés. et au pret.)
On notera les différences suivantes :
Do you have to ...?
mais : Have you got to ....?
You don't have to ....
mais: you haven't got to ....

PRÉSENT A VALEUR DE FUTUR
dans
PROP. SUB. TEMPORELLES

I'll join the Party when I'm older *(j'adhèrerai au Parti quand je serai plus âgé).*
He said he would join the Party when he was older *(il a dit qu'il adhèrerait .... quand il serait ....).*
Once you have joined the Party, you'll have to .... *(une fois que vous aurez ....).*
Donc : pas de futur, mais le présent, pas de condit. mais le prétérit, pas de futur antérieur, mais le parfait.

AS + NOUN

As a Frenchman, I can tell you that .... *(= en tant que Français, en ma qualité de Français...)* (article indéfini, *parce que je suis un Français parmi les Français)*
As Chairman, I must tell you that .... *(= en ma qualité de Président, ...)* (article zéro *car il n'y a qu'un président).*

11 ***Express in as many ways as you can the reasons why Jim wants to join the Party.***

He needs .... that's why ....
He wants .... that's why ....
If he wants to join .... it is because ....
He hopes that the Party will ....
He expects the party to ....
What he needs is ...., that's why ....
He wants to join .... so as (not) to ....
He wants to join .... in the hope of ....
To him, joining the party is a means (way) of ....

HOW TO EXPRESS REASON and PURPOSE

Voir p. 18

12 ***Drawing on the text, and using the following patterns, describe the mother's attitude to life and death:***

She was indifferent to ....
She seems to have been indifferent to ....
It looks as if she was indifferent to ....
It was quite indifferent to her whether ....
She didn't care whether/how/when ....
It didn't matter to her whether/who/when/how ....

HOW TO EXPRESS INDIFFERENCE

13 ***Show that it is not surprising that Jim should want to join the Party.***

No wonder he wants ....
It is quite understandable that he should ....
What else .... where else ....

14 ***Creative written work***

Compare the attitudes of the three characters to social injustice. (The action takes place between 1929 and 1933.)

15 ***Written or oral translation:***

From: *"Nilson poured the coffee cup full"* down to the end.

16 ***Could you suggest a suitable title for this passage?***

The cowboy in Hollywood

Heroes [ˋhiərəuz], villains [ˋvilənz], inevitable [inˋevitəbl], significance [sigˋnifikəns], cavalry [ˋkævəlri], rescue [ˋreskju:], familiar scenario [fəˋmiljə siˋnɑ:riəu], reenactment [ˋri:-iˋnæktmənt], stereotype [ˋstiəriətaip], irrelevant [iˋrelivənt], sojourn [ˋsɔdʒə:n], heroic [hiˋrəuik], ambiguous [æmˋbigjuəs], audiences'imaginations [ˋɔ:djənsizi,mædʒiˋneiʃənz], archetypal [ˋɑ:kitaipl], melancholy [ˋmelənkəli], unavoidably [,ʌnəˋvɔidəbli], combat [ˋkɔmbət].

The Western or cowboy movie has long been the most popular genre of American films around the world. Latterly, many local variants have appeared where heroes and villains face one another at the inevitable •showdown, hands reaching for guns at high noon in the center of a dusty town, not in the state of Kansas, but in Mexico, Spain, Italy, India. Mr. Pechter examines the appeal of the Western, and speculates about its significance.

A stagecoach •hurtles across the vast landscape. Indians suddenly stage a savage attack. All seems lost until a •bugle call signals the cavalry to the rescue! For many people this familiar scenario is the Western movie, a ritual reenactment of a •starkly simplistic morality play. Yet this stereotype of what the Western is seems •oddly •irrelevant •in view of the artistic power of the best Western movies, and their enormous popular appeal. Part of this appeal is another stereotype, the Western hero as a solitary rider, usually seen in a limitless landscape. One never quite knows where he came from, or where he is going. For a time in his journey he stops to sojourn at a town or camp on the prairie. But, though he seeks no quarrel, tranquility eludes him. He is challenged—insulted in a bar, his horse stolen—and that challenge must be faced though doing so will doubtless end in •bloodshed—and since the genre isn't rigid about this, it may even be his own. If he is successful, he will soon be riding off again. Though he's depicted almost always as heroic, the moral issues in his confrontations aren't always so clearly drawn. He may be strong, but he is often also ambiguous and, sometimes, •flawed.

Understanding this figure of the Western hero explains a lot about the Western itself and its persistent hold on audiences' imaginations. Probably the most ambitious and intelligent attempt to define the archetypal elements of the form remains that of critic Robert Warshow. In his essay, "The Westerner," Warshow compares the Western hero to the gangster hero who emerged in films of the 1930s, and whom he resembles "in being lonely and to some degree melancholy." But his melancholy comes from the "simple" recognition that life is unavoidably serious, not from the disproportions of his own temperament. Also, as Warshow points out, the two differ in the codes by which they kill. The gangster believes in seizing the advantage by shooting first, whereas for the Westerner "it is a crucial point of honor *not* to "do it first"; his gun remains in its holster until the moment of combat." Warshow then asks:

"What does the Westerner fight for? We know he is on the side of justice and order, and of course it can be said he fights for these things. But such broad aims never correspond exactly to his real motives; they only offer him his opportunity .... What he defends, at bottom is the purity of his own image—in fact his honor. This is what makes him invaluable .... The Westerner is the last gentleman, and the movies which over and over again tell his story are probably the last art form in which the concept of honor retains its strength."

William Pechter, *Dialogue*, Vol. II, 1978, n° 2

● **showdown** : *affrontement* ● **hurtles** : rushes ● **bugle** : *clairon* ● **starkly** : entirely, absolutely ● **oddly** : strangely ● **irrelevant** : has no importance ● **in view of** : when you consider ● **bloodshed** : *effusion de sang* ● **flawed** : il y a *une faille dans son caractère.*

TOWARDS COMPREHENSION

IN OTHER WORDS

1 ***Express the same ideas in simpler words :***

1. But, though he seeks no quarrel, tranquility eludes him (. . . . he can't . . . .).
2. . . . . though doing so will doubtless end in bloodshed (if he . . . .).
3. But his melancholy comes from the "simple" recognition that life is unavoidably serious (if he is melancholy, it is because he . . . .).

2 ***Pick out the words referring to :***

a. the appeal of the Western. b. its significance.

LANGUAGE PRACTICE

ALMOST ALWAYS ≠ HARDLY EVER

3 ***Express the same ideas, using :*** hardly ever :

Example : He is almost always heroic. He hardly ever lacks courage. *Or :* he is hardly ever cowardly.

1. He is almost always victorious.
2. The villain is almost always punished.
3. The Western hero almost always keeps his gun in its holster until the moment of combat.
4. He almost always waits for his opponent to shoot first.

Go on . . . .

HOW TO EXPRESS CONTRAST

4 ***Compare :***

He may be strong, but he is often also ambiguous.
Strong as he may be, he is often also ambiguous.
However strong he may be, he is often also ambiguous.
He is strong, and yet he is often also ambiguous.
He is strong, however he is often also ambiguous.
Although he is strong, he is often also ambiguous.

Give the other forms *(not all of them are possible in all cases) :*

1. He may be strong, he is also sometimes flawed.
2. He is heroic, and yet his motives are not always clearly analysed.
3. He behaves like a gentleman, however he may be rude to women.
4. He is depicted as heroic, however the moral issues he fights for are not always clear.

Go on . . . .

BOTH

s'emploie pour deux personnes ou deux choses lorsqu'on insiste sur l'association.
Sa place peut varier : he lost both his legs in the accident. Give me both these books. Both of them were killed. I'll take them both. He bought two books, both of which were interesting
Remarque : both peut être adverbe et signifier « à la fois » : this book is both cheap and interesting.

5 *Drawing on the text, make a few sentences showing the common points between the Western hero and the gangster hero.*

6 *Then recast your sentences, using the so-pattern :*

EXPRESSION DE LA SIMILITUDE

(moi aussi, moi non plus...)

a. Forme affirmative. Schéma : **so + auxiliaire + sujet.**
He is French—So am I *(moi aussi).*
They like Britain—So do we *(nous aussi).*
My brother will go to Britain next year—So will my sister.
He can speak English—So can I.

b. Forme négative. Schéma : **neither + auxiliaire + sujet.**
She isn't pleased—Neither am I *(moi non plus).*
He won't come—Neither shall I.
The French couldn't accept this treaty—Neither could the English.

TOWARDS APPRECIATION

7 *On the face of it, it can be said that .... resembles .... in so far as .... but actually ....*

8 *The popularity of the Western can be ascribed to the fact that ....*

9 *Those who don't like Westerns sometimes say : "If you've seen one, you've seen them all." Does this text provide you with arguments bearing out (confirming) this point of view?*

10 *What are the usual ingredients of the typical Western?*

(costume, setting, plot, good versus evil, a man on the run from the law, the bounty hunter = *chasseur de primes,* marshal, deputy, sheriff, trigger-happy = always ready to shoot, riding off alone etc. . . . .)

11 *Creative written work :*

a. How far does the Western give us a vision of America's westward expansion?

b. Some Westerns have been compared to tragedies in which character is fate. Can you think of any westerns that gave you this impression?

12 *Translation :* from : *the gangster believes in seizing* .... to the end.

IVORY
SOAP

The end of an era

Marines [mə'ri:nz], patriotic [,pætri'ɔtik], era ['iərə], heroically [hi'rəuikəli], lieutenant [lef'tenənt .U.S.: lu:'tenənt], athletic [æθ'letik], accurate ['ækjurit], campaign [kæm'pein], Vietnamese [,vjetnə'mi:z], dissolved [di'zɔlvd], atmosphere of disintegration ['ætməsfiərəv dis,inti'greiʃən], refugees [,refju:'dʒi:z], routed soldiers ['rautid 'səuldʒəz], numbing ['nʌmiŋ], ambivalent [æm'bivələnt], Marine Corps [mə'ri:n 'kɔ:], explicit gesture of protest [iks'plisit 'dʒestʃərəv 'prəutest], authorized ['ɔ:θəraizd], ominous ['ɔminəs], authorities [ɔ:'θɔritiz], episode ['episəud], career [kə'riə], idealism [ai'diəlizəm], purpose ['pə:pəs], missiles ['misailz .Am:'mislz], armada [ɑ:'mɑ:də .U.S.:ɑ:'meidə], Expeditionary Brigade [,ekspi'diʃnri bri'geid].

I joined the Marines in 1960, partly because I got swept up in the patriotic tide of the Kennedy era but mostly because I was sick of the safe, suburban existence I had known most of my life. [...]

That is what I wanted, to find in a commonplace world a chance to live heroically. Having known nothing but security, comfort, and peace, I hungered for danger, challenges, and violence.

I had no clear idea of how to fulfill this peculiar ambition until the day a Marine recruiting team set up a stand in the student union at Loyola University. •They were on a talent hunt for officer material and displayed a poster of a •trim lieutenant who had one of those athletic, slightly cruel-looking faces considered handsome in the military. He looked like a •cross between an •All-American •halfback and a Nazi tank commander. Clear and resolute, his blue eyes seemed to stare at me in challenge. Join the Marines, read the slogan above his white cap. Be a leader of men. [...]

An accurate description of the final month of North Vietnam's final campaign would require a book in itself. I am not even sure if what occurred could be called a campaign; a migration, rather. The North Vietnamese Army simply rolled over the countryside, driving on Saigon. Except for a brief, hopeless stand made by a single division at the provincial capital of Xuan Loc, the •ARVN offered no significant resistance. The South Vietnamese Army broke into pieces. It dissolved. There were terrible scenes of panicked soldiers beating and •trampling civilians as they fled from the advancing enemy. Late in the month, the atmosphere of disintegration became palpable. Not just an army, but an entire country was crumbling, collapsing before our eyes. The roads were jammed with refugees and routed soldiers. Some of the columns were twenty miles long, •winding out of the hills and rubber plantations toward the flat •marshlands around Saigon. They stretched along the roads for as far as we could see, processions that seemed to have no beginning and no end. [...]

There was so much human suffering in these scenes that I could not respond to it. It was •numbing. Regardless of the outcome, I wanted to see it end. At the same time, a part of me did not want to see it end in a North Vietnamese victory. I kept thinking about Levy, about Sullivan, about all of the others, and something in me cried out against the waste of their lives. The war was lost, or very nearly lost. Those men had died for no reason. They had given their all for nothing.

I think these ambivalent feelings were typical of American veterans who, like me, were both opposed to the war and yet emotionally tied to it. After my discharge from the Marine Corps in mid-1967, I had •drifted into the antiwar movement, though I was never passionately involved in it. I •eventually joined the Vietnam Veterans Against the War, but my most explicit gesture of protest was made in 1970, when I mailed my campaign ribbons to President Nixon, together with a long and bitter letter explaining why I was opposed to American policies in Indochina. I thought, naïvely, that such a personal, individual act would have more effect than mass marches. About a month later, I received in the mail an envelope bearing the return address "The White House." It contained my medals and a •curt note, written by some obscure functionary, which said that the Executive Branch of the United States government was not authorized to receive or hold military decorations; therefore, my ribbons were being returned to me. The writer concluded with the ominous phrase: "Your views about U.S. policies in South Vietnam have been noted and brought to the attention of the proper authorities." That episode sums up my career as an antiwar activist. [...]

My mind shot back a decade, to that day we had marched into Vietnam, •swaggering, confident, and full of idealism. We had believed we were there for a high moral purpose. But somehow our idealism was lost, our morals corrupted, and the purpose forgotten.

We reached the coast about twenty minutes later. We were out of danger, out of range of the missiles, removed from all possibility of being among the last Americans to die in Vietnam. [...] Swooping out over the South China Sea, over the thousands of fishing junks jammed with refugees, the •CH-53 touched down on the U.S.S. *Denver*, a helicopter assault ship that was part of the armada the Seventh Fleet had assembled for the evacuation. There was some applause as the aircraft settled down on the flight deck and as we filed out, a marine slapped me on the back and said, "Welcome home. Bet you're glad to be out of there." I was, of course. I asked him which •outfit he was from. "Ninth MEB," he answered. The 9th Expeditionary Brigade, the same unit with which I had landed at Danang. But the men who belonged to it now seemed a good deal more cynical than we who had belonged to it ten years before. The marine looked at the faint blue line marking the Vietnamese coast and said, "Well, that's one country we don't have to give billions of dollars to anymore."

PHILIP CAPUTO, *A Rumor of War*, 1977

After serving as a Marine in Viet Nam for 2 years, Philip Caputo left the Marine Corps in 1967 and became a journalist on the staff of the Chicago Tribune. In 1975, he was sent back to Saigon as the paper's war correspondent and in this way was present at the end of the war in Viet Nam.

• **they were on a talent hunt...** : *ils étaient en quête de graine d'officier* • **trim** : *bien sanglé dans son uniforme* • **a cross between** : a mixture of... • **All-American** : best (the élite of American football players) • **half-back** : *demi* • **ARVN** : The Army of South Vietnam • **trampling** : crushing underfoot • **winding out** : coming out in a sinuous column • **marshlands** : *marécages* • **numbing** : *paralysing* • **drifted into** : joined without great conviction • **eventually** : in the end • **curt** : *sec* • **swaggering** : self-satisfied • **CH-53** : helicopter • **outfit** : unit.

TOWARDS COMPREHENSION

1 ***Find the three correct answers among the following:***

This text is about the narrator's career:

a. as a war correspondent.
b. as a helicopter pilot.
c. as a White House functionary.
d. as an antiwar activist.
e. as a Marine officer.

1st part (down to: *"Be a Leader of Men."*)

2 ***Pick out the 2 words (an adjective and an adverb) which best sum up the reasons why he joined the Marines.***

2nd part (down to: *"They had given their all for nothing."*)

FROM THE CONTEXT

3 ***Show how the meaning of the key-sentence*** *"It dissolved"* ***is explained, clarified, made more precise by other words a little further down.***

4 ***Replace the words or phrases in italics by words or phrases from the text:***

1. This *account* of the end of the Vietnam war is *precise* enough for us to visualize what *happened.* 2. All those refugees *needed* help. 3. Soldiers and refugees *ran away* in disorder. 4. Towards *the end of the month,* the situation deteriorated. 5. *Paying no attention to* the consequences, I returned my campaign ribbons to President Nixon. 6. After *he left the Army,* he fought the American policy in Vietnam. 7. Do you think that personal acts of protest *are more effective* than *demonstrations?*

5 ***Right or wrong? Justify your answer.***

1. The war ended in a debacle.
2. The scenes the narrator saw revolted him.
3. The thought that men had died for nothing revolted him.
4. He threw himself whole-heartedly (with all his heart) into antiwar activities.
5. He sent back his decorations to President Nixon though he knew it would be without effect.

6 **3rd part** (down to the end).

The soldiers' mood (morale) has changed in the space of 10 years. Pick out the 2 words best expressing this change.

7 ***Sum up the whole text in 5 sentences.***

LANGUAGE PRACTICE

8 ***This text contains some information about the narrator's past. Ask (him, or the student next to you) as many questions as you can beginning with:***

When, how long, how long ago, etc. . . . .

COMMENT INTERROGER SUR LA DURÉE

How long are you staying?
How long did you stay in London two years ago *(combien de temps êtes-vous resté à Londres il y a 2 ans?)*
How long have you been waiting? *(depuis combien de temps attendez-vous?)*
Since when have you taken such an interest in social questions?
They're enemies. Since when? Since their first meeting.
How long ago, how long is it since...?
How long ago did you return your decorations? How long is it since you...? *(cela fait combien de temps que vous avez...?)*

9 ***Drawing on the text, make a few sentences beginning with:***

So far / Until then — he had led . . . .

So far / Until then — { he had had no chance of . . . . / he had had no opportunity { of . . . . / to . . . . } }

The Marines provided an opportunity for him to . . . .
The Marines provided him with an opportunity to . . . .
He must have thought: "It's the best chance I'll ever have of . . . ."
He must have thought it was . . . .

HOW TO EXPRESS DEGREE, INTENSITY, QUANTITY

so + adj. : his life was so dull that he was ready for any kind of adventure.
so much/so little + indénombrables : there is so much noise that we can't hear what he says. There is so little hope that you must be prepared for the worst.
so many/so few + dénombrables : there were so many refugees and so few junks that they could not all flee the country.

10 ***Fill in the gaps with:*** so, so much, so many, so little ***or*** so few:

1. He was . . . . sick of his safe existence that he joined the Marines.
2. There are . . . . refugees on this junk that it is bound to sink.
3. The Marines carried . . . . conviction and their propaganda was . . . . convincing that he enlisted right away.
4. The South Vietnamese Army offered . . . . resistance that the North Vietnamese Army soon reached Saigon.
5. There were . . . . helicopters that the evacuation took a long time.

11 ***Fill in the gaps as in the above exercise and complete:***

1. His disgust at American policies in Indochina was . . . . great that . . . .
2. The morale of the troops was . . . . low that . . . .
3. We had wasted . . . . money and lost . . . . men that . . . .

12 ***Make up a few more sentences on the same pattern.***

13 ***Drawing on the text, make a few sentences beginning with:***

He kept thinking about . . . . / (that) . . . .
He couldn't help thinking (that) . . . .
(=he couldn't avoid thinking, refrain from thinking).

THE GERUND

Voir p. 142

HOW TO EXPRESS ONE'S POWERLESSNESS *(son impuissance)*

It isn't much use, it's no use, it's no good, it isn't much good, what good is it, there is no point in, what's the point of + gerund.
It isn't much use protesting *(= ça ne sert pas à grand-chose de . . . .).* There's no point in protesting (= it won't help much).

14 ***React to the following statements, using some of the above phrases:***

Example: A. You should write a letter of protest.
B. Well, it isn't much use writing letters of protest.

A. You should send back your medals to the President. B. . . . .
A. You should write to your Senator. B. . . . .
A. Why don't you stage a protest march on the White House.
Go on . . . .

FORME D'INSISTANCE

Suj. + do, does, did + bv *(do...* accentué.*)*
S'emploie pour appuyer ce que vous dites et, assez souvent, pour contester le bien-fondé d'un reproche que l'on vous adresse.
I do want to go ! = How I want to go ! (Peut signifier selon le contexte : *Mais si, je veux y aller*).
Why didn't you protest? But I *did* protest *(= mais vous pensez bien que j'ai protesté).*
L'insistance peut également porter :
— sur l'auxiliaire d'une forme verbale : but I *have* seen him,
— sur un modal : you *must* work more,
— sur un auxiliaire placé en fin de phrase : he said he wasn't informed, but he *was*,
— sur une négation : « you tried to sap the morale of the troops ». « I did *not* »,
— ou sur tout autre mot dans une phrase.

15 ***Compose a few dialogues like this :***

A. You should have protested.
B. But I *did* protest, but there's no point in protesting, the proper authorities don't care a damn/who cares when you protest?/the authorities won't listen to you, etc. . . . .

A. The Vietnam Veterans should have launched an antiwar campaign B. . . . .
A. He should have joined the antiwar movement. B. . . . .
Go on . . . .

TOWARDS APPRECIATION

16 ***Complete the following :***

HOW TO EXPRESS ONE'S BITTERNESS

1. To think that . . . . 10 years ago.
2. Who would/could have thought, when we . . . ., that . . . .
3. Who cares how long . . . . / how many . . . . / how much . . . . / whether . . . .
4. They are cynical, and that's quite understandable . . . .
He/they is/are all the more bitter/cynical as . . . .
His/their bitterness is all the more understandable as . . . .

ALL THE + COMP.

Voir p. 161

17 ***Creative oral work :***

"The next day, April 30, the ship's captain announced that the Saigon government had surrendered to the North Vietnamese." Imagine how the narrator and the other evacuees took the news.

18 ***Paragraph-writing :***

"A diplomat from the American Embassy muttered to himself: it's the end of an era." Expand this comment into a paragraph of 10 lines.

19 ***Essay :***

A Rumor of War has been acclaimed as a classic of war, as the best book about Vietnam . . . .
Judging from this passage, can you guess why? Do you like war novels, war films? Why or why not?

I have a rendez-vous with death

I have a rendezvous with Death
At some disputed barricade,
When Spring comes back with •rustling shade
And apple blossoms fill the air—
I have a rendezvous with Death
When Spring brings back blue days and fair.
It may be he shall take my hand
And lead me into his dark land
And close my eyes and •quench my breath—
It may be I shall pass him still.
I have a rendezvous with Death
On some •scarred slope of •battered hill,
When Spring comes round again this year
And the first meadow flowers appear.
God knows 'twere better to be •deep
Pillowed in silk and scented down,
Where Love •throbs out in blissful sleep,
Pulse •nigh to pulse and breath to breath,
Where •hushed awakenings are dear . . . .
But I've a rendezvous with Death
At midnight in some flaming town,
When Spring •trips north again this year,
And I to my •pledged word am true,
I shall not fail that rendezvous.

Alan Seeger (1888-1916), an American poet, joined the Foreign Legion during World War I and was killed in action in July, 1916.

● **rustling** : *bruissant* ● **quench** : stop ● **scarred** : marked by battle ● **battered** : ravaged ● **deep pillowed...** : *que la tête s'enfonce dans un oreiller de soie et de duvet parfumé* ● **throbs out...** : *et l'amour palpitant s'apaise dans un sommeil béni* ● **nigh** (poetic) : near ● **hushed** : quiet ● **trips** : dances lightly ● **pledged** : given.

1 ***How does Seeger make the idea of death appear more poignant?***

2 ***Do the ideas expressed in this poem still seem valid to you or do they seem old-fashioned?***

SPOTLIGHT ON...

American cities

Columbia [kə'lʌmbiə], Maryland ['mɛəriland], Baltimore ['bɔ:ltəmɔ:], community [kə'mju:nəti], decade ['dekeid], purchase ['pə:tʃəs], terrain [te'rein], amenities [ə'mi:nitiz], architects ['ɑ:kitekts], engineers [,endʒi'niəz], developers [di'veləpəz], psychiatrists [sai'kaiətrists.U.S.:si'kai], psychologists [sai'kɔlədʒists], approximately [ə'prɔksimətli], oriented ['ɔ:rientid], cul-de-sac ['kuldə'sæk], utopia [ju:'təupjə], divorce [di'vɔ:s], idealists [ai'diəlists], actualization [,æktjuəlai'zeiʃən].

America does have one extraordinary success story in New Town creation. That is Columbia, Maryland, not far from Baltimore in the Washington-Baltimore corridor. While growing rapidly, it has kept its eye on the individual and his quest for community. It is dedicated to keeping everything it introduces to human scale.

It is the creation, primarily, of James Rouse, who has already bet $100 million (through his Rouse Company) that he can build a whole city of 100,000 people based on neighborhoods. It began about a decade ago when he managed to purchase a tract of rolling terrain of Maryland farmland and woodland about the size of Manhattan Island. More than a hundred and fifty separate negotiations were involved. [...] A major influence on his thinking was his wife, a remarkably appealing, thoughtful woman. [...]

At Columbia the Rouses are trying to combine the advantages of small-town life with the excitement and •amenities of city living. But how do you go about it? Rouse explains his approach this way: "If you want to plan out from the needs and •yearnings of the people the kind of community that will best serve and nourish their growth... where do you go? Whom do you ask? Architects, engineers, planners, bankers, and •developers are not the people who work intimately with people. Why not go to teachers and ministers and doctors, to psychiatrists, psychologists, and social scientists to plan a city?" [...]

Today Columbia is approaching 25,000 in population and by 1976, it is expected, will be approaching 75,000. But there are not now, and never will be if Mr. Rouse can help it, any of the familiar signs of urban •sprawl. This is because of the master plan. The plan calls for the center of the city to be separated by open greenery and water from the seven villages where people will live. And each village is being separated from its neighboring village by water, woodland, or a greenbelt. Four villages are already full or partially built. Columbia, incidentally, does not permit •billboards or •utility poles to •mar its landscape.

But the heart of the plan is that each village consists of approximately three neighborhoods built around the village center. The "neighborhood" is the basic building block of Columbia. It consists of from 800 to 1,200 families whose townhouses, detached houses, or apartments are oriented to a neighborhood center. Most of the homes are on cul-de-sac roads which are credited, among other things, with producing a low •burglary rate.

At each neighborhood center is an elementary school. It is within easy walking distance of most children in the neighborhood. Older children go to village schools within reasonable walking distance for them. Also at the neighborhood center is a •convenience store, a snack bar, a park, a playground, a swimming pool, and a meeting room. Some neighborhoods also have •day care centers. This kind of neighborhood is what James Rouse means when he talks about getting cities down to human scale. [...]

People have come to Columbia from more than forty states. Many are looking for a utopia. As a result, perhaps, the city has an above-average attraction for people who were having troubles where they came from and are seeking a fresh start. Some do not succeed in shedding their old problems—such as an ailing marriage, for instance—when they get to Columbia. This may help account for the fact that Columbia is believed to have a higher-than-average rate of divorce and separation. On the other hand it also attracts an above-average number of people who were lonely where they were. It is hard to stay lonely, unless it is an interior type of loneliness, in Columbia. The city also, at least in its early years, has attracted a large proportion of idealists questing for community and they are given an inviting place to seek actualization of their ideals.

VANCE PACKARD, *A Nation of Strangers*, © 1972

• **amenities** : parks, libraries, swimming pools and so on • **yearnings** : longings, desires • **developers** : *promoteurs* • **sprawl** : *étalement* • **bill-boards** : big boards used for publicity • **utility poles** : telegraph poles, electricity poles, etc. ; *poteaux* • **mar** : disfigure • **low burglary rate** : *avoir réduit le taux de cambriolages* • **convenience store** : shops open round the clock • **day care centre** : *crèche, maternelle.*

TOWARDS COMPREHENSION

1 ***Pick out the two words which best sum up the Rouses' purpose.***

2 ***Express the ideas differently, in several ways if you can.***

IN OTHER WORDS

1. While growing rapidly.
2. It has kept its eyes on the individual.
3. A major influence on his thinking was his wife.
4. Cul-de-sac roads which are credited with producing a low burglary rate (. . . . believed . . . . / . . . . supposed . . . . / . . . . in which the risks of . . . .).
5. It is within easy walking distance for most children in the neighborhood.
6. People who are seeking a fresh start (begin . . . . again).
7. Some do not succeed in shedding their old problems.

LANGUAGE PRACTICE

3 ***Make a few sentences on the following patterns:***

The Rouses'purpose is to . . . .
They're trying to . . . .
They're seeking to . . . .
He purchased a tract of land with a view to . . . . (+ gerund)
If so many people have come to Columbia, it is with a view to . . . ./in the hope of . . . .
The town has such good educational facilities that . . . .
The Rouses have created day care centers so that . . . .
. . . . in order to get away from it all.

HOW TO EXPRESS PURPOSE

Voir p. 151

THE PASSIVE VOICE

Voir p. 52

Compare

1. People think that he is right.
   It is thought that he is right.
   He is thought to be right.
2. People think that he was right.
   It is thought that he was right.
   He is thought to have been right.

On notera que si le verbe de la proposition complétive (introduite par **that**) *a une référence temporelle antérieure à celle du verbe de la proposition principale, on emploie l'infinitif passé* (have been right).

4 ***Give the two passive constructions:***

1. People say that Columbia is a success.
2. People believe that Mrs. Rouse played a major part in the creation of this town.
3. People think that the number of burglaries is decreasing.
4. People say that the rate of divorce is higher in Columbia than elsewhere.

5 ***Complete:***

1. It is considered that . . . .
2. It was proved that . . . .
3. It is expected that . . . .
4. It is presumed that . . . .
5. It is believed that . . . .

TOWARDS APPRECIATION

6 ***Is it surprising that Columbia should be a success?***

In Columbia they haven't made the mistake of . . . ./they have taken care not to . . . ./they have seen to it that . . . .

7 ***Why, in your opinion, is the quest for a utopia so widespread in the United States?***

If so many people . . . . it must be . . . .

8 ***Creative oral work.***

Is this town your idea of the ideal town?

9 ***Creative written work.***

You are polling those "idealists questing for community" to find out whether they are satisfied or disappointed (to poll people=to conduct a public opinion poll).

FOR FURTHER INFORMATION

A Texas City. That's busting out all over

Reprinted from "US News and World Report."

From refineries to cattle and fine arts, the oil capital of the world is spending its money in •headlong and noisy expansion unequaled anywhere else in the nation.

HOUSTON

This is not a city, It's a phenomenon [...]

An architectural critic once described Houston as "the city for the second half of the 20th century". An urbanologist, though, calls it "a pancake poured on a hot •griddle and trying to spread forever—and it can't be done".

Like it or hate it, no one questions Houston's vitality.

The downtown area glitters with new glass and steel monuments to commerce. Clustered along •freeways that •fan out from downtown are •soaring office parks and •sprawling shopping malls. A seemingly endless procession of suburbs and •housing developments blankets the flat prairie.

More than 1,000 people arrive each week, attracted by the hope of opportunity or by •the lure of a fast buck. The population now stands at 1.6 million. Another million live in the metropolitan area. The city has tripled in size since 1950 and will double again by 2000. Ninety-nine large firms have moved into Houston in the past seven years. [...]

Along with growth have come problems. Some •real-estate prices have tripled in only a few years. During rush hour, the freeway system looks like a vast parking lot.

While the crime rate is declining nationally, it is increasing in Houston, with a spectacular growth in murders and rapes. The •undermanned police force seems to spend more time defending itself from charges of corruption and brutality than fighting crime.

City leaders acknowledge these problems. But they admittedly place a higher priority on economic growth. [...]

All of this, says one official, keeps Houston "a city of open opportunity where anybody with work, imagination and •nerve can succeed".
Bankers claim that Houston's laissez-faire policies have helped to create more new millionaires and more new fortunes here in this century than in any other big city.

•A loan officer says that "anybody with a good idea and the •guts to put it into action can get the money to try".

Declares one newcomer: "I moved here six months ago with a wife, two kids and a used car. Now I owe a quarter of a million dollars".

Unlike many older cities, Houston takes pride in these newcomers and their success. "Most of us came here from the outside", explains banker Ben Love. "It would be selfish of us to close the door."

Newspapers are gorged with ads for job openings. Unemployment hovers around 4.5 percent. It would be even lower except that the boom has lured many •unskilled workers from elsewhere in the country. The skilled who want to work, however, usually are not unemployed for long.

Billed as the oil capital of the world, Houston has offices of 29 of the nation's 30 top oil companies, including the corporate headquarters of Exxon USA and Shell Oil Company. A fourth of the nation's refining capacity is in the area. The Houston Ship Channel is lined with 50 industrial •plants, most of them related to oil and petrochemicals. Oil •rigs are still •drilling in some parts of the city.

While oil is the lubricant that keeps the city •humming, there is a surprising diversity to Houston's economy. The port, third busiest in the nation, is the leading shipper of wheat and grain.

Houston's home county has one of the largest populations of cattle in the country. Rice fields that produce two crops yearly spread for miles just beyond the suburbs. [...]

Along with the investment opportunities have come 40 consulate offices, almost two dozen foreign banks and foreign businessmen by the thousands. A survey by the Houston school district found that 98 different languages—from Arabic to Yoruba—are spoken in the homes of school-age children.

"Houston went from a raw Texas city to an international city almost overnight", says Louie Welch, the five-time ex-mayor of Houston. "It became an international city without first becoming a national city, and that caught a lot of people in Boston, New York and Chicago by surprise."

Houston's economic explosion has produced a cultural explosion as well. The city's wealthy have long contributed heavily to the arts. Now, with additional funds from corporate newcomers, the city supports a symphony orchestra and repertory companies in ballet, opera and drama.

Art collecting has become a passion for some of Houston's newly rich. Private collections of painting and sculpture reportedly are among the most valuable in the world. •Sniffs a local art critic: "Artists may still show in New York, but they sell in Houston."

● **that's busting out all over** : *qui éclate de partout* ● **headlong** : thoughtless, hurried ● **griddle** : circular iron plate for cooking pancakes *(crêpes)* ● **freeways** : *autoroutes de dégagement (sans péage)* ● **fan out** : *se déploient en éventail* ● **soaring office parks** : high-rise office complexes ● **sprawling shopping malls** : *centres commerciaux tentaculaires* ● **housing developments** : *cités, lotissements* ● **the lure of a fast buck** (= dollar) : the irresistible attraction of making money fast ● **some real-estate prices** : *dans l'immobilier, certains prix...* ● **undermanned** : inadequate ● **nerve** : audacity ● **a loan officer** : *le responsable d'un bureau de prêt* ● **guts** : *assez de cran pour...* ● **unskilled workers** : not having training for a particular type of job ● **plants** : factories ● **oil rigs** : *derricks* ● **drilling**=drilling oil wells=*encore en activité* ● **that keeps the town humming** : that keeps the town in a state of activity ● **sniffs**=says with a sniff=in a disdainful tone.

SPOTLIGHT ON...

the energy crisis

Still a •Fuelish Paradise

With profound reluctance, the Wyoming •legislature last week abandoned its •drive to end the federally ordered 55-m.p.h. speed limit. No matter. Most U.S. drivers just laugh at the limit anyway. Meanwhile, homes and offices are overheated and empty skyscrapers are lit up like Christmas trees all night long. In short, five years after the Arab oil embargo, America remains a •profligate consumer and waster of energy. If all the barrels of oil that the U.S. uses in just one day were laid end to end, they would stretch from New York to Calcutta.

To reduce consumption will require not only heroic conservation but also costly development of domestic sources and a •switch to alternative fuels. Today's crisis may mean that needed reforms will get fresh attention and new support. "Congress now realizes the seriousness of the situation," says Energy Secretary James Schlesinger. "It is necessary to take advantage of short-term emergencies to •sell the need for unpopular measures."

Just about the most unpopular idea was Jimmy Carter's •thwarted proposal to impose a new tax on domestic •crude oil that would sharply raise the retail price. U.S. prices are low by world standards; a gallon of regular gas that sells in New York City for 78c costs $1.55 in Tel Aviv, $1.83 in Bonn and $2.09 in Paris. Economists, bankers and independent study groups like the Trilateral Commission agree that substantially higher prices would •drive home the reality of the energy crisis and the need to save. For that to occur, prices would have to rise drastically—probably to $1 or more a gallon for gasoline—and Congress is not yet willing to go that far.

Another unpopular measure to spare energy would be to moderate some antipollution regulations. The American Petroleum Institute estimates that the extra crude required to make •unleaded gas for new cars with catalytic converters amounts to 140,000 bbl. per day, and the Department of Energy figures that yet another 500,000 bbl. will be added to daily demand if the next legally mandated reduction in gasoline additives goes through as scheduled in October.

Restrictions on •strip mining will make it nearly impossible for the nation to meet Carter's goal of doubling production of coal to 1.2 billion tons a year by 1985. Demand for America's most plentiful fossil fuel is also being held down by expensive and rapidly changing regulations on the burning of coal. The Energy Department has tended to promote the use of coal, while the Environmental Protection Agency has been inclined to retard it. Nuclear power development has •slumped. A major reason: complex and long-drawn-out regulatory studies and hearings give a vocal minority a devastatingly effective forum for opposition and delay the building and licensing of new •plants for an average of twelve years or more.

At the same time, the U.S. has not fully exploited its domestic oil. Alaska's daily output could be increased from 1.2 million bbls. to 2 million, but there is not enough demand for the extra oil on the West Coast and it cannot be transported east easily or economically. The Jones Act requires that the oil be shipped on U.S. vessels and that jacks up the price to unacceptable levels. A pipeline to carry the oil across the country has been •stymied for six years. Initially the problem was just to get the necessary 700 federal, state and local permits. Now California environmental authorities are blocking construction of dock equipment to handle the crude, for fear that merely unloading and pumping it into the pipeline would pollute the air.

Other forms of alternate energy are •held up by the huge costs of development. This is particularly true of power from the sun, tides, waves and ocean currents, as well as oil from •tar sands and •shale. These sources stand to meet only a small part of the country's energy needs in the foreseeable future because the technologies are expensive, risks are high and immediate rewards are small. Progress may well require more Government grants, loan guarantees and tax incentives. What is needed to ease the nation's dependence on erratic foreign sources of oil is spending, sacrifice and compromise.

Time, February 26, 1979

● **Fuelish** : a pun on foolish. Think of a fool's paradise, to live in a fool's paradise = *se bercer d'un bonheur illusoire* ● **Fuel** : *carburant, combustible* ● **legislature** : *Congrès* (de l'état) ● **drive** : campaign ● **profligate...** : *le pays de la consommation effrenée et du gaspillage* ● **will require... a switch to...** : *implique que l'on se tourne vers des carburants de remplacement* ● **to sell the need for...** : to get people to agree to the need for... ● **thwarted** : *contrecarrée (par le Congrès)* ● **crude oil** : *pétrole brut* ● **drive home...** : *faire prendre conscience de...* ● **unleaded** = lead-free (lead : [led] *plomb*) *sans additif* ● **strip mining extraction** : *à ciel ouvert* ● **slumped** : has been slowed down, reduced ● **stymied** : *(le projet de construction est) bloqué* ● **held up** : temporarily stopped ● **tar sands** : *sables asphaltiques* ● **shale** : *schiste bitumineux.*

FOR FURTHER DISCUSSION

Individualisme et conformisme

Prise dans sa longueur et dans sa largeur — à plat — New York est la ville la plus conformiste du monde. A partir de Washington Square et si l'on excepte l'antique Broadway, pas une rue oblique ou tournante : une dizaine de longs sillons parallèles remontent tout droit de la pointe de Manhattan vers la rivière Harlem ; ce sont les avenues, elles sont traversées par des centaines de sillons plus petits qui leur sont rigoureusement perpendiculaires.

Ce quadrillage, c'est New York : les rues se ressemblent tant qu'on ne leur a pas donné de nom, on s'est borné à leur assigner, comme aux soldats, un numéro matricule.

Mais si vous levez le nez tout change : en hauteur, New York est le triomphe de l'individualisme. Les buildings échappent par le haut à toute réglementation urbaniste, ils ont vingt-sept, cinquante-cinq, cent étages, ils sont gris, bruns, blancs, mauresques, médiévaux, Renaissance ou modernes. Dans le bas Broadway ils se pressent les uns contre les autres, écrasant de minuscules églises noires et puis ils s'écartent, tout à coup, et laissent entre eux un trou béant de lumière. Vus de Brooklyn ils m'ont semblé avoir la solitude et la noblesse des bouquets de palmiers près des rivières dans le Souss marocain : des bouquets de gratte-ciel que l'œil cherche toujours à réunir et qui se défont toujours.

Ainsi l'individualisme américain m'est apparu d'abord comme une troisième dimension. Il ne s'oppose point au conformisme, il le suppose au contraire ; mais il est, au sein du conformisme, une direction nouvelle, en hauteur ou en profondeur.

D'abord il y a la lutte pour la vie — et elle est très âpre. Chaque individu veut réussir — c'est-à-dire gagner de l'argent. Mais il ne faudrait pas y voir l'avidité ou seulement le goût du luxe. L'argent n'est aux États-Unis, me semble-t-il, que le signe nécessaire mais symbolique de la réussite. On doit réussir parce que la réussite prouve les vertus morales et l'intelligence et aussi parce qu'elle indique qu'on bénéficie de la protection divine.

Et puis on doit réussir parce que, seulement alors, on pourra se poser, en face de la foule, comme une personne. Voyez les journaux américains : tant que vous n'avez pas réussi, il est vain d'espérer que vos articles paraîtront comme vous les avez remis. On coupera, on taillera. Mais si vous avez un nom qui fait de l'argent, alors tout est changé : on passera sans coupures ce que vous écrivez, vous avez acquis le droit d'être vous-même.

De même au théâtre : une dame très versée dans la littérature française et connue dans les milieux d'édition, me demandait si, éventuellement, j'aurais plaisir à ce qu'une pièce de moi fût jouée aux États-Unis. Je lui répondis que j'en serais heureux, si à ce qu'on m'avait dit, les metteurs-en-scène n'avaient pas l'habitude de remanier d'eux-mêmes le texte qui leur était soumis. Elle parut fort étonnée et « s'ils ne le font pas, dit-elle, qui le fera ? Ce que vous avez écrit est fait pour être lu. Mais ils doivent travailler dessus pour qu'on puisse l'entendre ».

Ainsi l'individualisme en Amérique, dans la lutte pour la vie, est surtout l'aspiration passionnée de chacun vers l'état d'individu. Il y a des individus comme il y a des gratte-ciel en Amérique, il y a Ford, il y a Rockefeller, il y a Hemingway, il y a Roosevelt. Ils sont des modèles et des exemples.

Jean-Paul SARTRE, *Situation III*,

1 ***Doesn't this text seem to be about two different subjects? And yet can't you find a connection between them?***

On the face of it . . . . there is no connection between the criss-cross pattern of . . . . and yet when we reach the conclusion . . . .

2 ***What does this text teach us about the American conception of life goals and life values?***

3 ***Sum up in 2 or 3 sentences from*** *"D'abord il y a la lutte pour la vie"* ***down to*** *" le droit d'être vous-même".*

4 ***What relationship is there between individualism and conformity? Are they two conflicting aspirations?***

5 ***Why do so many Americans want to achieve success? Is it out of love of gain? Is it to conform to*** *"the law of the fast buck"* ***(money easily and quickly earned)? Is it to acquire prestige?***

6 ***Why do so many Americans want to gain recognition and to make a name for themselves? Is it the same in France?***

7 ***What most surprised Sartre as a writer and a playwright?***

8 ***Can you see some differences between French individualism and American individualism?***

A. Choose the right answer :

1. He was .... tired that he had no strength left to talk.
   a) so. *b)* so much. *c)* so little. *d)* so far.
2. There were .... cars that they had to go on foot.
   a) so. *b)* so many. *c)* so little. *d)* so few.
3. He was arrested .... he was not guilty.
   a) as if. *b)* as though. *c)* whereas. *d)* although.
4. He behaved .... he had not recognized me.
   a) although. *b)* as though. *c)* while. *d)* whereas.
5. They are people .... it can be said that they are the victims of the system.
   a) of which. *b)* of whom. *c)* whose. *d)* whom.
6. There have been a number of local strikes .... were opposed by the national officers.
   a) all of whom. *b)* all of which. *c)* whose. *d)* none of whom.
7. From 1800 to 1914 some fifty million people left Europe, ... almost thirty five million came to the U.S.
   a) of which. *b)* all of whom. *c)* of whom. *d)* among which.
8. I'll join the union when .... 21.
   a) I'll be. *b)* I was. *c)* I am. *d)* I'd be.
9. He said he .... the union when he .... 21.
   a) joined .... is. *b)* had joined .... is. *c)* will join .... was. *d)* would join .... was.
10. The public authorities claim that the crime rate .... decreasing for the last few months.
    a) was. *b)* had been. *c)* has been. *d)* is.

B. Re-cast the second sentences, using the patterns : so/neither + aux (do, be, etc. ....)

1. "I'd hate to live in such a town." "I'd hate it too."
2. The soldiers fled the country. The refugees fled the country too.
3. She was bitterly disappointed. The other women were bitterly disappointed too.
4. "I'm not going to put up with racism." "I'm not going to put up with racism either."
5. "I don't think I could live in the South." "I don't think I could either."

C. Dans l'exercice suivant, vous proposerez le plus de solutions possible :

1. Vous demandez la permission d'organiser une réunion syndicale.
2. Vous tenez à parler au patron : d'abord vous formulez votre demande poliment, puis vous insistez.
3. Vous aimeriez savoir combien de temps la réunion va durer.
4. Vous demandez à l'un de vos amis depuis combien de temps il est membre du parti et quand il y est entré.
5. On vous accuse à tort de ne pas avoir assisté à un cours ou une réunion. Vous protestez.
6. Vous pensez que ça ne vaut pas la peine d'essayer de persuader vos parents de changer d'avis. Vous le dites.

ON YOUR OWN

I was going to do a fine job

It was a very cold night, the first night of the year, January Ist, and I had just come out of the Astor Place subway stop and was approaching the theatre where Kevin McCarthy and I were appearing in an off-Broadway production of *Marching Song*. It was my first play and we'd opened the week before. I was shivering from the snow blown down my neck by the bitter wind and also from spasms of fear, the first palpable fear I'd ever known. Twenty minutes earlier, I'd called my stepfather from a phone booth in Grand Central Station, clumsily pouring •change into all three slots because he was in New Haven and I didn't want him to think I was so cheap as to •call collect. I wanted to talk to him and, with luck, to Mother, or at least send her my love if she couldn't come to the phone; she was starring in a play that was trying out there before its New York engagement. He told me that she'd just died.

Mother dead. Impossible. I had called to say Happy New Year just in time to learn she was dead.

The vast dome of Grand Central Station closed down over me in the glass telephone booth like one of the jars in which we'd caught •fireflies as children, only without any holes punched out in the lid, so that I seemed to go deaf. There was absolute silence: the beating of my heart, the •static on the telephone, my stepfather asking me between sobs to take the next train to New Haven, and me saying no, I had to be at the theatre in a few minutes and would come up by late train that evening—all silent—and even when I pushed open the door for air, no sound anywhere in the entire huge space of the station with its magazine stands and hotdog stands and shoe-polishing stands and waiting rooms and information booths and entrances and exits filled as before with people, but people moving noiselessly, without echoes. I moved with them, my own footsteps on the worn marble floor... My mother, my very own mother, beautiful, warm, always more alive than anyone else in the world—alive in ways that nobody else dared to be—my mother, with her special gift for living and for giving that life to all the people who knew her and many who didn't, dead. There was only one other person in my subway car, a drunk swinging like a monkey from •pull to pull. He stopped right in front of me and leaned down, suspended by both arms. "Why," he asked in a •slur, puncturing the dense membrane of silence with such ease that I looked up at him as if he were a •wizard, "why would you be looking so sad, little lady? It's New Year's Day." He peered more closely. •"Drink up your cup fer auld lang syne. Here's to you—"

"Are we the only two people on this whole subway tonight?" I asked him as if it were the most profound question in the whole world, desperately wanting him to go on, to tell me everything about his life before we got to my stop.

"Everyone's home with friends," he said. "Celebrating."

"Why aren't you?"

"Well, you see, I'll ride to the end of the line. They let me sleep here."

"My mother died tonight," I informed him because he was a stranger. Water began to rise in his red eyes, and then he sat down quietly next to me, shaking his head. I was grateful he was there. We both waited until my stop came, and he stood up with me as I got off.

Then I climbed swiftly up to the street, my mind beginning to burn like a newspaper. First there was the energizing reassurance that I was on my way somewhere specific and solid and important. I was already •wound up to play my role before the phone call, and after the shock that followed, my instincts were sharpened by the freezing air; I was supposed to give a performance, and it would have to be an excellent performance. I kept sucking in air until my lungs hurt and then coughing it out like a steam engine; it reminded me that I was alive. It was much too soon for anyone involved with the play to have heard about her death, and I wouldn't have to say anything until afterward, if then. So I concentrated as Lee Strasberg had taught us, whispering over and over in a litany, "I must *use* this, I must *use* this," and finally arrived at the Gate Theatre, rather proud of myself, knowing, as seldom if ever one does, that I was going to do a fine job. Standing at the entrance of the theatre were the producer, the director, and the stage manager of the play, an unusual but not unreasonable place for them to be. Before I could say hello, Peter Kass, the director, •blurted out something to the effect that Father had just called the theatre to tell them what had happened, and to have them •cancel tonight's performance.

"What?" I remember asking, waves of anger striking me. "What?" He's got no right to do that, he's not the producer: it's *your* play."

BROOKE HAYWARD, *Haywire*

● **change** : *monnaie* ● **call collect** : *appeler en P.C.V.* ● **fireflies** : *lucioles* ● **static** : *parasites, grésillements* ● **pull** : *poignée* ● **in a slur** : in an indistinct voice ● **wizard** : magician ● **Drink up...** : (old Scottish song) : *(videz votre verre, buvez) « au bon vieux temps ».* ● **wound up** : tense and ready ● **blurted out** : suddenly said ● **cancel** : *annuler.*

1 ***What information would you choose from the following list in order to tell someone the main facts of the story?***

1. *Marching Song* was my first play.
2. I was shivering from spasms of fear.
3. My stepfather asking me between sobs to take the next train to New Haven, and me saying no, I had to be at the theatre in a few minutes and would come up by late train . . . .
4. I seemed to go deaf . . . .
5. My mother, my very own mother, beautiful, warm, always more alive than anyone else in the world . . . . dead.
6. "My mother died tonight," I informed him because he was a stranger.
8. I was grateful he was there.
9. There was the energizing reassurance that I was on my way somewhere specific and solid and important.
10. I was supposed to give a performance, and it would have to be an excellent performance.
11. I concentrated . . . . whispering, "I must *use* this," . . . .
12. I arrived, rather proud of myself, knowing that I was going to do a fine job . . . .
13. Father had just called . . . . to have them cancel tonight's performance . . . . "What?"" I remember asking, waves of anger striking me. "What? He's got no right to do that . . . ."

2 ***What might give the impression that the heroine is hard-hearted, putting her career before her family?***

3 ***What, on the contrary, shows that she is sensitive and acts out of delicacy?***

4 ***What shows that she, like everyone in show business, has a strong sense of duty?*** (Her mother was also an actress.)

In Mississippi : the K.K.K. suits up

In the room at the Holiday Inn in Tupelo, Miss., there are no towels. But there is a •fly swatter with a sign on its handle that reads FOR EMERGENCY USE ONLY. A visitor in Tupelo gets told again and again, "This town could be the model for all other Southern towns." On normal Saturday mornings, the main street fills up peaceably with shoppers, black and white, from all over Lee County, plus a •sprinkling of reverent tourists looking for Elvis Presley's birthplace.

On this Saturday morning, seven Ku Klux Klansmen are sitting at a table in the Holiday Inn coffeeshop eating •grits and scrambled eggs. Wives and children have been put at smaller tables. Out behind the inn, a dozen Mississippi state highway patrolmen are clustered around the •trunk of a car, joking and passing out bullets like jelly beans as they draw a day's supply of ammunition. "Did you count 'em? I give you 18, didn't I?" says one. "Now, you *know* I can't count," comes the reply. One of them tells me they are going to shoot •skeet. "Yeah, down at the •skeet march," adds another. Everyone finds this hilarious.

But the people of Tupelo, torn between •sheer incredulity and cold fear, do not find their situation funny. Tupelo (pop. 26,500) managed to tiptoe all the way through the '60s without any •civil rights trouble. Ever since spring, though, local blacks have been boycotting stores, first to protest the failure of the city to •fire two white policemen accused of beating a black prisoner, then, when the two resigned, to demand more jobs. And here is the Ku Klux Klan threatening a rally and •cross-burning outside town on the very day that the United League of North Mississippi, a black civil rights group, has scheduled a protest march. Both groups are •headed for the county courthouse. All week little Southern Airway's 18-seat Metros, have been pumping in from Memphis and Atlanta, loaded with Klansmen and league supporters from as far away as San Francisco.

In the Waffle House coffeeshop on Gloster Street, Jerry Rice groans, "I think there're a lot of people like me who just can't believe these guys are still running around in sheets. This is 1978." Walter Christian, a local insurance man, grumbles, "Why did they pick Saturday, anyway? Saturday is our busiest shopping day." Most people have a deeper fear. They are pretty sure there will be a shooting. "Life is cheaper down here than in the North," says Mel Blatt, who migrated to Mississippi from New York a few years back. "You don't have to do much to get yourself shot."

Just before noon, 600 blacks step out from the Springhill Missionary Baptist Church on Green Street and head silently for the courthouse, walking three abreast and carrying signs reading SMASH THE KLAN. A police helicopter whirls overhead. The 65-member Tupelo police force is stationed along the route. [...] "I walked •point for 31 days in a row in Viet Nam," says a young black marcher. "I was tense, but not scared. That's how I feel today."

Meanwhile, down at the auto center, 50 Klansmen are suiting up, clumsily pulling robes and •floppy •hoods on over their street clothes. Imperial Wizard Bill Wilkinson, has arrived in his long gray Chrysler. He likes to tell people it once belonged to President Nixon, and he usually adds regretfully that it is not bulletproof. A shotgun leans against the front seat. •Boasts Klansman Gene West of San Antonio: "We've got a whole arsenal of guns here today, *all* of them concealed."

The number of KKK members, of course, is secret. No wonder. Most of these Klansmen are older men, and the Klan's recent attempts to pretend that it is a political lobby like any other have been a transparent failure. "Let's face it," Wilkinson later tells me privately. "We had a couple of million members in the '20s, but we haven't got anywhere near that now. We just want to get the same attention from the press that the blacks get." Finally, 50 robed Klansmen set out for the courthouse, just as the United League is leaving it. Only a few minutes separate them, but it is enough to avoid a confrontation. "It's damned hot in here," one Klansman admits from under his hood. Many marching Klansmen are swinging •clubs, and some are carrying Instamatics and snapping pictures of the people, black and white together, packed three deep on the sidewalks. The jewelry store down the street suddenly closes up as the Klansmen approach.

At the courthouse, Mississippi Grand Dragon Douglas Coen, a •shipping executive from nearby Saucier, tells the crowd, "The Klan is here today, it was here yesterday, and it will be here tomorrow." Applause. "The Klan will be here forever!" Coen screams, and a few spectators hoot. Wilkinson takes the podium and is saying the KKK is basically a Christian organization when a white man yells, "You symbolize hatred! How can you call yourselves Christians?" Suddenly the crowd rolls forward as several Klansmen rush the •heckler. The police grab him quickly. A local newspaperman is arrested too, for taking pictures of the arrest, and both prisoners are •whisked off to jail.

The KKK evening rally starts at 7:30 in the auditorium at the edge of town. Police and Klansmen guard the entrance. A country band is playing old •stand-bys. Klan ladies in robes are selling hot dogs and Pepsi. Sometimes they sell KKK Tee shirts ($5) and belt buckles ($6), but tonight they simply hand out the KKK gift catalogue ("We have 400 items").

At dark everyone goes outside, where a 25-ft. cross swathed in kerosene-soaked rags stands in a field. •Rifle-toting Klansmen guard the perimeter. The others button up the face panels on their hoods. Wilkinson •rehearses them, but they are awkward at the ritual... Some cannot see too well through those eyeholes. Slowly they circle the cross, throwing torches at its foot. The flames race upward, and all salute by raising both arms, as if crucified.

JANICE CASTRO, *Time*, June 26, 1978

• **suits up** : *se costume* • **fly swatter** : a device for killing flies *(tapette)* • **sprinkling** : handful • **grits** : a sort of porridge • **trunk**=boot (G.B.) : *malle, coffre* • **skeet** : clay pigeon • **the skeet march** : the black protest march • **sheer** : *pure* • **civil rights trouble** : problems over desegregation, etc. • **fire** : dismiss, sack *(renvoyer, vider)* • **cross-burning** : see the end of the passage • **headed for** : the destination of both groups is... • **walked point** : (presumably) at gunpoint • **floppy** : hanging down looseley • **hoods** : *cagoules* • **boasts...** : **Klansman** Gene West boasts... =says proudly • **clubs** : *matraques* • **shipping executive** : *agent maritime* • **heckler** : a person who interrupts a speaker to ask embarrassing questions • **whisked off to jail** : *embarqués en quatrième vitesse* • **stand-bys** : *le vieux répertoire* • **rifle-toting** : carrying rifles • **rehearses them** : teaches them their roles.

■ ***You have been asked to give an account of this article to the other students.***

a. select the essential information (imagine the title you would choose for the article rather than the one given; what subtitles would you choose for the different parts of the article . . . .)

b. rephrase—in your own words—the most significant sentences.

c. Give the main facts (cut out unessential details!) and then try to bring out the general meaning. Does Janice Castro express her own opinion? Can we imagine whose side she is on from the way she writes up these events?

Taming a guide

In this place I may as well jot down a chapter concerning those necessary nuisances, European guides. Many a man has wished in his heart he could •do without his guide; but knowing he could not, has wished he could get some amusement out of him as a remuneration for the affliction of his society. We accomplished this latter matter, and if our experience can be made useful to others they are welcome to it.

Guides know about enough English to •tangle everything up so that a man can make neither head nor tail to it. They know their story by heart—the history of every statue, painting, cathedral, or other wonder they show you. They know it and tell it as a parrot would—and if you interrupt and throw them off the track, they have to go back and begin again. All their lives long they are employed in showing strange things to foreigners and listening to their bursts of admiration. It is human nature to take delight in exciting admiration. It is what prompts children to say •"smart" things, and do absurd ones, and in other ways •"show off" when company is present. It is what makes •gossips turn out in rain and storm to go and be the first to tell a startling bit of news. Think, then, what a passion it becomes with a guide, whose privilege it is, every day, to show to strangers wonders that throw them into perfect ecstasies of admiration! He gets so that he could not by any possibility live in a soberer atmosphere. After we discovered this we *never* went into ecstasies any more—we never admired anything—we never showed any but impassible faces and stupid indifference in the presence of the sublimest wonders a guide had to display. We had found their weak point. We have made good use of it ever since. We have made some of those people savage, at times, but we have never lost our own serenity.

The •doctor asks the questions, generally, because he can keep his countenance, and look more like an inspired idiot, and throw more imbecility into the tone of his voice than any man that lives. It comes natural to him.

The guides in Genoa are delighted to secure an American party, because Americans so much wonder, and deal so much in sentiment and emotion before any relic of Columbus. Our guide there •fidgeted about as if he had swallowed a spring mattress. He was full of animation, full of impatience. He said:

"Come wis me, genteelmen!—come! I show you ze letter-writing by Christopher Colombo!—write it himself!—write it wis his own hand!—come!"

He took us to the municipal palace. After much impressive fumbling of keys and opening of locks, the stained and aged document was spread before us. The guide's eyes sparkled. He danced about us and tapped the parchment with his finger:

"What I tell you, genteelmen. Is it not so? See! handwriting Christopher Colombo! write it himself!"

We looked indifferent, unconcerned. The doctor examined the document very deliberately, during a painful pause. Then he said without any show of interest:

"Ah—Ferguson—what—what did you say was the name of the •party who wrote this?"

"Christopher Colombo! ze great Christopher Colombo!"

Another deliberate examination.

"Ah—did he write it himself, or—or how?"

"He write it himself!—Christopher Colombo! he's own handwriting, write by himself!" Then the doctor laid the document down and said:

"Why, I have seen boys in America only fourteen years old that could write better than that."

"But zis is ze great Christo—"

"I don't care who it is! It's the worst writing I ever saw. Now you mustn't think you can impose on us because we are strangers. •We are not fools by a good deal. If you have got any specimens of penmanship of real merit, •trot them out!—and if you haven't, drive on!"

We drove on. The guide was considerably shaken up, but he made one more venture. He had something which he thought would overcome us. He said:

"Ah, genteelmen, you come wis me! I show you beautiful, oh, magnificent bust of Christopher Colombo!—splendid, grand, magnificent."

He brought us before the beautiful bust—for it *was* beautiful—and sprang back and struck an attitude:

"Ah, look, genteelmen!—beautiful, grand—bust, Christopher Colombo!—beautiful bust, beautiful pedestal!"

The doctor put up his eyeglasses—procured for such occasions:

"Ah—what did you say this gentleman's name was?"

"Christopher Colombo!—ze great Christopher Colombo!"

"Christopher Colombo—the great Christopher Colombo. Well, what did *he* do?"

"Discover America!—discover America, oh, ze devil!"

"Discover America. No—that statement •will hardly wash. We are just from America ourselves. We heard nothing about it. Christopher Colombo—pleasant name—is—is he dead?"

"Oh, *corpo di Baccho!*—three hundred year!"

"What did he die of?"

"I do not know!—I cannot tell."

•"Smallpox, think?"

"I do not know, genteelmen!—I do not know *what* he die of."

•"Measles, likely?"

"Maybe—maybe—I do *not* know—I think he die of somethings."

"Parents living?"

"Im-posseeble!"

"Ah—which is the bust and which the pedestal?"

"Santa Maria!—*zis* ze bust!—*zis* ze pedestal!"

"Ah, I see, I see—happy combination—very happy combination indeed. Is—is this the first time this gentleman was ever •on a bust?"

That joke was lost on the foreigner—guides cannot master the subtleties of the American joke.

We have made it interesting for this Roman guide. Yesterday we spent three or four hours in the Vatican again, that wonderful world of curiosities. We came very near expressing interest, sometimes—even admiration—it was very hard to keep from it. We succeeded though. Nobody else ever did in the Vatican museums. The guide was •bewildered—•nonplussed. He walked his legs off, nearly, hunting up extraordinary things, and exhausted all his ingenuity on us, but it was a failure; we never showed any interest in anything. He had reserved what he considered his greatest wonder till the last—a royal Egyptian mummy, the best-preserved in the world, perhaps. He took us there. He felt so sure, this time, that some of his old enthusiasm came back to him:

"See, genteelmen!—Mummy! Mummy!"

The eyeglasses came up as calmly, as deliberately as ever.

"Ah,—Ferguson—what did I understand you to say the gentleman's name was?"

"Name?—he got no name!—Mummy!—'Gyptian mummy!"

"Yes, yes. Born here?"

"No! '*Gyptian* mummy!"

"Ah, just so. Frenchman, I presume?"

"No!—*not* Frenchman, not Roman!—born in Egypta!"

"Born in Egypta. Never heard of Egypta before. Foreign locality likely. Mummy—Mummy. How calm he is—how •self-possessed. Is, ah—is he dead?"

"Oh, *sacré bleu*, been dead three thous' year!"

The doctor turned on him savagely:

"Here, now, what do you mean by such conduct as this! Playing us for Chinamen because we are strangers and trying to learn! Trying to impose your vile, secondhand carcasses on *us*!—thunder and lightning, I've a notion to—to—if you've got a nice *fresh* corpse, fetch him out!—or, by George, we'll •brain you!"

We make it exceedingly interesting for this Frenchman. However, he has paid us back, partly, without knowing it. He came to the hotel this morning to ask if we were up, and he endeavored as well as he could to describe us, so that the landlord would know which persons he meant. •He finished with the casual remark that we were •lunatics. The observation was so innocent and so honest that it amounted to a very good thing for a guide to say.

MARK TWAIN, *Innocents Abroad*

● **do without** : *se passer de* ● **tangle** : *emmêler* ● **smart** : *astucieuses* ● **show off** : *à se rendre intéressants* ● **gossips to turn out...** : *les commères à sortir par tous les temps...* ● **the doctor** : he is one of the tourists ● **fidgeted about** : *ne tenait plus en place* ● **party** : person, individual ● **we are not fools by a good deal** : we are far from being... ● **trot them out** : =let's see them ● **will hardly wash** : *ne tient pas debout* ● **smallpox** : *variole* ● **measles** : *rougeole* ● **go on a bust** : (a play on words) *faire la noce* ● **bewildered** : *dérouté* ● **nonplussed** : perplexed ● **self-possessed** : calm, self-assured ● **brain you** : hit you hard on the head ● **he finished with...** : *pour terminer, il déclara d'un ton détaché...* ● **lunatics** : madmen.

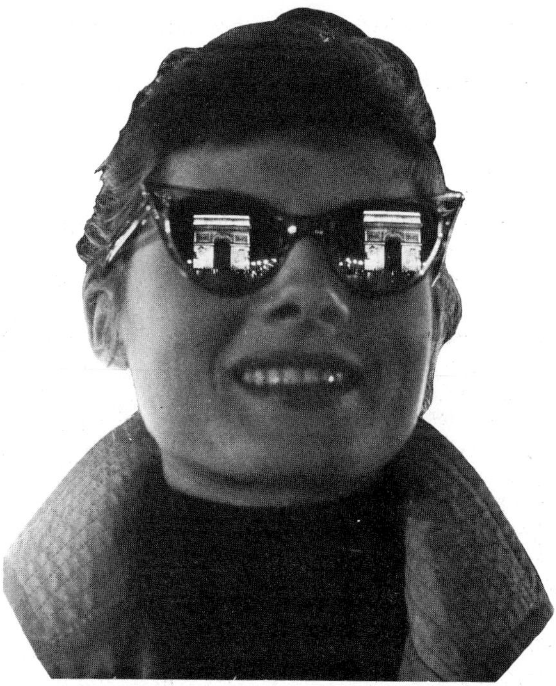

Good times, bad times

FIRST ENCOUNTERS WITH THE FRESHMAN EXPERIENCE

When college freshmen return home for Christmas, many tell their high school friends exotic tales of monstrous •midterms, •stadium-sized lectures, and •creepy roommates. Their stories may well be true. Freshman year is quite a challenge, and the first few months are usually the roughest. On the other hand, •survival rates are high, and most college students look back on that freshman year with pleasure—and a certain sense of triumph. To find out what it's really like, we asked freshmen on campuses across the country to •pinpoint some of the most typical trials, traumas and experiences of starting college.

If you've never been away from home before, living with a pack of •rowdy students can be quite a •jolt. Even for veterans of boarding school or summer camp, dormitory life requires compromises and adjustments.

The average dorm room consists of two •closets, two beds, two dressers, two bookshelves, two desks, two lamps and two roommates. Each unit comes complete with ceiling, floor, walls, a window and a door leading to endless other identical units. Some freshmen take one look and start thinking about off-campus apartments, but there are definite advantages to living in the dorm when you first come to college. It's easier to meet people, get involved in activities and find out what college life is all about.

One item conspicuously missing in most dorm rooms is the simple but vital clothes hanger. "I had to stuff my clothes under the bed for two weeks," confesses Betsy Murphy from the University of Denver. "All the stores in the area were out of hangers because everyone else had forgotten to bring them, too."

Roommates often pool their worldly goods—borrowing and lending hangers, clothes, records and typewriters. When things look worst, a good roommate can supply Kleenex, class notes, a shoulder to cry on. Yet living •that closely with a person whose habits don't match your own can cause major problems.

"My first roommate liked •acid rock and •being cool," recalls Betsy Murphy. "Unfortunately, I liked classical music and fine art. We just didn't mesh. One morning she played Peter Frampton at full blast at six o'clock. It was then that we realized it was just not going to work." Betsy promptly changed roommates, a very common practice in the first few months of the year.

Some students find a friend or high school classmate who is going to the same college and arrange to share a room. Many schools separate smoking and nonsmoking residents, while some try to match students by the likes and dislikes they listed on their application forms. In most cases, roommates have •a few squabbles but eventually end up getting along. [...]

The larger freshman classes are often conducted in arena-sized auditoriums that hold three or four hundred bodies. Terrified students frantically scribble notes while the far-off figure of the professor makes •garbled noises into a microphone. Fortunately, students quickly begin to make sense of all this. Large classes are split into sections run by Teaching Assistants (TA's), who are graduate students assigned to help students with questions and •projects.

There's a good bit of strategy involved in class attendance. Most professors drop hints about key points in their lectures that will appear, almost word-for-word, on the exam. Some profs repeat a point twice, say "this is important" or use the ever-popular "this will be on the test." Students learn to keep their ears open. Textbooks have their own clues; a common sight in college libraries is rows of students hunched over textbooks underlining the key words and phrases that appear in bold print or italics.

Back in the classroom, freshmen soon realize that they must race to take notes fast enough to keep up with their professors. " Learning how to take notes is important," observes Aggie Syracuse of Northwestern University. She found that at midterm time, her biggest problems stemmed from having incomplete notes.

This is one reason that so many students share their lecture notes and study in groups. In almost any dorm, there will be several students who are taking the same course and can band together to review class materials and assignments. "We get together and discuss things because there's no chance to talk in the big lectures," explains Susan Matteucci of Northwestern. "If you have never talked about the work before the test, it's hard to know whether your own thinking makes any sense." Each professor has his own style and expects something different from his students, so the main idea is to figure out what kind of research and thinking is required for each course. This is tricky, but most students learn to handle it within a few months. Dorm residents often vote certain hours in which there can be no loud music or noise. In general, students enforce these rules out of self-interest, because everybody has to study.

Despite careful planning and good intentions, however, there are times when preparing for a big exam means pulling an all-night study session. Some dorms keep 24-hour coffee percolators going during midterms and •finals, while college libraries extend their hours. •Propped up at the library tables you can find heavy-lidded students whose eyes are bloodshot from reading 438 consecutive pages of William Faulkner for an English Lit exam. Other students wander aimlessly around the campus, mumbling poetry or equations or both. Dozens of freshmen consider becoming plumbers or joining the Foreign Legion. It's •hectic, and a bit hysterical, but you get a lot of sympathy from fellow sufferers. Everybody lives through it, and usually celebrates the end of exams with •massive bouts of partying and solemn oaths that NEXT TIME they'll begin to study a whole lot earlier.

CHIP BERLET, Reprinted with publisher's permission from *Summer* © 1978 13-30 Corporation, 505 Market St., Knoxville, TN 37902.

Chip Berlet is a Chicago-based journalist who frequently writes on student topics.

• **midterms** : series of examinations at the middle of a school term • **stadium-sized lectures** : lectures, *(cours/conférences)* in an auditorium as big as a stadium • **creepy** : *un peu bizarres* • **survival rates** : *le pourcentage des rescapés* • **pinpoint** : pick out • **rowdy** : noisy • **jolt** : shock • **closet** : *placard, penderie* • **that closely** : as closely as that • **acid** : suggestive of psychedelic experience • **cool** : « *décontracté* », « *relax* » • **have a few sqabbles** : *se chamaillent un peu* • **garbled** : incomprehensible • **projects** : « dossiers » • **finals** : examinations at the end of the year at college • **propped up** : *s'appuyant sur leurs coudes* • **it's hectic** : *on est sous pression* • **massive bouts...** : *orgies.*

An interesting cure

Coming down on the subway last Tuesday, I noticed a man sitting on the seat opposite who appeared to be in a high state of nervous excitement. He was staring wide-eyed at one of the advertising cards in the car. I took my stethoscope and rushed over to him . . . .

The patient, whom we shall call Mr. X., was forty-four, and one of ten or fifteen children. His maternal grandfather had fought in the Civil War and after going through two battles developed a pronounced case of ennui and left the army. The patient's mother had suffered from Hodgkin's disease, Pott's disease, Alexander F. Detwiller's disease... The patient's retina reacted favorably to light...

Well, I wouldn't be too much alarmed about my condition, if I were you,' I told the patient. 'I can tell definitely, without even a detailed examination, that your condition is not serious. You are a trifle neurasthenic, perhaps. You know, America is getting to be a land of neurasthenics . . . . Now, you think that the morbid sensations you experience are peculiar to yourself. My dear man,' I told him, adjusting my glasses," there are many like you . . . . I am treating another man who is mortally afraid of closed places, such as the subway, or a crowded theater. We call that claustrophobia, for lack of a better name. Isn't it remarkable how far medical science has progressed? Now another very common fear is the fear of insanity. What makes you think you are going crazy?

He pointed a shaking hand at a •car advertisement telling about the virtues of a certain collar.

"It will not •wilt, •shrink, crack or •wrinkle," proclaimed the ad.

"Yes,' I said, sympathetically, what about it?"

"It's got me," he moaned. "I can't say it. Oh, my God, I can't say it! Take me away."

"Tut, my dear man, " I assured him. "You can say it, of course you can. You simply have a psychoneurosis. You have panic hysteria. You must have regular exercise, plenty of good, plain food, and eight hours' sleep at night. Now try and say it."

"It - it will not wilt, crink, wack or shrinkle," he said, and with a cry of despair flung his head into his arms.

"Come now, again," I urged.

"It's no use," he cried, "I've been trying to do it all the way down from Dyckman Street and I can't."

"Oh, now, be yourself!" I encouraged him. "Ready now. . . . . GO!"

"It will not wilt, kink, shack or winkle," he cried, and burst into a flood of tears.

It was rather a strange case. I asked him what dreams he had dreamed the preceding night. He said he hadn't slept. I saw that he had a marked Œdipus fixation. I thought I saw a way to help him. I would set an example for him, and leave the rest to suggestion. Suggestion is very powerful.

"Listen to me," I told him, "and learn how perfectly simple the whole thing is, when you have rid yourself of your inhibitions."

I continued in a firm tone: "It will not wink, shink, wack or crinkle."

Odd, I thought, but due, of course, to the power of suggestion. He had actually communicated a bit of his hysteria to me.

"Pardon me, my error," I told him, "I'll try again. It will not wilt, kink, wack or shinkle." Damn!

A faint smile played about Mr. X.'s mouth. His pulse was much better, his respiration was normal ....

"Now I'm going to try again," I told him, •briskly, "and this time watch me get it."

But I didn't.

Mr. X. was laughing heartily now, and appeared to be in a greatly improved frame of mind ....

•"Why, •it's a cinch," he told me. "All you have to do is to get rid of your psychoneurosis, and just read plain English. Listen: It will not wilt, shrink, crack, or wrinkle."

I was delighted. The man was cured. The passengers crowded about me, shaking my hand. Several lifted me to their shoulders and began singing "For He's a Jolly Good Fellow!" .... I consider the cure of Mr. X. one of the great triumphs of my career.

FRANK SULLIVAN (Abridged), *An interesting Cure*, From *An Encyclopedia of Modern American Humor*
Edited by Bennet Cerf. Doubleday & Company, Inc.

• **car advertisement** : an advertisement in the subway car (compartment) • **wilt** : *s'avachir* • **shrink** : *rétrécir* • **wrinkle** : *plisser* • **briskly** : *vivement* • **why** : *voyons !* • **it's a cinch** : *pas de problème.*

LOCAL 302 F.I.S.T. WORKERS ON STRIKE FOR A LIVING WAGE AND A UNION SHOP
WE ARE PICKETING CONSOLIDATED DON'T BE A SCAB F.I.S.T.
UNITED WITH F.I.S.T.

F.I.S.T.

Johnny Kovak, the son of a poor Hungarian immigrant, was so revolted by working conditions in Cleveland in the 1930s, and by the methods used to break strikes in spite of the N.R.A., (see A.B.C.), that he tried to organize a union of transport workers called the Federation of InterState Truckers (F.I.S.T.). He and his friends were brutally attacked by men in the pay of the bosses, the strike organized by F.I.S.T. was broken and one of Johnny's friends killed. On the day of the funeral, a gunman acting as an agent provocateur caused the death of four people in the procession and, in his rage, Johnny killed him by beating his head on the floor of a •boxcar. Finally, Johnny decided to ally himself with Vince Doyle and Babe Milano, both members of the underworld. Thanks to the support of their gang, F.I.S.T. became a powerful union and after some years Johnny was elected president. Senator Cole Madison is an ambitious man in search of an •issue that will give him enough publicity to run for the White House some day. As chairman of the Senate Rackets Committee he decides to investigate the links between F.I.S.T. and the world of organized crime. He begins by questioning Doyle, who "takes the Fifth" (see A.B.C.) Meanwhile, in order to put pressure on the White House, members of F.I.S.T. organize a monster traffic jam, paralysing Washington. The following week, it is Johnny's turn to be questioned by Cole Madison.

When Johnny walked into the Senate •Caucus Room with John Howard Harper and Bernie Marr, many of the spectators cheered. A few people had signs that said, "Stop the Railroad!" and "Senate •Scab Committee". A •trucker went up to Johnny and said, "They ain't gonna •push us." Johnny •grinned. "Goddamn right they ain't." He walked to the •witness table and sat down. Harper and Bernie Marr sat behind him in the first row. Johnny looked at Cole Madison and smiled. He took his coat off and draped it over an empty chair next to him.

"May we have quiet, please?" Cole Madison said. He banged his •gavel. "I'm sure we all want to hear every single word Mr. Kovak has to say."

The spectators fell silent. Johnny grinned.

Cole Madison smiled. "First, I'd like to thank Mr. Kovak, since it seems this •city is free this morning of the many truck breakdowns which took place the day Mr. Doyle testified." He paused and looked at Johnny. "It's nice of you to permit the nation's capital to go about its business today, Mr. Kovak."

Johnny grinned. "Anything I can ever do to help you with the law and order, senator. I'm always happy to do."

Madison smiled. "Thank you."

"Sure. Anytime you need help, senator, call me."

The spectators laughed.

"For the record," Cole Madison said, "can you state your full name, please?"

"John Joseph Kovak. But I've never gone by all that formality stuff, senator. Johnny sounds okay."

The spectators laughed.

"And where were you born, Mr. Kovak?"

"On •Ellis Island, right off the boat."

"Then you're a citizen of this country?"

"I got the birth certificate put up and framed on my wall."

"Your occupation?"

"I'm the national president, Federation of Interstate Truckers."

Some of the truckers in the audience cheered. Johnny smiled.

"Thank you," Cole Madison said. "That takes care of the formalities."

"You mean we can cut the •crap," Johnny said, "and get down to what we're here for."

The spectators roared.

Madison looked at him and smiled. "Yes, Mr. Kovak, we can." He paused until the room was silent.

"Mr. Kovak, how many members do you have in your union?"

"We've got more than 700,000 guys."

"And exactly what is the scope of your authority as president?"

"We represent the guys that drive your cabs, •haul your furniture, pick up your •garbage, and deliver anything else."

Madison smiled. "Is that all?"

"Everything that's on the road is mine."

"Yours, Mr. Kovak?"

"I get •raises for all of 'em."

"Doesn't it frighten you," Cole Madison said, "to think of all this power—in the hands of one man?"

"No."

"Why not, Mr. Kovak?"

•"I don't scare that easy, senator."

The spectators laughed.

"And the reason is that it's in *my* hands."

The spectators laughed.

"It might be bad if it got in the wrong hands," Johnny smiled.

"But your hands are the right hands?"

"My hands are the ones that got the guys the eight percent •hike."

The spectators laughed.

"I see," Cole Madison said. He smiled and paused, looking at his notes. "Now isn't it a fact, Mr. Kovak, that in your hands the Federation has gained a reputation for •strong-arm tactics?"

"All the guys in the union got strong arms, senator."

The spectators laughed.

"Please answer the question," Cole Madison said.

"I don't know what you mean, senator," Johnny said. "I'm just a street kid from the slums. Nobody's gonna put me down on my knees, I got a reputation for that. Nobody's gonna put my union on its knees, we got a reputation for that."

The truckers in the audience cheered.

"But isn't it a fact, Mr. Kovak," Madison said, "that many of your members, especially many of your business agents, have •criminal records?"

"Yeah, that's a fact, senator." Johnny smiled.

"You admit that?" Cole Madison said.

"Sure. Any union man that went out on strike in the 30s, 40s—he's got a criminal record. The policemen in those days didn't have nothin' to do except put us in jail. You •wanna find a good union man, senator, all you gotta do is make sure he's got an arrest record." The spectators laughed.

"Isn't it a fact," Cole Madison said, "that you've paid the •legal fees and continued to pay the salaries of those business agents arrested for criminal offenses?"

"Absolutely, senator. If he's a union man •in good standing, we'll pay those things, Every man is presumed innocent, until he's proven guilty. It's part of our Declaration of Independence, senator. You don't want me to start giving you civics lessons, do you. senator?"

The spectators laughed.

"No, I really don't want you to do that, Mr. Kovak," Cole Madison smiled.

The spectators laughed again.

"Why do you keep criminals—convicted criminals—in your union?" Madison said.

"I don't know what you're talkin' about, senator. I threw the Communists out."

"I'm talking about former •bootleggers, armed robbers, extortionists, musclemen—"

"Guys that lift weights?" Johnny said.

The spectators roared.

"Answer the question, Mr. Kovak," Cole Madison said.

"As long as they've done a good job for this union, senator, that's all I care about."

"Has Vincent Doyle done a good job for your union?" Cole Madison said.

•"Top notch." Johnny smiled. "The best."

"He's an official of your union?"

"General vice president."

"Mr. Kovak, do you believe a union official should be suspended from office if he refuses to answer questions on the grounds of self-incrimination?"

"That's right."

"If he •takes the Fifth?"

"It's part of the Declaration of Independence and the Bill of Rights. The whole package, right, senator? A guy's got a right to refuse to answer somethin' if he don't want to and I ain't gonna •can him for it."

"Why not, Mr. Kovak?"

"Why not? What kinda question is that, senator? You want me to •screw around with George Washington and Thomas Jefferson and all those guys that thought up that stuff?"

The spectators laughed.

"Mr. Kovak," Cole Madison said, "do you know Anthony Milano?"

"Yes I do."

"You're friends?"

"I know him."

"And your union recently gave one of Mr. Milano's concerns, Aquacade Entertainment Corporation of Las Vegas, a •loan of $1.2 million from your •pension fund?"

"That's right."

"Did Mr. Milano ask you to give him the loan as a favour to him?"

"He talked to the •trustees, senator."

Cole Madison smiled. "Did he now?"

"Yes he did, senator."

"You're one of the pension fund trustees, aren't you, Mr. Kovak?"

"That's right."

"And you voted to give him the loan?"

"Along with the other eleven trustees."

Madison smiled. "How long have you known Mr. Milano?"

"A long time."

Madison grinned. "Have you and Mr. Milano ever been involved in previous business transactions?"

Johnny hesitated. "I don't remember one."

"Let me try to refresh your memory," Cole Madison said. "What about the Haley Jukebox Company of Pontiac, Michigan?"

"I don't know nothin' about that firm," Johnny said slowly.

"Isn't it a fact, Mr. Kovak, that when you headed the midwest council of your union, you forced businessmen to buy Haley jukeboxes?"

Johnny grinned. "How could I force any businessman to do that?"

Madison smiled and looked at him. "By telling bar-owners that unless they used Haley jukeboxes, your drivers wouldn't deliver liquor to them."

There was a buzz among the spectators. Johnny looked slightly uneasy.

"No," he said, "that's not true."

"Isn't a fact," Cole Madison said, "That the Haley Jukebox Company was at the time owned by Mr. Anthony Milano—"

"I don't know nothin' about—"

"And Mr. Shondor Elik Gerky?" Madison said.

"I don't know nothin' about who owned some company I don't know nothin' about," Johnny said forcefully.

Madison grinned. "And isn't it true that to convince you to help his firm—Mr. Milano paid you a •bribe?"

There was a lot of noise among the spectators. Johnny looked startled.

"That's a lie," he said.

Madison paused. "A bribe in the form of a wedding present?"

Some reporters ran from the room. Johnny looked preoccupied. Madison banged his gavel for silence.

"It's a lie you dreamed up for your headlines," Johnny said.

"You're under oath here," Madison said sharply.

•"I don't give a damn what I'm under. I never took nothin' in my life."

Madison grinned at him. John Howard Harper got up from the front row, sat down next to Johnny, and whispered to him. Johnny did not acknowledge his presence. He stared at Madison and waited.

Madison looked up from his notes. "Have you ever killed anyone, Mr. Kovak?" he said. There was •pandemonium in the hearing room.

"You know goddamn well," Johnny said, "if you asked me that outside this room, I'd •sue you for everything you got."

"Is your answer no?"

"That's right."

"What's right?"

"That's right," Johnny said angrily. "I never killed nobody."

"You're sure?" Madison said.

Johnny said nothing. He glared at Cole Madison.

There was a long pause. Madison looked at his notes.

"Isn't it a fact," Madison said loudly, his voice crisp, "that you once killed a man with your own hands?"

Johnny looked •stunned. Several reporters ran from the room. Madison banged his gavel for silence.

"Isn't it a fact," he said, "that in the strike against Talbot's Consolidated Trucking, you beat a man's head against the floor of a boxcar and left him in a pool of blood?"

Johnny stared at Madison. Harper talked excitedly to Johnny. There was •bedlam in the room.

"Answer the question, Mr. Kovak!" Madison said.

Johnny kept staring at him.

"Answer the question!"

"I'm not gonna sit here," he shouted, "and be called all kindsa names and be accused of all kindsa things without—"

"Answer the question!"

"—•a shred of evidence. I tried to give you the truth. That's not what you want—"

"You're not answering the question!" Madison said.

"You wanna see your name in the paper tomorrow next to a •buncha crazy •charges!"

"We can hold you in •contempt," Madison said.

Johnny got up from the table. "The hell with you! Do anything you want! On my lawyer's advice, I'm not gonna answer nothin' more."

He turned and walked out of the hearing room as Madison pounded the gavel for order and the photographers tried to take his picture. Bernie Marr and Harper helped him through the crowd. Johnny looked dazed.

Madison watched him. "This meeting is adjourned," he said. "We will reconvene next Tuesday, July the 7th."

JOE ESTERHAS, F.I.S.T.

Joe Esterhas was born in Hungary but has lived in the United States since 1951. F.I.S.T. is his fourth book.

• **boxcar** : *wagon de marchandises (couvert)* • **issue** : *affaire* • **Caucus** : committee • **scab** : *« jaune »* • **trucker** : *camionneur* • **... push us** : *nous marcher sur les pieds* • **grinned** : *eut un large sourire* • **witness** : *témoin* • **gavel** : *marteau de président* • **this city is free** : see introduction • **Ellis Island** : in New York harbour, an island where immigrants had to wait before being admitted in the U.S. • **crap** : *foutaises* • **haul** : transport • **garbage** : *ordures* • **raise, hike** (U.S.) : rise (G.B.), a pay increase • **I don't scare that easy** : *il en faut plus pour me faire peur* • **strong-arm tactics** : use of force • **criminal records** : *casier judiciaire* • **wanna** : want to • **legal fees** : *frais du procès* • **in good standing** : having kept all the rules • **bootleggers** : traffickers in illegal liquor (whisky, gin...) during Prohibition (see A.B.C.) • **top notch** : *de première* • **takes the Fifth** : the Fifth Amendment (see A.B.C.) • **can him** : throw him out • **... screw around with...** : *c'est quand même pas à moi d'en remontrer à...* • **loan** : *prêt* • **pension fund** : *caisse de retraites* • **trustess** : *conseil d'administration* • **bribe** : *pot-de-vin* • **I don't give a damn...** : *je me fiche pas mal...* • **pandemonium** : noise and confusion • **sue...** : *j'intenterais un procès en diffamation* • **stunned** : stupefied • **bedlam** : tumult • **a shred of evidence** : an atom of proof • **a buncha** : a bunch of = a lot of • **charges** : accusations • **hold you in contempt** : *poursuivre pour outrage à la cour.*

The departure of Emma Inch

Emma Inch looked no different from any other middle-aged, thin woman you might glance at in the subway or deal with across the counter of some small store in a country town, and then forget forever. Her hair was •drab and unabundant, her face made no impression on you, her voice I don't remember—it was just a voice. She came to us with a letter of recommendation from some acquaintance who knew that we were going to Martha's Vineyard for the summer and wanted a cook. We took her because there was nobody else, and she seemed all right. She had arrived at our hotel in Forty-fifth Street the day before we were going to leave and we got her a room for the night, because she lived •way uptown somewhere. She said she really ought to go back and give up her room, but I told her I'd fix that.

Emma Inch had a big •scuffed brown suitcase with her, and a Boston bull terrier. His name was Feely. Feely was seventeen years old and he grumbled and growled and •snuffled all the time, but we needed a cook and we agreed to take Feely along with Emma Inch, if she would take care of him and keep him out of the way. It turned out to be easy to keep Feely out of the way because he would lie •grousing anywhere Emma put him until she came and picked him up again. I never saw him walk. Emma had owned him, she said, since he was a •pup. He was all she had in the world, she told us, with a mist in her eyes. I felt embarrassed but not touched. I didn't see how anybody could love Feely.

I didn't lose any sleep about Emma Inch and Feely the night of the day they arrived, but my wife did. She told me next morning that she had lain awake a long time thinking about the cook and her dog, because she felt kind of •funny about them. She didn't know why. She just had a feeling that they were kind of funny. When we were all ready to leave—it was about three o'clock in the afternoon, for we had kept putting off the packing—I phoned Emma's room, but she didn't answer. It was getting late and we felt nervous—the Fall River boat would sail in about two hours. We couldn't understand why we hadn't heard anything from Emma and Feely. It wasn't until four o'clock that we did. There was a small rap on the door of our bedroom and I opened it and Emma and Feely were there, Feely in her arms, •snuffing and snaffling, as if he had been swimming a long way.

My wife told Emma to get her bag packed, we were leaving in a little while. Emma said her bag *was* packed, except for her electric •fan, and she couldn't get that in. "You won't need an electric fan at the Vineyard," my wife told her. "It's cool there, even during the day, and it's almost cold at night. Besides, there is no electricity in the cottage we are going to." Emma Inch seemed distressed. She studied my wife's face. "I'll have to think of something else then," she said. "Mebbe I could let the water run all night." We both sat down and looked at her. Feely's asthmatic noises were the only sounds in the room for a while. "Doesn't that dog ever stop that?" I asked, irritably.

"Oh, he's just talking," said Emma. "He talks all the time, but I'll keep him in my room and he won't bother you none." "Doesn't he bother you?" I asked. "He *would* bother me," said Emma, "at night, but I put the •electric fan on and keep the light burning. He don't make so much noise when it's light, because he don't •snore. The fan kind of keeps me from noticing him. I put a piece of cardboard, like, where the fan hits it and then I don't notice Feely so much. Mebbe I could let the water run in my room all night instead of the fan." I said "Hmmm" and got up and mixed a drink for my wife and me—we had decided not to have one till we got on the boat, but I thought we'd better have one now. My wife didn't tell Emma there would be no running water in her room at the Vineyard.

"We've been worried about you, Emma," I said. "I phoned your room but you didn't answer." "I never answer the phone," said Emma, "because I always get a shock. I wasn't there anyways. I couldn't sleep in that room. I went back to Mrs. McCoy's on Seventy-eighth Street." I lowered my glass. "You went back to Seventy-eighth Street last *night?*" I demanded. "Yes, sir," she said. "I had to tell Mrs. McCoy I was going away and wouldn't be there any more for a while—Mrs. McCoy's the landlady. Anyways, I never sleep in a hotel." She looked around the room. "They burn down," she told us. It came out that Emma Inch had not only gone back to Seventy-eighth Street the night before but had walked all the way, carrying Feely. It had taken her an hour or two, because Feely didn't like to be carried very far at a time, so she had had to stop every block or so and put him down on the sidewalk for a while. It had taken her just as long to walk back to our hotel, too; Feely, it seems, never got up before afternoon—that's why she was so late. She was sorry. My wife and I finished our drinks, looking at each other, and at Feely.

Emma Inch didn't like the idea of riding to Pier 14 in a taxi, but after ten minutes of cajoling and pleading she finally got in. "Make it go slow," she said. We had enough time, so I asked the driver to take it easy. Emma kept getting to her feet and I kept pulling her back onto the seat. "I never been in an automobile before," she said. "It goes awful fast." Now and then she gave a little squeal of fright. The driver turned his head and grinned. "You're O.K. wit' me, lady," he said. Feely growled at him. Emma waited until he had turned away again, and then she leaned over to my wife and whispered. "They all take cocaine," she said. Feely began to make a new sound—a kind of high, •agonized yelp. "He's singing," said Emma. She gave a strange little giggle, but the expression of her face didn't change. "I wish you had put the Scotch where we could get at it," said my wife.

If Emma Inch had been afraid of the taxicab, she was terrified by the *Priscilla* of the Fall River Line. "I don't think I can go," said Emma. "I don't think I could get on a boat. I didn't know they were so big." She stood rooted to the pier, clasping Feely. She must have squeezed him too hard, for he screamed—he screamed like a woman. We all jumped. "It's his ears," said Emma. "His ears hurt." We finally got her on the boat, and once aboard, in the salon, her terror abated somewhat. Then the three parting blasts of the boat whistle rocked lower Manhattan. Emma Inch leaped to her feet and began to run, letting go of her suitcase (which she had refused to give up to a porter) but holding onto Feely. I caught her just as she reached the •gangplank. The ship was on its way when I let go of her arm.

It was a long time before I could get Emma to go to her •stateroom, but she went at last. It was an inside stateroom, and she didn't seem to mind it. I think she was surprised to find that it was like a room, and had a bed and a chair and a washbowl. She put Feely down on the floor. "I think you'll have to do something about the dog," I said. "I think they put them somewhere and you get them when you get off." "No, they don't," said Emma. I guess, in this case, they didn't. I don't know. I shut the door on Emma Inch and Feely, and went away. My wife was drinking straight Scotch when I got to our stateroom.

The next morning, cold and early, we got Emma and Feely off the *Priscilla* at Fall River and over to New Bedford in a taxi and onto the little boat for Martha's Vineyard. Each move was as difficult as getting a combative drunken man out of the night club in which he fancies he has been insulted. Emma sat in a chair on the Vineyard boat, as far away from sight of the water as she could get, and closed her eyes and held onto Feely. She had thrown a coat over Feely, not only to keep him warm but to prevent any of the ship's officers from taking him away from her. I went in from the deck at intervals to see how she was. She was all right, or at least all right for her, until five minutes before the boat reached the dock at Woods Hole, the only stop between New Bedford and the Vineyard. Then Feely got sick. Or at any rate Emma said he was sick. He didn't seem to me any different from what he always was—his breathing was just as abnormal and irregular. But Emma said he was sick. There were tears in her eyes. "He's a very sick dog, Mr. Thurman," she said. "I'll have to take him home." I knew by the way she said "home" what she meant. She meant Seventy-eighth Street.

The boat tied up at Woods Hole and was motionless and we could hear the racket of the deckhands on the dock loading freight. "I'll get off here," said Emma, firmly, or with more firmness, anyway, than she had shown yet. I explained to her that we would be home in half an hour, that everything would be fine then, everything would be wonderful. I said Feely would be a new dog. I told her people sent sicks dogs to Martha's Vineyard to be cured. But it was no good. "I'll have to take him off here," said Emma. "I always have to take him home when he is sick." I talked to her eloquently about the loveliness of Martha's Vineyard and the nice houses and the nice people and the wonderful accommodations for dogs. But I knew it was useless. I could tell by looking at her. She was going to get off the boat at Woods Hole.

"You really can't do this," I said, grimly, shaking her arm. Feely snarled weakly. "You haven't any money and you don't know where you are. You're a long way from New York. Nobody ever got from Woods Hole to New York alone." She didn't seem to hear me. She began walking toward the stairs leading to the •gang plank, •crooning to Feely. "You'll have to go all the way back on boats," I said, "or else take a train, and you haven't any money. If you are going to be so stupid and leave us now, I can't give you any money." "I don't want any money, Mr. Thurman," she said. "I haven't earned any money." I walked along in irritable silence for a moment; then I gave her some money. I made her take it. We got to the gangplank. Feely snaffled and gurgled. I saw now that his eyes were a little red and moist. I know it would do no good to summon my wife—not when Feely's health was •at stake. "How do you expect to get home from here?" I almost shouted at Emma Inch as she moved down the gangplank. "You're way out on the end of Massachusetts." She stopped and turned around. "We'll walk," she said. "We like to walk, Feely and me." I just stood still and watched her go.

When I went up on deck, the boat was clearing for the Vineyard. " How's everything?" asked my wife. I waved a hand in the direction of the dock. Emma Inch was standing there, her suitcase at her feet, her dog under one arm, waving goodbye to us with her free hand. I had never seen her smile before, but she was smiling now.

● **drab** : *terne* ● **way uptown** : a long way from the town centre ● **scuffed** : *éraflée* ● **snuffled** : breathed noisily ● **grouse** : *grogner* ● **pup** : young dog ● **she felt kind of funny about them** : *ils lui avaient paru un peu bizarres* ● **snuffling and snaffling** : *reniflant et renâclant* ● **electric fan** : *ventilateur électrique* ● **snore** : *ronfler* ● **agonized yelp** : *jappement déchirant* ● **gangplank** : *passerelle* ● **stateroom** : private cabin ● **crooning** : singing softly ● **... at stake** : *s'il y allait de.*

The third day after Christmas

Donald Efaw, who was six years old plus three months, was standing on the corner of 3rd Avenue and 37th Street where his angry father Harry had asked him an hour ago to wait a minute while he stepped into the store for some stuff for Alice who was sick in bed, coughing and crying. Alice was three and she had kept everybody awake all night. Donald's angry father Harry hadn't liked the noise at all and he'd blamed it on Mama. Mama's name was Mabelle. "Mabelle Louisa Atkins Fernandez before I married Harry Efaw," the boy had once heard his mother say to a man who had come to fix the broken window in the kitchen. "My husband is part-Indian on his mother's side, and I'm part-Indian on my father's. Fernandez sounds more Spanish or Mexican than Indian, but my father was part-Indian just the same. We never lived among them, though, the way some part-Indians do. We always lived in cities."

The boy wore overalls and an old •checkered coat his father had outgrown that might have been an overcoat for him if it hadn't been so ill-fitting. The sleeves had been cut to fit the boy, but that was all. The pockets were out of reach, so the boy rubbed his hands to keep them warm. It was eleven o'clock in the morning now.

Donald's father had gone into the place, and pretty soon he would come out and they'd walk home and Mama would give Alice some of the stuff—milk and medicine—and she'd stop crying and coughing and Mama and Papa would stop fighting.

The place was Haggerty's. It had an entrance on the corner and another on the side street. Harry Efaw had used the 37th Street exit five minutes after he had gone in. He hadn't *forgotten* the boy in the street, he had just wanted to get away from him for awhile, and from the rest of them, too. He had had one little •shot of rye that had cost too much and that was all. It had cost a quarter and that was too much for one little shot of rye. He had gulped the drink down and hurried out of the place and walked away, planning to come back after a few minutes to pick the boy up and then buy the food and medicine and go back home to see if something could be done about the little girl's sickness, but somehow or other he had gone right on walking.

At last Donald stepped into the place and saw that it was not like any other store he had ever seen. The man in the white coat looked at him and said, "You can't come in here. Go on home."

"Where's my father?"

"Is this boy's father in the house?" the man called out, and everybody in the place, seven men, turned and looked at Donald. They looked only a moment and then went back to their drinking and talking.

"Your father's not here," the man said, "whoever he is."

"Harry," Donald said. "Harry Efaw."

"I don't know anybody named Harry Efaw. Now, go on home."

"He told me to wait outside a minute."

"Yes, I know. Well, a lot of fellows come in here for a drink and then go. I guess that's what he did. If he told you to wait outside, you'd better do it. You can't stay in here."

"It's cold outside."

"I know it's cold outside," the bartender said. "But you can't stay in here. Wait outside like your father told you to, or go home."

"I don't know how," the boy said.

"Do you know the address?"

The boy obviously didn't know the meaning of the question, so the bartender tried to put it another way.

"Do you know the number of the house and the name of the street?"

"No. We walked. We came for medicine for Alice."

"Yes, I know," the bartender said patiently. "And I know it's cold outside, too, but you'd better get out of here just the same. I can't have small boys coming into this place." A sickly man of sixty or so who was more than half-drunk and half-dead got up from his table and went to the bartender.

"I'll be glad to get the boy home if he can show me the way."

"Sit down," the bartender said. "The boy doesn't know the way."

"Maybe he does," the man said. "I've had children of my own and the street's no place for a small boy. I'll be glad to get him home to his mother."

"I know," the bartender said. "But just go sit down."

"I'll take you home, sonny," the old man said.

"Sit down," the bartender almost shouted, and the old man turned in astonishment.

"What do you take me for, anyway?" he said softly. "The boy's scared and cold and needs his mother."

"Will you please sit down?" the bartender said. "I know all about the boy. And you're not the man to get him home to his mother, either."

"*Somebody's* got to get him home to his mother," the old man said softly, and then •belched. He was in the kind of worn and •lumpy clothing the bartender knew had been given to him by a charitable institution. He probably had another thirty or forty cents to spend for beer, money he'd gotten by begging, most likely.

"It's the third day after Christmas," the old man went on. "It's not so long after Christmas any of us has got right to forget trying to help a small boy home."

"Ah, what's the matter?" another drinker asked from his chair.

"Nothing's the matter," the bartender said. "This boy's father asked him to wait for him outside, that's all." The bartender turned to Donald Efaw. "If you don't know how to get home, just wait outside like your father told you to— and pretty soon he'll be back and he'll take you home. Now, go on and get out of here."

The boy left the place and began standing where he had already stood more than an hour. The old man began to follow the boy. The bartender swung himself over the bar, caught the old man by the shoulders at the swinging doors, twisted him around and walked him back to his chair.

"Now sit down," he said softly. "It's not your place to worry about the boy. Keep your worry for yourself. I'll see that nothing happens to him."

"What do you take me for, anyway?" the old man said again.

At the swinging doors for a look up and down the street the bartender, a short, heavy Irishman in his early fifties, turned and said, "Have you had a look at yourself in a mirror lately? You wouldn't get to the next corner holding the hand of a small boy."

"Why not?" the old man demanded.

"Because you don't look like any small boy's father or grandfather or friend or anything else."

"I've had children of my own," the old man said feebly.

"I know," the bartender said. "But just sit still. Some people are allowed to be kind to children and some aren't, that's all."

He took a bottle of beer to the old man's table and set it down by the old man's empty glass. "Here's a bottle •on me," he said. "I'm allowed to be kind to old men like yourself once in awhile, and you're allowed to be kind to bartenders like me •once in awhile, but you're not allowed to be kind to a small boy whose father is some place in the neighborhood, most likely. Just sit still and drink your beer."

"I don't want your dirty beer," the old man said. "You can't hold *me* prisoner in your dirty saloon."

"Just sit still until the boy's father comes and takes him home, and then you can get out of here as fast as you like."

"I want to get out of here *now*," the old man said. "I don't have to take insults from anybody in this whole world. If I told you a few things about who I am I guess you wouldn't talk to me the way you've been talking."

"All right," the bartender said. He wanted to •keep things from getting out of hand, he didn't want •a fuss, and he felt he might be able to •humor the old man out of his wish to be helpful to the boy. "Tell me a few things about who you are and maybe I won't talk to you the way I've been talking."

"I'll say you won't," the old man said.

The bartender was glad to notice that the old man was pouring beer into his glass. He watched the old man drink the top third of the glass, and then the old man said, "My name is Algayler, that's what it is."

He drank some more of his beer and the bartender waited for him to go on. He was standing at the end of the bar now, so he could keep his eye on the boy in the street. The boy was rubbing his hands together, but it was all right. He was a boy who had been •toughened by hard times of all kinds, and this waiting in the street for his father wasn't going to be too much for him.

"Algayler," the old man said again, and he went on softly. The bartender couldn't hear what he was saying now, but that didn't matter because he knew the old man would be all right from now on. He was back in himself altogether again where he belonged.

A woman who had been coming to the saloon every day now around noon for a week or so came in with a fox-terrier on a leash and said, "There's a small boy standing out front in the cold. Now, whose boy is he?"

The woman •clamped her false teeth together as she looked over the drinkers, and her dog danced around her feet getting used to the warmth of the place.

"He's all right," the bartender said. "His father's gone on an errand. He'll be back in a minute."

"Well, he'd *better* be back in a minute," the woman said. "If there's one thing I can't stand it's a father who leaves a boy standing in the street."

"Algayler," the old man turned and said in a very loud voice.

"What did you say to me, you drunken old •bum?" the woman said. Her dog moved toward the old man, tightening the leash, and barked several times.

"It's all right," the bartender said politely. "He only said his name."

"Well, it's a good thing he didn't say something else," the woman said, clamping down on her false teeth again.

The dog calmed down a little, too, but still had to dance about because of the warmth. He was wearing the coat she always strapped on him in the cold weather, but it never did his feet any good, and it was his feet that felt the cold the most.

The bartender poured beer into a glass for the woman and she began to drink, standing at the bar. Finally, she got up on a stool to take things easy, and the dog stopped dancing to look around the place.

The bartender took Algayler another bottle of •free beer and without a word, or even a glance, they were agreed that they could get along on this basis.

A man of thirty-five or so whose face and neatly trimmed moustache seemed faintly familiar came in from the 37th Street entrance and asked for a shot of bourbon, and after the drink had been poured, the bartender said very quietly so that no one else would hear him, "That wouldn't be your son standing outside, would it?"

The man had lifted the small glass to his lips, looking at it, but now, having heard the question, he looked away from the glass to the bartender, then swallowed the drink quickly and without a word moved to the front window to have a look at the boy. At last he turned to the bartender and shook his head. He wanted another and had it and then went out and walked past the boy, hardly noticing him.

After finishing the second free bottle of beer Algayler began to •doze in his chair, and the woman with the fox-terrier began to tell the bartender something about her dog.

"I've had Tippy all his life," she said, "and we've been together the whole time. Every minute of it."

A fellow under thirty in pretty good clothes came in at a quarter after twelve and asked for Johnny Walker Black Label over ice with a •water chaser, but quickly settled for

Red Label, and after finishing the drink said, "Where's the television?"

"We don't have any."

"No television?" the man said cheerfully. "What kind of a bar is this, anyway? I didn't know there was a bar in New York that didn't have a television. What do people look at in here, anyway?"

"All we've got is the phonograph."

"Well, O.K., then," the man said. "If that's all you've got, that's all you've got. What would you like to hear?"

•"Suit yourself."

The man studied the titles of the various records that were in the machine and then said, "How about Benny Goodman doing •*Jingle Bells*?"

"Suit yourself," the bartender said.

"O.K.," the man said, putting a nickel into the slot. "*Jingle Bells* it is."

The machine began to work as the man sat at the bar again and the bartender fixed him another Red Label over ice. The music began and after listening a moment the man said

"That ain't *Jingle Bells*, that's something else."

"You pressed the wrong number."

"Well," the man said pleasantly, "no matter. No matter at all. That ain't a bad number, either."

The boy came in again but the machine was making too much noise for the bartender to be able to tell him to get out without shouting at him, so he went to the boy and led him out to his place in the street.

"Where's my father?" Donald Efaw said.

"He'll be back in a minute. You just stay out here."

This went on until half past two when snow began to fall. The bartender chose an appropriate moment to go out and bring the boy in. He began to make trips to the kitchen fetching the boy things to eat. The boy sat on a box, behind the bar, out of sight, and ate off the top of another box.

After eating, the boy began to fall asleep, so the bartender fixed him a place to stretch out on some empty beer cases, using his overcoat for a mattress and three old aprons out of the laundry bag and his street coat for covering. He and the boy hadn't said a word since he had brought the boy in, and now, stretched out, on the verge of falling asleep, the boy almost smiled and wept at the same time.

The morning drinkers were gone now, including Algayler and the woman with the false teeth and the fox terrier and the •trade changed once again while the boy slept.

It was a quarter to five when the boy sat up. He remembered the bartender after a moment, but again they didn't speak. He sat up, as if he were in his bed at home, and then, after dreaming with his eyes open for ten minutes, stepped down.

It was dark outside now and it was snowing the way it does in a storm. The boy watched the snow a moment and then turned and looked up at the bartender.

"Did my father come back?" he said.

"Not yet," the bartender said.

He knelt down to talk to the boy.

"I'll be through work in a few minutes, and if you can show me your house when you see it, I'll try to get you home."

"Didn't my father come back?"

"No, he didn't. Maybe he forgot where he left you."

"He left me right here," the boy said, as if that were something impossible to forget. "Right out front."

"I know."

The night bartender came out of the kitchen in his white coat and noticed the boy.

"Who's that, John? One of your kids?"

"Yeah," the bartender said because he didn't want to try to tell the other bartender what had happened.

"Where'd he get that coat?"

The boy •winced and looked at the floor.

"It's one of *my* old coats," the bartender said. "He's got his own of course, but this is the coat he *likes* to wear."

The boy looked up at the bartender suddenly, •amazed.

"Yeah, that's the way it is with kids, John," the night bartender said. "Always wanting to be like the old man."

"That's right," the other said.

He took off his white coat and got into his street coat and overcoat, and took the boy by the hand.

"Good night," he said, and the night bartender answered him and watched him step out into the street with the boy.

They walked together in silence three blocks and then stepped into a drug store and sat at the counter.

"Chocolate or vanilla?"

"I don't know."

"One chocolate, one vanilla ice cream soda," the bartender said to the soda jerk, and when the drinks were set down on the counter the bartender went to work on the vanilla. The boy did all right on the other, and then they stepped out into the snow again.

"Now, try to remember which way you live. Can you do that?"

"I don't *know* which way."

The bartender stood in the snow, trying to think what to do, but the •going was tough, and he got nowhere.

"Well," he said as last, "do you think you could spend the night at my house with my kids? I've got two boys and a little girl. We'll make a place for you to sleep, and tomorrow your father will come and get you."

"Will he?"

"Sure he will."

They walked along in the silent snow and then the bartender heard the boy begin to cry softly. He didn't try to comfort the boy because he knew there was no comforting him. The boy didn't let himself go, though, he just cried softly, and moved along with his friend. He had heard about strangers and he had heard about enemies and he had come to believe that they were the same thing, but here was somebody he had never seen before who was neither a stranger nor an enemy. All the same it was awful lonesome without his angry father.

They began to go up some steps that were covered with snow and the boy's friend said, "This is where we live. We'll have some hot food and then you can go to bed until tomorrow when your father will come and get you."

"When will he come?" the boy said.

"In the morning," his friend said.

When they stepped into the light of the house the bartender saw that the boy was finished crying, perhaps for the rest of his life.

William Saroyan « *The third day after christmas* » in *The Assyrian*

• **checkered coat...** : *veste à carreaux qui était devenue trop étriquée pour son père* • **one little shot of rye** : *un petit verre/coup de whisky* • **belched** : *rota* • **lumpy** : *informes* • **on me** : I'm paying for this bottle • **once in awhile** : from time to time • **keep things from getting out of hand** : keep control of the situation • **he didn't want a fuss** : *il ne voulait pas d'histoires* • **humor the old man out of...** : *amener le vieil homme, sans le brusquer, à renoncer à...* • **toughened** : *endurci* • **clamped her false teeth together** : *fit claquer son dentier en serrant les mâchoires* • **bum** : *clochard* • **free** : *gratuite* • **began to doze** : *commença à s'assoupir* • **water chaser** : some water to drink after it • **suit yourself** : whatever you like • **Jingle Bells** : a Christmas song • **trade** : *clientèle* • **winced** : *se crispa* • **amazed** : astonished • **the going was tough** : it was a difficult problem.

THE A.B.C. OF THE U.S.A.

American Dream : symbolic image of liberty, material prosperity and upward mobility.
American Federation of Labor : (A.F.L.) : founded by Samuel Gompers in 1886. He believed that the interests of the workers were closely connected with those of the capitalist system. The A.F.L. was a federation of craft unions *(syndicats professionnels)* and there was no attempt to unionize unskilled workers, blacks or immigrants.

Bill of Rights : the first ten amendments to the American Constitution ; designed to guarantee individual liberties (freedom of speech, assembly and so on).
Bus(s)ing : a Supreme Court decision in 1971 designed to ensure a better racial balance in schools by transporting black children by bus to schools in predominantly white neighbourhoods and vice versa. This aroused fierce opposition throughout the country.

Checks and balances : (see Government).
Congress : (see Government).
Congress of Industrial Organizations (C.I.O.) founded in 1934 by rebellious members of the A.F.L. who were in favor of industrial unions. The C.I.O. was merged with the A.F.L. in 1955.
Civil Rights Bill of 1964 : a comprehensive bill designed to remove all traces of segregation from American life and to provide equal access to public facilities, job opportunities, housing, schools, etc.
Crash : the Wall Street Crash of 1929 was caused by too much speculation. On Black Thursday (October 24) panic swept the Stock Exchange. Eleven speculators are said to have committed suicide.

Depression : the Great Depression of the thirties was due to the Wall Street crash. It has been calculated that in 1932 there were 15 to 17 million unemployed.
Dixie : the Southern States of the U.S. 'Dixie' is thought to be a corruption of 'Mason-Dixon Line', that is the imaginary line separating free and slave states.

Fifth : the Fifth Amendment (see Bill of Rights) allows a witness to refuse to answer a question if the answer may compromise the witness himself. During the McCarthy political witch-hunt, 'taking the Fifth' was considered to be a tacit admission of guilt.
Founding Fathers : refers to the delegates of the states who came to Philadelphia in 1787 to draw up the Constitution.
Frontier : wild, virgin lands of the west behind the cultivated, settled territories. As the U.S. expanded, the frontier moved progressively westward for more than two centuries until, towards the end of the 19th century, all the land up to to the Pacific had been settled and the Frontier had disappeared.
Frontier (or pioneer) spirit : spirit of endurance, enterprise and self-help.

Gold Rush : gold was found in California in 1848. In 1849 more than 50,000 'fortyniners' traveled 2,000 miles, partly in wagons, partly on foot, from Missouri to California. Many died of cold, hunger and thirst, and most of them arrived too late to profit from the discovery of gold in the mountains.
Government (U.S.) : the separation of powers between 3 branches: the Executive (the President), the Legislative (Congress) and the Judiciary (the Supreme Court) is designed to protect the country against totalitarianism. The separation is not absolute, however, and the overlapping *(chevauchement)* of certain powers constitutes a system of "checks and balances" allowing the three bodies to counter-balance one another. Thus articles of impeachment *(mise en accusation)* were brought by Congress against President Nixon who resigned rather than face conviction.
President (or Chief Executive) : is head of the executive branch of the Federal Government. He can only serve two terms of 4 years each. His powers have been increased in recent years to enable him to cope with the complexity of 20th century life. They include supervision of the administration and enforcement of the law. The President is also Commander-in-Chief of the armed forces.
Congress : the legislative branch of the Federal Government. It consists of the Senate and the House of Representatives and all laws are passed by a majority vote of both Houses. The Senate is the more powerful of the two. Each state is represented by 2 senators, whereas the number of state representatives depends on the population of the state. Both the Senate and the House of Representatives can set up committees to examine proposed legislation or investigate special problems.
the Supreme Court : the highest court in the U.S. Although the Constitution did not give the Supreme Court the power to nullify unconstitutional Acts of Congress, in practice it has been allowed to do so. Its 9 members are appointed for life by the President with the Senate's approval.
Government (State) : Most of the States have governments based on the Federal model.

Homestead Act (1862) : by giving free grants of 160 acres of land to anyone proving 6 years residence, the Act opened up the prairies and Great Plains to the farmers but restricted the activities of the ranchers.

Immigration : nearly 50 million people have been admitted to the U.S. since 1820. In the 1840s and 1850s there was a wave of Irish immigration due to the potato famine. The failure of the 1848 revolutions in Europe brought a wave of Germans in search of political freedom followed by a wave of Scandinavians attracted by cheap land in the Middle West. After the assassination of Czar Alexander II and the subsequent persecutions in 1881 there was a wave of Jewish immigration. In the first decade of the 20th century, 8 million immigrants arrived from Hungary, Italy and Russia. (For further information see p. 56.)
Inauguration Day : on January 20th, the new President is officially inaugurated and swears to defend the Constitution of the U.S.

KuKlux Klan : a secret society founded in 1866. Wearing white hooded costumes to frighten Negroes, members of the Klan would ride by night, terrorizing Negroes who forgot their 'place', pro-Republicans, etc., resorting to torture and murder. The Klan was revived in 1916 and it has been calculated that several thousand Negroes were lynched between the middle of the 19th century and the 1950s when Negro protest created a new militancy that put pressure on the Federal Government to outlaw such activities.

Lobby : a political pressure group organized to influence members of Congress on a particular issue. Since 1946 they have had to register and declare their purpose and income. They are an accepted feature of American political life.

Manifest Destiny : an article attributed to John O'Sullivan in 1845 claimed that 'it is our manifest destiny to overspread the continent allotted by Providence for the free development of our multiplying millions'.
McCarthyism : during the period between 1947 and 1952 the Cold War created a 'Red Scare' in the U.S. and Senator Joseph McCarthy launched a campaign against people whom he suspected of having Communist sympathies. Soon he was leading a full-scale 'witch-hunt' *(chasse aux sorcières)* by means of the Senate committee of which he was chairman. Large numbers of innocent people, including writers, actors and scientists, fell under suspicion and some well-known books were actually burnt in public.
Melting Pot : term invented in 1909 by a Jewish Immigrant, Israel Zangwill; America was seen as a melting pot *(creuset)* in which many different races were mixed to form a new people : the Americans. Ethnic links have, however, remained stronger than was then supposed and ethnic plurality in which different traditions and cultures exist side by side (a Multi-Racial Society) has replaced the concept of the Melting Pot.

New Deal : term used by Roosevelt to describe his program to help the American people. On taking office in 1933 he launched a series of measures concerning banking, business, industry, agriculture and, above all, relief for the victims of the Depression.
National Industrial Recovery Act (the) : (also called **the Blue Eagle Act** because of its emblem) included a huge relief program designed by the Roosevelt Administration to provide jobs in public works for nearly 4 million people. The N.R.A. (National Recovery Administration) tried to establish business codes and working conditions; it also recognized the workers' right to organize.

President : (see Government U.S.).
Prohibition : the 18th Amendment prohibiting the manufacture, sale or transportation of alcohol was passed in 1919. It proved ineffective since traffic in alcohol was promptly organized by gangs, the most famous of which was Al Capone's. The Act was repealed (annulled) in 1933.
Protestant (or Puritan) Work Ethic : a belief in work for work's sake, since "Satan findeth mischief still for idle hands to do". As in the Old Testament, success was thought to be a sign of Divine approbation.
Puritans : originally so called because they wanted to purify the Church of England. They founded the colony of Massachusetts: the Pilgrim Fathers were Puritans. Each community was to be a "city of God". Although Puritanism has become synonymous with narrow-mindedness and bigotry, and is associated with the Salem witch-hunts of 1692, the Puritans also had a positive influence on American life, introducing some measure of self-government and making education compulsory (obligatory). (Harvard University was founded in 1636.)

Senate : (see Government, U.S.).
Sit-in : the occupation of a public place as a form of protest. The first sit-in was a spontaneous demonstration against segregation. It took place in Greensboro, North Carolina in 1960. A handful of black students refused to move from a snack-bar where Negroes were refused service.
Supreme Court : (see Government, U.S.).

Teamsters : founded originally as a union of truck drivers *(camionneurs)* in 1898. Today the Teamsters form a federation of unions covering workers in many different sectors of activity. The Teamsters are generally held to be the most conservative, the most powerful and also the most corrupt of the American labor organizations. They were expelled from the A.F.L. - C.I.O. in the 1950s.
Thanksgiving Day : celebrated on the fourth Thursday of November. It is a national holiday and commemorates the Pilgrims' thanksgiving for their survival in the autumn of 1621.

Unions : an American union is made up of workers in one particular sector of activity (e.g. steel, construction, etc.). Most unions belong to a federation such as the A.F.L. - C.I.O. Unionized workers are represented by a delegate called a "shop-steward". The "closed-shop" system prevents employers from taking on workers who are not members of the appropriate union. Although various trends of opinion co-exist within the different federations, the unions are generally conservative in spirit.

WASP : abbreviation for White Anglo-Saxon Protestant. The first census of 1790 showed that 75% of the American population was of British origin. Immigrants from Holland, Germany or Scandinavia had a very similar culture and outlook and so were easily assimilated. Thus the white Anglo-Saxon Protestants remained a privileged caste and until after the Second World War they provided a model to which the other groups were expected to conform.

REFERENCES PHOTOGRAPHIQUES

ATLAS-PHOTO : Petit : 152. KEYSTONE : 110, 112, 206. MAGNUM : Erwitt : 131 ; Harbutt : 35, 193 ; Kalvar : 121 ; Manos : 76 ; Uzzle : 47 ; Webb : 14, 92, 196. RAPHO : Blackstar : 155 ; Bonnay : 176 ; Doisneau : 201 ; Gerster : 54, 106, 175, 186, 189 ; Heyman : 108 ; Spiegel : 104.
Couverture : MAGNUM : Erwitt.

IRREGULAR VERBS

On ne trouvera dans cette liste que les plus fréquents. La traduction n'est donnée qu'à titre indicatif. Elle peut varier selon le contexte.

be [bi:]	was [wɔz; wəz]	been [bi:n; bin]	*être*
beat [bi:t]	beat [bi:t]	beaten [bi:tn]	*battre*
become [biˈkʌm]	became [biˈkeim]	become [biˈkʌm]	*devenir*
begin [biˈgin]	began [biˈgæn]	begun [biˈgʌn]	*commencer*
bite [bait]	bit [bit]	bitten [bitn]	*mordre*
blow [bləu]	blew [blu:]	blown [bləun]	*souffler*
break [breik]	broke [brəuk]	broken [brəukn]	*casser*
bring [briŋ]	brought [brɔ:t]	brought [brɔ:t]	*amener ; apporter*
build [bild]	built [bilt]	built [bilt]	*construire*
burn [bə:n]	burnt [bə:nt]	burnt [bə:nt]	*brûler*
buy [bai]	bought [bɔ:t]	bought [bɔ:t]	*acheter*
catch [kætʃ]	caught [kɔ:t]	caught [kɔ:t]	*attraper*
choose [tʃu:z]	chose [tʃəuz]	chosen [tʃəuzn]	*choisir*
come [kʌm]	came [keim]	come [kʌm]	*venir*
cost [kɔst]	cost [kɔst]	cost [kɔst]	*coûter*
cut [kʌt]	cut [kʌt]	cut [kʌt]	*couper*
deal *(with)* [di:l]	dealt [delt]	dealt [delt]	*s'occuper (de)*
do [du:]	did [did]	done [dʌn]	*faire*
draw [drɔ:]	drew [dru:]	drawn [drɔ:n]	*dessiner*
dream [dri:m]	dreamt [dremt]	dreamt [dremt]	*rêver*
drink [driŋk]	drank [dræŋk]	drunk [drʌŋk]	*boire*
drive [draiv]	drove [drəuv]	driven [drivn]	*conduire (voitures, etc.)*
eat [i:t]	**ate [eit]**	eaten [i:tn]	*manger*
fall [fɔ:l]	fell [fel]	fallen [fɔ:ln]	*tomber*
feel [fi:l]	felt [felt]	felt [felt]	*(se) sentir*
fight [fait]	fought [fɔ:t]	fought [fɔ:t]	*se battre*
find [faind]	found [faund]	found [faund]	*trouver*
fly [flai]	flew [flu:]	flown [fləun]	*voler*
forbid [fəˈbid]	forbade [fəˈbæd]	forbidden [fəˈbidn]	*interdire*
forget [fəˈget]	forgot [fəˈgɔt]	forgotten [fəˈgɔtn]	*oublier*
forgive [fəˈgiv]	forgave [fəˈgeiv]	forgiven [fəˈgivn]	*pardonner*
freeze [fri:z]	froze [frəuz]	frozen [frəuzn]	*geler*
get [get]	got [gɔt]	got [gɔt]	*obtenir ; devenir*
give [giv]	gave [geiv]	given [givn]	*donner*
go [gəu]	went [went]	gone [gɔn]	*aller*
grow [grəu]	grew [gru:]	grown [grəun]	*croître ; pousser*
hang [hæŋ]	hung [hʌŋ]	hung [hʌŋ]	*suspendre*
have [hæv; həv]	had [hæd; həd]	had [hæd; həd]	*avoir*
hear [hiə]	heard [hə:d]	heard [hə:d]	*entendre*
hide [haid]	hid [hid]	hidden [hidn]	*(se) cacher*
hit [hit]	hit [hit]	hit [hit]	*frapper*
hold [həuld]	held [held]	held [held]	*tenir*
hurt [hə:t]	hurt [hə:t]	hurt [hə:t]	*faire mal (à)*
keep [ki:p]	kept [kept]	kept [kept]	*garder*
know [nəu]	knew [nju:]	known [nəun]	*savoir ; connaître*
lay [lei]	laid [leid]	laid [leid]	*poser ; étendre*
lead [li:d]	led [led]	led [led]	*conduire ; mener*

learn [lə:n]	learnt [lə:nt]	learnt [lə:nt]	*apprendre*
leave [li:v]	left [left]	left [left]	*laisser ; quitter*
lend [lend]	lent [lent]	lent [lent]	*prêter*
let [let]	let [let]	let [let]	*laisser ; permettre*
lie [lai]	lay [lei]	lain [lein]	*être couché*
light [lait]	lit [lit] ; *(lighted)*	lit [lit] ; *(lighted)*	*allumer*
lose [lu:z]	lost [lɔst]	lost [lɔst]	*perdre*
make [meik]	made [meid]	made [meid]	*faire ; fabriquer*
mean [mi:n]	meant [ment]	meant [ment]	*vouloir dire ; signifier*
meet [mi:t]	met [met]	met [met]	*rencontrer*
pay [pei]	paid [peid]	paid [peid]	*payer*
put [put]	put [put]	put [put]	*mettre ; poser*
read [ri:d]	read [red]	read [red]	*lire*
ride [raid]	rode [rəud]	ridden [ridn]	*aller à cheval*
ring [riŋ]	rang [ræŋ]	rung [rʌŋ]	*sonner*
rise [raiz]	rose [rəuz]	risen [rizn]	*s'élever ; se lever (soleil)*
run [rʌn]	ran [ræn]	run [rʌn]	*courir*
say [sei]	said [sed]	said [sed]	*dire*
see [si:]	saw [sɔ:]	seen [si:n]	*voir*
sell [sel]	sold [səuld]	sold [səuld]	*vendre*
send [send]	sent [sent]	sent [sent]	*envoyer*
sew [səu]	sewed [səud]	sewn [səun]	*coudre*
shake [ʃeik]	shook [ʃuk]	shaken [ʃeikn]	*secouer*
shine [ʃain]	shone [ʃɔn]	shone [ʃɔn]	*briller*
shoot [ʃu:t]	shot [ʃɔt]	shot [ʃɔt]	*tirer (fusil)*
show [ʃəu]	showed [ʃəud]	shown [ʃəun]	*montrer*
shut [ʃʌt]	shut [ʃʌt]	shut [ʃʌt]	*fermer*
sing [siŋ]	sang [sæŋ]	sung [sʌŋ]	*chanter*
sink [siŋk]	sank [sæŋk]	sunk [sʌŋk]	*couler ; sombrer*
sit [sit]	sat [sæt]	sat [sæt]	*être assis*
sleep [sli:p]	slept [slept]	slept [slept]	*dormir*
smell [smel]	smelt [smelt]	smelt [smelt]	*sentir (odeurs)*
speak [spi:k]	spoke [spəuk]	spoken [spəukn]	*parler*
spell [spel]	spelt [spelt]	spelt [spelt]	*épeler*
spend [spend]	spent [spent]	spent [spent]	*passer (temps) ; dépenser (argent)*
spread [spred]	spread [spred]	spread [spred]	*étaler*
stand [stænd]	stood [stud]	stood [stud]	*être debout*
steal [sti:l]	stole [stəul]	stolen [stəuln]	*voler (dérober)*
stick [stik]	stuck [stʌk]	stuck [stʌk]	*coller*
strike [straik]	struck [strʌk]	struck [strʌk]	*frapper*
swear [sweə]	swore [swɔə]	sworn [swɔ:n]	*jurer*
sweep [swi:p]	swept [swept]	swept [swept]	*balayer*
swim [swim]	swam [swæm]	swum [swʌm]	*nager*
take [teik]	took [tuk]	taken [teikn]	*prendre*
teach [ti:tʃ]	taught [tɔ:t]	taught [tɔ:t]	*enseigner*
tear [teə]	tore [tɔə]	torn [tɔ:n]	*déchirer*
tell [tel]	told [təuld]	told [təuld]	*dire ; raconter*
think [θiŋk]	thought [θɔ:t]	thought [θɔ:t]	*penser ; croire*
throw [θrəu]	threw [θru:]	thrown [θrəun]	*jeter ; lancer*
understand [,ʌndə'stænd]	understood [,ʌndə'stud]	understood [,ʌndə'stud]	*comprendre*
wake (up) [weik]	woke (up) [wəuk]	woken (up) [wəukn]	*(se) réveiller*
wear [weə]	wore [wɔə]	worn [wɔ:n]	*porter (vêtements)*
win [win]	won [wʌn]	won [wʌn]	*gagner*
write [rait]	wrote [rəut]	written [ritn]	*écrire*

Imprimé en France par l'Imprimerie Gaston MAILLET 93400 St-OUEN
N° d'impression 7646 - Cde n° 1338 - N° d'éditeur C 33 556 XIII (PC.c. VII) - Mars 1983